The memory [of the tornado is etched in the] minds of those [who lived in Oklahoma] City at that time. I saw it from a distance. Carolyn experienced it in all its horror and devastation. She lived to tell us the story, a story of God's grace and healing. Let me warn you: once you start reading this book, you won't be able to put it down.

—Marty Grubbs, senior pastor,
Crossings Community Church

To look at Carolyn today and imagine what she endured then is an inspiration. But to know her story and witness how she survived and thrived is an epiphany.

—Mick Cornett, mayor of Oklahoma City

Having seen first-hand the devastation of the mother of all tornadoes, it is miraculous that anyone survived to tell about it. Thankfully, in Twist of Faith, Carolyn does so honestly and movingly. Her optimism, grace, resilience, and resolve strengthen my own faith.

—Frank Keating, former governor of Oklahoma

As the lieutenant governor of Oklahoma at the time of the May 3 tornado, I was one of the first to arrive on the scene of the devastation of the homes and neighborhoods along with my highway patrol escort. I can still remember walking up to the remains of the homes and visiting with the families who had lost everything and were in total shock. It was like a scene out of the movie *Twister* that had been filmed in Oklahoma. I had known Carolyn Stager as a friend and business associate, but I had no idea I had a friend in the path of tornado or of the tremendous injuries she had sustained as I walked through the devastation. Since that time, I have witnessed her tremendous strength on her road to recovery as well as the perseverance and faith that has lead her back to a normal life. One would never know all she has overcome by meeting her. She has a positive outlook on life, has continued to climb the corporate ladder, and is an inspiration to all.

—U.S. Congresswoman Mary Fallin

Carolyn is a woman of grace and grit - a true Oklahoman. Despite the tremendous hardships she and her daughter Christi endured on May 3, 1999, and in the days following, they have persevered. Carolyn Stager's incredible story of survival is an inspiration to us all.

—Oklahoma Lt. Governor, Jari Askins

I remember when Carolyn first came to my office days after the tornado, I did not recognize her. The beautiful, stylish, energetic woman who had been my patient for several years was replaced by a stranger in a donated housedress. Her head was swathed in bandages and she leaned heavily on a walker. I watched her over the next many years as she dealt with the physical and emotional aftermath of this devastating natural disaster. She endured countless surgeries and still emerged a beautiful person - both inside and out. Her story is truly one of courage and faith.

—Mary Ann Bauman, MD

On May 3, 1999, when the most powerful tornado on record in U.S. history hit my friend's home while she and her daughter clung to each other in a closet under the stairs, the storm did not know that it had struck a pillar. That pillar was Carolyn Stager, one of God's strongest children with faith to move mountains as well as determination and tenacity that surpass all human understanding. I watched Carolyn go into survival mode, and she didn't stop until God brought her completely through the storm after several years of medical treatment and rebuilding all that she had lost. As her long-time friend and business partner, I have watched her touch the lives of hundreds of people, and I know she will continue to touch lives by sharing her story. Carolyn sets the bar on faith…and faith looks up!

—Cheryl Willie, friend and business partner

Carolyn's story is captivating and inspiring. Her memoirs of what happened in Oklahoma on May 3, 1999, offer the reader an opportunity to see the human spirit at its best. It's a story everyone can relate to and be better for it.

—Ann Dagg, friend (Oklahoman, and
  wealth management advisor)

March 2012

To: Shawn

Twist of Faith

Thank you for sharing this day with me & allowing me to share my story —
Always believe & have faith!
Hebrew 11:1
♡ Carolyn Stayer

Twist of Faith
A Tornado Survivor's Spiritual Journey to Recovery

Carolyn Stager
with Kimberly Lohman Suiters

TATE PUBLISHING & *Enterprises*

Twist of Faith
Copyright © 2009 by Carolyn Stager and Kimberly Lohman Suiters. All rights reserved.

No part of this publication may be reproduced, stored in a retrieval system or transmitted in any way by any means, electronic, mechanical, photocopy, recording or otherwise without the prior permission of the author except as provided by USA copyright law.

Scripture quotations marked "NAS" are taken from the *New American Standard Bible* ®, Copyright © 1960, 1962, 1963, 1968, 1971, 1972, 1973, 1975, 1977, 1995 by The Lockman Foundation. Used by permission. All rights reserved.

Scripture quotations marked "NIV" are taken from the *Holy Bible, New International Version* ®, Copyright © 1973, 1978, 1984 by International Bible Society. Used by permission of Zondervan Publishing House. All rights reserved.

Scripture quotations marked "NRSV" are taken from *The Holy Bible: New Revised Standard Version* / Division of Christian Education of the National Council of Churches of Christ in the United States of America, Nashville: Thomas Nelson Publishers, Copyright © 1989. Used by permission. All rights reserved.

Several names, descriptions, entities, and incidents included in the story are based on the lives of real people and on actual events. However, some names and incidents have been changed.

The opinions expressed by the author are not necessarily those of Tate Publishing, LLC.

Published by Tate Publishing & Enterprises, LLC
127 E. Trade Center Terrace | Mustang, Oklahoma 73064 USA
1.888.361.9473 | www.tatepublishing.com

Tate Publishing is committed to excellence in the publishing industry. The company reflects the philosophy established by the founders, based on Psalm 68:11,
"The Lord gave the word and great was the company of those who published it."

Book design copyright © 2009 by Tate Publishing, LLC. All rights reserved.
Cover design by Tyler Evans
Interior design by Stefanie Rooney

Published in the United States of America

ISBN: 978-1-60799-597-5
1. Biography & Autobiography, Religious
2. Biography & Autobiography, Personal
09.04.07

"He performs wonders that cannot be fathomed, miracles that cannot be counted" (Job 5:9, NIV).

For the Great Physician, Jesus Christ, all my earthly physicians, family, co-workers, colleagues, and friends who inspired me through this journey.

Table of Contents

Introduction
— 13 —

End Times
— 15 —

Goodbye
— 39 —

A Mother's Son
— 51 —

Two Hospitals
— 61 —

Code Black
— 70 —

Code Gray
— 81 —

Born Again
— 95 —

Angels
— 106 —

Found
— 111 —

Hellhole
— 127 —

Surprise
— 132 —

Home
— 137 —

Together
— 145 —

Miracles
— 167 —

One by One
— 184 —

Pieces
— 201 —

Broken Hearts
— 214 —

Dr. Walker's Rejection
— 223 —

Good Gifts
— 231 —

Beautiful
— 246 —

Surgery One
— 252 —

Surgery Two
— 271 —

Surgery Three
— 283 —

Surgery Four
— 300 —

With This Ring
— 315 —

The Last Cut
— 331 —

Revelations
— 343 —

One Decade Later
— 353 —

Epilogue
— 363 —

Introduction

May 3, 1999 is a date that will forever be imbedded in so many hearts and minds in the Heartland. I love that Oklahoma is referred to that way. Our spirit, our resilience, and our hearts sustain us, no matter what comes at us.

At times, writing this book was a painful and delicate process. Some names of places, people, and things were altered for the sake of privacy. I wanted this story to be honest and true without being disrespectful to anyone. Above all, I wanted to honor God. Although we humans often fail to each other, God *never* fails us.

Even though this book is the story of what my family went through during this time, there are countless others who experienced and continue to live with the repercussions of that dreadful May day.

Many family members, friends, and co-workers are mentioned in the book. It is impossible to name all of the people across the country who reached out to me and other tornado victims through everyday help, financial support, and prayer. They number in the thousands.

Two people who are not referenced directly, but without whom there would be no book, are Ann Dagg and Kimberly Lohman Suiters. This book would have never happened if not for Kimberly's generous labor of love. God has blessed my life richly by having her, Tyler, and Sloane as a forever part of my extended family. Throughout the past three years on our journey together, we spent countless hours traveling to relevant locations; interviewing my children, friends, colleagues, and physicians; and pouring over my three-year long journal.

Of course, my connection with Kimberly would have never happened if not for the introduction by my precious friend, Ann Dagg. We all know it was a divine appointment carried out by this beautiful woman. Ann and I initially met at a business function and had both arrived early. We struck up a conversation, and she was admiring my hair (which was actually a wig). That exchange was all it took for Ann to quickly become a best friend forever. I thank her for her love, support, encouragement, and for always being there.

My prayer is that this book will serve you as a modern-day Job story and bear witness to God's goodness, his timing, his healing power, and *his* faith—his promise to never leave us.

Carolyn Stager
March 3, 2009

End Times

Now, brothers, about times and dates we do not need to write to you, for you know very well that the day of the Lord will come like a thief in the night. While people are saying, "Peace and safety," destruction will come on them suddenly, as labor pains on a pregnant woman, and they will not escape.

1 Thessalonians 5:1–3 (NIV)

But a different thief in the night was on his way. A murderous one. Hell-bent and furious, roiling and powerful, spun to life only to unravel it. Carolyn did not know where he was, how close he was, or that he even existed at all. Had she known all of this, would she have been afraid?

The air where she stood on her front porch hung thick and heavy around her body, pressing down on her chest like a wet wool coat in the heat of summer. She noticed the birds had stopped chirping, and she couldn't find them fluttering around the redbud trees. She wondered where they had gone. *Have they sought shelter somewhere?* She pictured them sleeping while standing, huddled together under the eaves of rooftops, two hours before their natural bedtime. *Or have they deemed this place unsafe and deserted it?* The big blue sky that had always inspired her was now a hue she had never seen before. Pale gold—or was it sickly yellow?

Strange, she thought.

Stillness infiltrated everything around her, down to the tiniest particle of air.

I am not afraid. So why am I talking to myself about not being afraid?

A few hours earlier the weather had been lovely, cloudless, and sunny; a perfect May morning. Turning off of Lincoln Boulevard at ten, Carolyn caught the dome-less state capitol in the rearview mirror. She furrowed her brow, wondering when the state would pony up the money to match the inferior exterior of the building with the elegance of the interior. At least she had a moment to step away from the madness there: a mid-morning break to tutor a fourth-grader at one of the inner city schools.

After reading a stack of books together, Carolyn's tiny tutee left her with a demure smile that lingered in her mind. As she crossed the school's parking lot, she felt the warmth of the late morning sun on her skin. She opened the sunroof of her fire-engine red Acura Legend and zipped over to the office to check in. After running through messages with her secretary, answering a few e-mails, and returning one legislator's call, she crossed town to the Cowboy Hall of Fame. Officially it had a much longer and more culturally inclusive name, one that reflected the rich collection of Native American paintings and sculptures housed there, but as long as she'd been in Oklahoma—and that was her whole life—everyone called it the Cowboy Hall of Fame.

Carolyn looked forward to the luncheon at the museum. It was the birthday of her friend, Susan Cochran, another excuse to get together with the girls of the Clematis Club. Just like a bouquet of clematis flowers, they considered themselves a group of elegant ladies in mid-bloom who worked mostly in the good ole boy-dominated state senate. That was the official explanation. Unofficially, they would giggle, even blush, any time they said "clematis" out loud, knowing full well it was only three letters off a very different word, the very same female organ that Georgia O'Keefe was suspected of painting within the folds of her flowers.

On her way out, Carolyn ducked into the Grand Hall, a spacious room that made her aware of how small she was; how small they all were in the scheme of life. Looking up at the series of giant triptychs of sunsets over western landscapes, she felt smaller still, but not diminished. What a privilege it was to be a twinkle on this beautiful Earth. Carolyn never tired of those sunsets: their sweet pink and baby blue hues, the way the sunlight streamed across the mountains as if God himself opened the curtains that morning.

The rest of the afternoon, Carolyn tied up loose ends at the state capitol building. Session was just about over, meaning a much-needed summer break was within reach for lobbyists like her who wore the rubber off their heels down to the nails every spring. She often thought that if she were to wear one of those pedometers, she would clock hundreds of miles of brisk walking up and down the capitol's marble floors and stairs between January and May. The louder her heels echoed down the hall, the later in the session it was, the longer the midnight oil burned, the greater the need for a vacation. Carolyn only had to hold out a few more days and she'd be sunning herself on a beach in Cancun. She and her dear friend, Nancy Nichols, a lobbyist with the city of Edmond, had planned the trip months earlier, knowing just how much they would want an escape in May.

Carolyn's purse rattled and rang some sort of disco tune. She picked up the metallic red cell phone and looked at the display:

Mother
May 3, 1999
4:10 p.m.

Caller ID was an invention Carolyn could not imagine living without. It meant she could preempt a feisty legislator looking for a fight with a sugary sweet welcome, or she could ignore him. Since in this case it was her mother, she picked up right away.

"Hello, Mother."

"Have you been watching the weather?"

"Not really. I've been running around town."

"Carolyn, you might want to check it out. Two bitty tornadoes in Comanche County already."

Of course, if you were listening to the conversation, you wouldn't think Carolyn's mother sounded quite like that. People had varying degrees of difficulty understanding her, often asking if she were from another country. Sarah Leona was profoundly deaf and had been since Carolyn was born. Sarah Leona never learned sign language (she said they didn't have it way back then), preferring to master the art of lip-reading. In return, her family learned to read not only her lips but her sounds. Carolyn was fluent in Mother's language, even if friends and strangers struggled to follow along. Growing up, Carolyn and her siblings would scream bloody murder and Mother would never hear them. When they needed her help, they would pound on the walls of their home, and Mother sensed those vibrations. She sensed something else now, and was in something of a panic about it. Sarah Leona wanted to know her daughter's plans for the night, in case the weather turned severe.

"I need to swing by the office. Then I'm going to do my deal on the treadmill. I'm supposed to have dinner—"

"Carolyn, you need to go home..."

Even though she had never been able to hear a tornado siren, Mother was notoriously worried about the weather. Carolyn was not—a trait she may have inherited from her grandfather. The strong push and the gentle pull between mother and daughter this time were no different. Sarah Leona had a deep respect for her daughter's ability to think that stemmed back to preschool, but you wouldn't know it if the weather was bad.

Sarah Leona was a little girl when she survived her first tornado. Every time it rained, Sarah Leona's mother, Vertie, would take her into the storm cellar, but her father, Bert Frances, after whom Carolyn was named, would refuse to go. (Carolyn was his first granddaughter and he liked to call her "Prissy.") Bert was out milking cows in their barn when it came. When he was a child growing up in Arkansas, tornadoes were as common as Christmas. He was unfazed by them. By contrast, Sarah Leona was scared enough for both of them.

So Mother repeated the TV meteorologists' warnings that a tornado outbreak was possible and urged her child of one divorce, two children, and forty-five years to go straight home and prepare to take cover.

Carolyn rolled her eyes as she listened to Mother's concerns and walked out to her coupe. She kept the roof closed this time—a small concession—and drove a quarter mile to the office. Most of her colleagues were gone. But her assistant, KD, was standing by a small television set in their break room.

"Favorable," KD repeated what she had heard. "They're saying conditions are *favorable* this time, as if we want to have our houses blown to bits."

"Makes for good TV, right?" Carolyn answered, not entirely convinced.

The two women watched the news coverage for a few minutes. The meteorologists were preempting all the afternoon shows.

"The whole state's under a warning. I guess I'd better cancel my dinner plans. Mother wants me to crawl into a cellar yesterday."

"I don't even have a 'fraidy hole. Never have, never will. Have you called your kids?"

Carolyn had not—not yet. Typically she talked to

each of them once a day, but she thought she knew exactly where they were—Nathan doing his chores and Christi headed to her own house after work. Nathan was still a full-time student at Oklahoma State University's Oklahoma City campus but living at home. *I'll be supporting this kid forever,* Carolyn often worried. When she would ask him what he wanted to do after college, he would always say he did not know. But he could not get the dream of becoming a firefighter off his mind.

Thinking about both of her children, Carolyn smiled to herself, finding it ironic that she had been so protective of her only daughter. But Christi had a steady job at the Oklahoma Department of Health, a husband, and a baby on the way. Carolyn resolved to call her kids on her drive home, which wouldn't happen until she checked all of her e-mails and returned another senator's call.

One of Carolyn' colleagues, Diane, stopped by her office. Carolyn was on the phone, so Diane just waved as she headed out to the parking lot.

On her way home, Carolyn sent Nathan a page. Then her cell phone rang. She expected to hear Nathan on the line.

Christi
May 3, 1999
5:25 p.m.

"Hey, Mom."

Christi's voice was tense. Like her grandmother,

she was nervous when it came to storms, but she felt doubly vulnerable in pregnancy.

"Hi, Sissy. How's it looking where you are?"

"Weird. They say Chickasha just got hit."

"Do you want to come over?" Carolyn asked.

Carolyn raised both of her children in a two-story home on Del Aire Place, just a stone's throw to Tinker Air Force Base in Del City, a suburb of Oklahoma City. She and her former husband, Don Stager, had bought it in 1977 to be close to the base, where they had both been employees at one time or another. When Christi moved away, it was only half a mile down the road. And *her* husband, Roman, worked at the Dayton Tire Plant just west of the base.

"Roman called from the plant. He wants me to go to his uncle's place. But I've got Jake. Why don't you come to my house? I want to show you my new maternity clothes."

Christi had planned to go over to her dad's house after dinner to cut his hair, but she called him earlier in the day to cancel. Don did not mind the change. He was used to the kids bouncing between Carolyn and him ever since they divorced nine years earlier. Christi explained that she had gone shopping during her lunch hour earlier in the day, picking up seven new outfits to cover her expanding bump, and was eager to let her mom see them. The last one she had tried on was simple enough, a soft white t-shirt and black cotton pants with Velcro above the belly for easy adjustment as she ballooned over the last two months of her pregnancy. But of the seven, it would be the only new outfit she would get the chance to wear.

Jake was Christi's six-month-old puppy, part yellow Labrador Retriever and part German Shepherd. He went everywhere with Christi, from the shopping mall to the bank. He even slept in between her and Roman. In their short time together, Christi clung to him as though he were her firstborn.

It was coming up on six o'clock in the evening, just about the time mothers would swing open unlocked front doors to call in the kids for dinner. They still did that in the Del Aire neighborhood. But this night there were no children to call. The bikes were stored away, the trampolines still. No one was jogging or chatting over front yards. The early evening resembled early morning when nothing stirs and the headlights of those on the third shift at the base are the last light anyone sees between moonshine and sunrise. As she drove down her street, Carolyn couldn't help but feel that the family-friendly neighborhood was devoid of life—a ghost town under a darkening sky.

Christi's voice over the phone startled Carolyn out of her daydream.

"Mom? So, are you coming?" Christi sounded annoyed.

"No, Sis, come to my house. You're in a little frame house. The big bad wolf could blow yours down. Mine's brick. If this storm pops out a window or knocks down a tree, we'll be safe. Just bring Jake with you."

By the time Christi gathered her puppy and her maternity clothes, a heavy rain fell from black storm clouds.

She leaned forward over the steering wheel to get a better view of the road. Tiny hailstones made clicking sounds on her windshield. A few seconds later, it sounded like someone was punching the roof of her red Jeep Cherokee. She didn't know it at the time, but Christi was driving through the tell-tale precursors of a tornado.

Strange.

Carolyn repeated it under her breath, not wanting to believe that this storm would be different from any other she'd ever lived through. Carolyn Frances Crump was born in 1953 in a small town called Wewoka. The Crumps always had an underground cellar in the backyard, a concrete box in the ground about ten feet wide where you had to walk outside to get into it and pull the metal door closed overhead. Her whole life, every time she went in that cellar, it was a false alarm. When she had to go, it was an annoyance. But when she chose to go, it was an adventure.

Sometimes on the calmest of nights, Carolyn and her girlfriends would grab their pillows, stuffed animals, snacks, and flashlights and run under the stars, crawl down into the cellar, and giggle the hours away with a slumber party. Even as they got older, the girls enjoyed the escape into the backyard. There was never any thought of misbehaving either—no cigarette puffs or swigs of alcohol. The Crumps were Pentecostal, and the kids knew where they would go straightaway if they crossed the line. Everybody called it a 'fraidy hole, but Carolyn was never afraid down there. She found it peaceful.

Carolyn left the front porch and headed into the kitchen to make two tomato and bacon sandwiches and poured one glass of water for Christi and a Coke for herself.

Christi, Jake, and the maternity clothes were already coming through the front door before Carolyn noticed her daughter's Jeep parked in the driveway.

Carolyn met her in foyer.

"BoPeep! I'm sorry; I didn't see you pull up."

Jake the lumbering Lab made a beeline for the small water bowl belonging to Carolyn's dachshund, Little Miss Muffin, who whined. Christi didn't see a good place to secure Jake, so she tied his leash to the handle of the front door. Carolyn gathered up the clothes from Christi and put an arm around her. She gave her a squeeze and both of them smiled. Christi was overjoyed at being seven months pregnant. In her cheerleading days, when Christi was a natural blonde with sparkling blue eyes and a body that was always tanned and toned, it was hard to imagine a girl being any happier. Now her long hair looked bushy from the humidity and dishwater dark as she took a hiatus from highlighting, her blue eyes tired, and her body thick and expecting. But none of those aesthetics mattered. Just being pregnant was the fulfillment of a lifelong dream for her.

"How's my precious grandbaby, Abby Dawn?"

"Growing."

"Let me see those cute little outfits you got yourself."

Carolyn had already developed a sweet-sounding grandma voice, as if the baby were already there. Christi slipped into the bathroom off the laundry room and tried on the t-shirt and black pants.

Her mother approved.

"Very comfy, Sissy. You'll wear that a lot. Are you hungry?"

Carolyn handed Christi half a sandwich, feeling harmlessly smug that her children still wanted to be near her, even though they were old enough to be parents themselves. In two months, Carolyn would become a bona fide grandmother. She caught a glimpse of herself in the kitchen mirror: her wavy blonde hair up in a high pony tail, cut-off jean shorts, and a white "Keep Oklahoma Beautiful" t-shirt with pink and gray print—she was president of the civic club at the time. She was also barefoot and braless. It was her post-work, pre-workout uniform.

I look a mess, she thought.

This was quite the contrast to her public presentation: a reliable combination of candy-apple red lipstick, glittery eye shadow, something in rhinestones, likely something in animal print, two-inch heels at minimum, and not only a bra but a designer one that matched her underwear. Her jewelry was well-appointed but simple and always the same—a favorite gold watch, a set of diamond earrings, and a sapphire and diamond ring. Part of her disrobing routine was to tuck away those precious pieces into a blue athletic sock in her top drawer. It was also the place she stashed another sock filled with twenty-five thousand dollars in emergency funds. She figured no thief would think to steal socks.

"Mom, I drove through baseball-size hail near my house. They're ringing the sirens. Let's clean out your hall closet, just in case."

Not wanting to upset Christi, Carolyn started clearing out a small hall closet under the staircase. It was the centermost part of her house, the best she could do for a tornado shelter. She found it comical to see such a small space stuffed with rain coats, winter jackets, and picture frames. The top shelf housed all kinds of seasonal trinkets that gathered a thin layer of dust on top when they were off the holiday decoration rotation. On the floor, old eight millimeter film reels captured Christi and Nate on vacation at Disney World, Thanksgiving dinners, and Christmas mornings. Everything she ever had on film—the record of their lives to this point—was in that little closet.

"Gosh, I really need to convert these to DVD," Carolyn said aloud as she walked down the hall, headed for her bedroom closet.

"We *need* to get the glass out."

Christi grabbed the picture frames first.

"And what are—awww, these are so sweet."

Carolyn thought Christi had come across some old photos of her and her brother, but instead she carried in three newborn-sized dresses with the tags still on. Carolyn had hung them in the closet, meaning to save them as a surprise. In just sixty days, those dresses would wrap around a tiny, beautiful baby. But for the next few minutes, mother and daughter removed anything that might whack them on the head.

The television set in the living room was turned up much louder than normal, so that if they did need to hide in the closet, they would know when it was safe to come out. Carolyn was only half-listening to the weatherman doing his what-to-do-if-a-tornado-hits routine. If you have never witnessed it before, you might worry that Armageddon was imminent. But she had heard it hundreds of times throughout her life in Tornado Alley.

"Bridge Creek, you need to be in your shelters now. If you're in a house, get to the lowest possible point. Put as many walls between you and the outside—" said the weatherman. The urgency in his voice through the television was no greater than the last storm that blew over.

"It looks like it's heading north, Mom. Right toward the city. Gosh, think of all those windows downtown. Maybe it will miss us."

"I'm going to peek outside for a second."

The TV weatherman continued. "Cover your head with blankets, pillows, and a bike helmet if you have it. If you're in a mobile home, get to a sturdier shelter or a even a ditch—"

Carolyn tried to open the front door. The wind slammed it back in her face. Strange had been kicked out by violent. Carolyn looked out a west-facing window. The view bore no resemblance to the serene paintings of tender pastels in the Great Hall. No one dared brave the conditions outside now.

I've never seen anything like this.

For the first time in her life, she gave a second

thought to the tornadoes that were predicted to tear apart the homes, lives, and loves of innocent people that day. Blackness descended like the door of a giant casket closing on top of the world. Carolyn felt the intensity of the storm in her gut.

We should already be in the closet.

Mother
May 3, 1999
6:15 p.m.

Sarah Leona, who lived ten miles to the east, wanted to make sure that Carolyn and Christi had adequate shelter. Earlier in the day, she had encouraged Christi to go to her mother's house. The TV was not running closed captioning, so Sarah Leona relied on the meteorologists' maps and her husband to tell her where the storm was headed. He didn't mention Del City, but Sarah Leona sensed danger. Like hives on skin, she knew storm clouds could bubble up unannounced all over the state and send a twister through anyone's backyard.

After she hung up with Carolyn, Sarah Leona walked out to her enclosed patio where she often said her prayers and looked to the southwest. She saw one strange-looking cloud in the sky, but everything around her was unnaturally still—quieter than what even she was used to.

Don
May 3, 1999
6:34 p.m.

Christi's dad and his wife, Sue, were in their house in Moore, about ten miles south of Carolyn's home in Del City.

He wanted to know where Christi and Nathan were, so Carolyn passed her phone to Christi. Don did not mean to scare his daughter, but he did.

"Baby, I'm standing in my backyard, and I can't even see the whole tornado. It's filling up my peripheral vision."

"Are you kidding me, Dad?"

"Serious as a heart attack. There are semis flying in the air. Bridge Creek was just wiped off the map."

Dad, Granny, and the entire family feared for Carolyn and her children. Everyone seemed terribly afraid, except for Carolyn, who was on the phone, calmly exploring all of their options. She had called two neighbors from the kitchen phone, asking them if they had room in their shelters. None of them even had shelters, so she decided they would stay put.

Then the call Carolyn had been waiting for finally came.

Nathan
May 3, 1999
7:00 p.m.

"Sorry to call so late, Mom."

Nathan explained his pager had fallen to the bottom of his golf bag and he did not check it until that moment.

"Ah. I thought you might be grocery shopping," Carolyn said sarcastically, as she now understood why none of Nathan's chores had been done. Although she wanted him home, she was not angry. It took a lot more to rile Carolyn than that. "Where are you?"

"Sal's. Thought we'd hang here."

"Okay, baby. Stay safe. Call me when it's over."

She hung up, and her cell phone rang again.

Patty & Charlie
May 3, 1999
7:20 p.m.

"You know you're in the target, right?" Charlie, married to Carolyn's younger sister, could be the family jokester.

"I'm fine."

The weatherman interrupted them. "Radar indicates a tornado may form at any time. Take cover now."

"Carolyn," Charlie said with intensity, "kiss your butt goodbye because you're not going to survive. Moore is flat out gone." He was trying to frighten her into action.

But Carolyn laughed.

"You're a dern fool, Charlie. I've got another call."

She looked at her phone before clicking over.

Danny
May 3, 1999
7:38 p.m.

It was Carolyn's boss. She knew why he was calling, but teased him anyway.

"Hungry for some chicken spaghetti?"

"Very funny, Ms. Carolyn. Do you have time to get out of there?"

"Isn't it heading toward Oklahoma City?"

"Carolyn, it's turning east."

At the same time, Christi shouted from her spot a few inches from the television set.

"Mom! Del City at 7:45!"

Carolyn pulled her phone away from her ear and looked at the time. She had two minutes left.

"I'd better go, Danny," she said, calmly walking toward Christi.

"You don't have a shelter. Do you have time to go to a neighbor's or something?"

Christi tugged on her mother's t-shirt.

"Mom! It turned right! It turned right! We're in the path!"

"Del City, you must take cover. Midwest City, you must take cover. Tinker Air Force base, Choctaw, in your shelters now—"

"Danny, I think it's too close—"

"Get low, Carolyn. Make sure to cover your he—"

"I will. Gotta go."

Carolyn hung up the phone, slipped it back into

her pocket, and helped Christi squat down on the carpeted closet floor. Carolyn knelt down beside her, stuffing pillows, blankets, and Christi's new maternity clothes all around them.

"There's too much stuff. This isn't going to work." Carolyn groaned.

"Mom, we're not moving."

Over the booming voice of the meteorologist, Carolyn heard the phone in the kitchen ring. She made a move to get it.

"Mom! You are not getting out there to answer that phone!"

It occurred to Carolyn that the call might be from J.R., her boyfriend for the last year. He was just about the only person she knew whom she had not spoken to in the last hour. The week before, J.R. had taken Nathan on a fishing trip to Lake Fork, a chance for the two of them to bond. Tonight, J.R. planned to pick up his daughter from the Tulsa airport after returning from an overseas trip. Carolyn intended to dine with Scott Mitchell, a friend and political consultant. In the back of her mind, Carolyn pictured the whole storm blowing over, making it possible for her to join him for a foamy decaffeinated cappuccino sometime before 9 p.m.

"Abandon mobile homes, cars, and trucks. Get to an interior room. Keep away from windows." The weatherman had said it a million times before, and a million times before the storm had missed them.

Carolyn pulled the closet door shut. In the dark, crowded space, she could not see her daughter's eyes, but she could sense her fear. Christi was young, pregnant, and hormonal—all those things added to her anxiety. Carolyn's maternal instinct had told her not to worry her daughter.

Stay calm. Don't overreact. Everything will be fine. Christi yelled out. Carolyn jumped.

"Oh no! Jake!"

In all the commotion, Jake was left behind, still tied to the front door. Christi looked for something to hoist herself up, but Carolyn beat her to it. She dashed out and unhooked his leash as he bounded for the closet all in one motion. Like any Lab Carolyn had ever met, he wanted to be as close as possible to the excitement and his "mother." Jake leaped into Christi's arms, and she held him like a baby. He licked her chin, snuggled against her chest, his thin white body covering her belly. His muscular tail knocked rhythmically against the closet door. Christi looked up at her mother.

"What about Little Miss Muffin?"

Carolyn poked her head out of the door and scanned the hallway as far as she could see. No sign of Miss Muffin. She figured her sweet old dog was in her favorite spot—curled up on the couch under a blanket. She clapped her hands and called out her name.

"Come here, Muffins! Come here, Muffins!"

"Mom, just go grab her. Hurry!"

Carolyn found her twelve-year-old dachshund right where she expected. She saw her nose first, the rest of her body buried under covers on the couch. Carolyn ran back to the closet with Muffin, the blanket, and a couch cushion in her arms. She closed the door for the last time.

The house phone rang again, but Carolyn did not move.

Even with the door closed, they could hear the TV meteorologist's voice, muffled though it was, coming through the entertainment center on the other side of the wall. In the darkness Carolyn felt a heavy pressure, like a G-force, weighing down her body.

"Mom, can you breathe?"

"Sissy, we're going to be okay. Let's pray."

"Already there, Mom."

Mother and daughter bowed their heads and closed their eyes, the knuckles of their clasped hands nearly fused together. Carolyn thought about Matthew's gospel account where Jesus directs the faithful to go into a room, close the door, and pray in secret as opposed to the hypocrites who pray standing where they can be seen. Pray the Lord's Prayer, he instructs. So Carolyn did, and then kept going. She asked for God's protection through the storm. She gave thanks for her children and unborn grandchild. She prayed for forgiveness for...

Her prayer was interrupted by the most startling sound she had ever heard.

Something hit the house. A car had hit the house and bounced off.

"Oh my God, Mom, we're in it."

A tremendous roar—louder than a train on the front porch or a Tinker jet engine in the kitchen, more like the mouth of a monster—enveloped them.

Pop! Crash! Pop, pop, pop, pop, pop! Crash! Crash! One after another, the double-paned windows of the house blew out, as if someone were shooting at them.

The TV in the living room exploded.

Mother and daughter could not hear each other scream.

The tornado chewed up the walls of the house and spit them out, one at a time, closer and closer to the closet under the stairs.

They could not hold on to their dogs. Carolyn had no power over this wind; she cried out as she felt it snatch Little Miss Muffin right out of her arms and rip the carpet and tile out from under her body. Christi yelled for Jake, but whether he was thrust against her or stolen away, she could not tell.

Carolyn and Christi grabbed for each other, but their arms were overpowered. Darkness descended on them. The walls of the closet were ripped away, and so were they. Carolyn and Christi wanted to open their eyes, but their reflexes took over, forcing their lids to shut tight against the raging sandstorm. Their bodies were beaten and whipped, thrashed and torn open like rag dolls in the jaws of a blood-thirsty beast. Their senses were overloaded by everything and nothing. Nightmares and flashbacks flooded their thoughts. As her body was seized from the ground, Carolyn felt sick to her stomach. Like a violent puppeteer, the force yanked her up steeply, and then dropped her suddenly before jerking her in every direction. Her screams could no longer escape her throat; that exit was blocked. Her small, athletic body could not sus-

tain the abuse for much longer. The dirt of the earth piled up on top of her, burying her alive.
I'm being run over.
I'm being crushed.
Lord, please take me...
Heaven heard the same prayers coming from mother and daughter.
I can't take any more.
Christi's thoughts turned from the pain and punishment of her beating to the next certain seconds.
I love you, Lord. I'll see you any minute.
Suddenly, everything stopped. Christi tried to sit up and lift her head.
Could it be?
For a moment, there was quiet—no light, no movement, no sound, no feeling, only stillness.
It was a false reprieve.
A massive section of plywood rammed into the back of her neck, and Christi plunged into darkness.
Carolyn saw whiteness and in that space, she prayed for mercy. Her lips did not move. Her body disengaged from itself.
She did not know whether Christi was with her, uncertain herself about where she was, or what she was. *Alive? Dead? Somewhere in between?*
Her mind spun in slow motion as a familiar face emerged from the whiteness. The face of her friend, Jeanna, who had died a terrible and tragic death three months earlier, drifted into her consciousness.
Young in her early forties, Jeanna had left behind a husband and daughter. She had been Carolyn's busi-

ness partner years back when they owned a children's clothing store called Klassy Kids. On one rainy day, an eighteen-wheeler plowed into her car, but she did not die right away. It took a full month.

The memory of the last time they saw each other had faded, but Carolyn saw her clearly now. Jeanna was blinking as if she were alive, as if she understood.

Dear God, am I so close?

The thief grabbed Carolyn by the throat and sucked her breath away.

Goodbye

I am forgotten, out of mind like the dead; I am like a shattered dish.

I hear the whispers of the crowd; terrors are all around me. They conspire against me; they plot to take my life.

But I trust in you, Lord, I say, "You are my God."

My times are in your hands; rescue me from my enemies; from the hands of my pursuers. Let your face shine on your servant; save me for your mercies' sake.

Psalm 31: 13–17 (NAB)

"Help me! Someone help me!"

Christi blinked to clear the dirt and tears from her burning eyes and yelled again.

At first, she heard nothing—not a footstep, a whisper, nor a hint of wind. Her mother was gone. Her puppy was gone. There were no cries except her own.

Where am I?

Christi could not get up, so she surveyed the war zone while lying on her back. She saw no houses, just heaps of splintered lumber, broken brick, shattered glass, and twisted metal strewn across the ground. Piles and piles of rubble surrounded her. One car was wrapped so completely around a tree that the front bumper touched the back. An overturned truck was flat as if a child-giant had flipped it then stomped on it. Toppled and torn trees littered the ground. The handful that remained standing had lost their tops, leaving behind jagged trunks. Surviving branches were stripped of their leaves and bark. Shredded clothing and blankets clung to their naked, bony structures like ghosts. There was nothing to indicate to Christi that she was still in her mother's backyard.

I made it through this, and I'm going to die right here.

"Help! *Help!*"

Out of the corner of her eye, Christi saw a sign of life limp slowly across the wasteland. She heard crunching under the paws of a black dog, and as she turned to look squarely at him, she felt a sharp pain deep in her neck.

"Jake? Puppy?"

The black dog paused, looked back at the lumps of brown, pink, and red flesh and dipped his head. He made a sniffing sound, more an exhale than an inhale, as if he were clearing his nostrils. The scent of the ground was vaguely familiar, but not enough to make him stay.

I've lost my mind.

Christi struggled to clear her thoughts.

Jake's yellow not black.

But she wanted the dog to be Jake more than anything at that moment. She needed something familiar, something to hold on to. As the puppy hobbled away, Christi heard a whimper. But it didn't come from the dog. Gingerly, she turned her head around toward the sound. A life-sized doll lying a few feet away came into focus.

The mannequin's head was blood red, and her lips were white. She lay rigid and lifeless, slightly propped up on her back by a mass of shattered wood. She had no shoes. Her clothes were muddied and torn. Her right leg was contorted in an unnatural and—had she been alive—terribly painful position.

That must be a doll from one of the shop windows down the road.

Staring at the doll took Christi's mind off the pain in her own leg.

God only knows how it got here.

"Oh my God," Christi whispered as she put her earth-covered hand to her mouth.

That can't be a mannequin.

Blood seeped from the doll's head.

The eyes of the mannequin gazed left, but the rest of her body remained motionless. Another stream of blood trickled down her cheek. Suddenly, Christi recognized the doll's face as her own mother's.

"Mom?" Fear filled Christi's voice. "Mom?"

It took Carolyn a moment to register the voice she knew with the unfamiliar vision in front of her. Christi was covered in mud from head to toe. Her shirt was torn and no longer white. Her long, curly hair had been furiously twisted like tumbleweed, a knotted web of red mud, splintered wood, and shattered glass.

"BoPeep," Carolyn whispered.

I need to go help my child. I need to go help my child.

As strong as her will and instinct were, Carolyn's body would not move.

"Mom! We should holler for help."

"I can't."

There's sand in my throat.

Carolyn made a choking sound. A dam of dirt, insulation, and other debris had piled up in her mouth. With one finger, she began to dig the stuff out. She retched and spat weakly on the ground, unaware of the blood soaking her hair and face.

Overhead, Carolyn heard the rhythmic tapping of a helicopter's rotors. Like Christi, she did not know where she was. Her neighborhood had green leafy trees, cars in the driveways, and pretty homes. This place had none of that. It resembled the black and white photographs of war-torn cities that Carolyn had seen in newspaper stories over the decades. Surreal as it was to be in such a strange place now, she felt certain someone would find them.

We don't have to yell. They're coming to save us.

Christi turned her eyes to the sky and screamed at the top of her lungs for both of them.

"Help us! Somebody please help us!"

But no one came. No one came for what felt like the longest time.

Christi began to cry softly, complaining about throbbing in her leg. Still wearing the black maternity pants, her right pant leg appeared wet. It was soaked in blood. Carolyn looked helplessly at her daughter and reached out toward her. Christi winced as she inched closer to her mother. A few feet separated them from touching each other, but it was too excruciating to move any more.

I need to help my child.
I need to help my mom.
God, please help my child.

They had survived the storm so far. But they knew they were injured badly enough that they needed help right away. The longer they waited for help, the less they believed they would be rescued in time. Carolyn's head and right hip swelled with each passing second; Christi's right leg was turning blackish purple. Mother and daughter were lost at sea and bleeding out rivers.

"Sissy, I love you. So proud of you."

"Mom, I love you, too."

Christi needed to be closer. She gritted her teeth and edged over one last time. It was enough to touch her mother's hand.

"Are you saying goodbye, Mom?"

Carolyn didn't answer.

Tears streaked down Christi's muddy face as she screamed for help once more, but Carolyn was not crying. If this were her end, she wanted to see her daughter clearly.

Carolyn felt herself fading. Her hand lay limp in Christi's.

"I'm not going to make it, Sis," she said weakly.

"Mom," Christi said sternly, as she gathered herself and squeezed her mother's hand.

"You *are* going to make it. Promise me you'll stay with me. Promise, Mom."

The ring of a cell phone startled Christi and Carolyn. It was close by—Carolyn's phone. Neither of them had imagined that a cell phone was within reach. Carolyn slowly slipped her hand into her pocket to retrieve it. She had no idea what time it was. She didn't bother to look at the caller ID.

"Carolyn! I can't believe I got through. Circuits are jammed. Where are you?"

It was her boss, Danny, calling again.

"I'm not sure," Carolyn answered in a daze. "No one's here. Me and Christi. Can you send help?"

Danny lived close to an hour away from Carolyn's house, but she was not thinking straight. It had not even occurred to her to call 911. She just knew she had spoken with someone familiar, someone who was not where she was.

Danny assured her.

"I will. Don't worry. I will."

Someone else was trying to call Carolyn, so she hung up with Danny. It was J.R.

"Hey, baby, are you okay?"

"No!" Carolyn yelled feebly. "We need help! Christi's hurt. It's really bad. It's so bad."

"Please help us!" Christi shouted again.

"It's going to be okay," J.R. said reassuringly, although he talked himself into believing that it could not be as bad as it sounded. He wondered but did not ask, *who the heck is screaming?*

Carolyn hit the off button angrily.

It's not okay. This is not okay.

J.R. was panicked. In their year-long love-hate

relationship, Carolyn had never hung up on him before. But thoughts of his first and beloved wife Patti, who died of cancer, flashed in his brain and stung his heart. He resolved to get to Carolyn's house as soon as possible.

Exhausted, Carolyn closed her eyes.

Suddenly, mother and daughter heard shouting around them. They didn't recognize the voices, but their urgency was obvious.

"We've got one over here...one—no, two here! Two here!"

As the women realized that some measure of help had arrived, they both felt something very strange happening. The adrenaline that had kept them somewhat lucid immediately after the tornado began to run out. Knowing they were actually being rescued sent them into full-blown shock.

"We need doors! Two doors!"

A man crouched down next to Carolyn.

"What's your name, honey? Can you tell me your name?"

Carolyn watched the man's mouth. His questions were designed to keep her focused. She could not place his face, even though the man knew her very well. It was too late for Christi, who had gone unconscious.

"When were you born?"

Another man's voice sounded like Carolyn's neighbor, Phil, but she could not be sure. He and his wife, Mindy, were a young couple who lived one house to the north. They had a sixteen-month-old baby, and the three of them rode out the storm in a closet too.

The difference between his house and Carolyn's was that behind a thick tree wrapped with Christi's jeep one wall had remained. It was the reason his family survived.

She didn't answer him. She couldn't answer him. All she could say was her daughter's name.

"Christi—"

Carolyn turned her shoulders slightly as if she were going to get up. Another man, this one with broad shoulders, touched her shoulder gently. The truth was she couldn't move anyway.

"Carolyn, you need to stay just where you are," he said.

He was not looking at Carolyn's eyes as people normally do.

"There are lots of folks helping Christi."

He was fixated on her head.

"You just stay right where you are."

Why is he staring at me like that?

Carolyn's head definitely did not feel normal. She sensed that something was lodged in her skull.

Are there wood chips stuck in my head? Glass?

As she bled, the color drained from her skin.

"Am I going to die?" Carolyn asked the broad-shouldered man.

"I'm not going to lie to you, Carolyn." He said her name again as if he had said it many times before. "It's not looking good." He could not believe she could actually talk to him. Her head was a red, black, and gory mess.

"Everybody run for your lives! It's going to blow!"

Another man ran shouting from the scene, but the rescuers had no intention of following. The man helping Carolyn tried to restore calm.

"We're in too deep to worry now," he said. "You can either stand there and watch or help. Right now, I need another door to get her out of here."

"Steve, are you sure we should move her?" someone asked. Steve was the name of the man with big shoulders, but it did not register with Carolyn.

"On a bad accident like this, we don't move unless there's danger. And I don't mean to scare you like that idiot just did, but there is danger," Steve said. He did not say what the danger was, although he continued to glance at Carolyn's head. Instinctively, she wanted to be moved. In her mind, being moved meant being rescued, and she trusted the man they called Steve.

"Careful, she's pregnant..." It was the voice of a long-haired woman.

The conversation a few feet away turned Carolyn's mind away from her own state and back to the rescue effort surrounding her daughter. *How did she know that Christi had a baby inside?*

Someone was trying to get Carolyn's attention.

"I'm Libby, just like a can of green beans. Can you hear me?" Carolyn could hear her but she was not able to answer. "Try and remember this name: Libby." She would remember the name, but for now the only name that mattered in her world was Christi.

Carolyn watched the chaotic movement as a half-dozen or so strangers lifted Christi onto a large door that the wind had sucked off its hinges but left intact. The woman with long hair appeared to be in charge. She seemed to care deeply for Christi, as if she knew her—even loved her. Christi was the saddest-looking thing Carolyn had ever seen, utterly helpless. Truthfully, at this point, Carolyn could not distinguish between what was real and what was imagined. Christi's sadness, the woman's strength, and the man's orders appeared and then disappeared as they do in dreams or nightmares.

Perhaps it was for her own protection that Carolyn could not see the lashing her daughter and unborn granddaughter had taken. Under Christi's clothing, her body looked as though she'd been beaten with a bat and ripped to shreds by shrapnel. As for inside her body, only God could know whether her baby had survived.

Carolyn prayed to him.

Just save her. Please save her.

She wondered whether she would live to see her daughter again.

Christi's crew was off and before long another set of footsteps brought a young man short of breath and full of panic. It was Roman, who was shouting, "Are they alive? Are they alive?"

Christi could not see him as the hazy world swirled around her. She turned her head to look in the direction of her husband's voice, but instead she focused on the outline of a roof.

"Ro? See that house?"

"What house, baby?"

"Over there. Call someone. Get us out. Hospital."

"Christi, there's nothing, no houses left."

"Just use their phone. Just go."

"There's nothing, baby. It's just a mirage."

A few more men circled Carolyn, and she felt a tugging on her shorts but not pain. Her right leg was numb. As they cut back her blue jean shorts, a geyser of blood shot into the air. A man ripped off his shirt and pressed it against her leg. Someone else swathed her head with a t-shirt.

They lifted Carolyn as carefully as they could onto another door, then up toward an overcast sky. A few dark storm clouds lingered harmlessly.

I am not afraid.

"Oh God..." someone said.

I am not afraid.

"Watch her head, watch her head. Easy..."

I am not afraid to die.

Carolyn closed her eyes and heard shouts like darts fly over her from several directions. She felt as though she were riding in the back of a bumpy wagon. The commotion faded in and out. She was in the heart of a search and rescue operation.

If her eyes had been open, the view from her makeshift gurney through ground zero would have been grim. She would have understood why rescuers had to shuttle the injured and the dying out, and leave the dead behind for now. There were no streets to be followed or landmarks to guide them. They could not tell where pavement started and grass began. The roadway was covered in fractured pieces of furniture, houses, and cars. Water poured and gas hissed from broken pipes. Ambulances could not get close to them. There were no addresses to give.

"The road's that way! Sooner's that way!" A man pointed east through the chaos to the nearest open road.

Had she opened her eyes, she would have seen the stripped trees, overturned cars, and pieces of houses strewn everywhere. She would have seen people she knew crawling out from under caves of broken beams as rescuers dug for them. She would have recognized the man who coordinated her rescue as Steve, a career firefighter and father to Roman. And she would have known instantly that the strong woman by Christi's side was Roman's mother, Mydonna. She would have seen men and women in military uniforms from nearby Tinker Air Force Base running to and fro. She would have seen countless people digging themselves out of would-be graves. She would have seen a team of people lift a car that had flipped over, revealing the bodies of her neighbor and his girlfriend, two of six people who died that evening in the Del Aire addition. The thief in the night had claimed many victims. He would claim more.

Carolyn would have known this and seen this and many horrible things, had she been awake. She was not exactly asleep, more sinking, sinking, sinking down to the bottom of an unknown vortex. Suddenly, something stopped her from disappearing and called her back from the depths of darkness. It was a scream of utter terror that sounded vaguely familiar. It was Nathan's voice, the voice of her son.

A Mother's Son

Sons are a heritage from the Lord,
children a reward from him.
Like arrows in the hands of a warrior
are sons born in one's youth.
Psalm 127:3–4 (NIV)

The note on the kitchen table had let Nathan know the "home" work of the day: clean bedroom, unload dishwasher, get groceries—penance for still living at home at age eighteen.

So, naturally, as good sons do, when Nathan's high school buddy, Sal, called him to play golf, he declined the tempting offer.

"I can't. I've got chores."

"Mama's boy. You're kidding me, right? Have you seen how blue the sky is today?"

It did not take Sal much longer to convince Nathan that chores could wait. The sun was shining, the sky was blue, and when else in his life would he be so free to just pick up and play golf with his best amigo?

Sal swung by the house a few minutes later. Nathan grabbed his pager out of the seat of his Ford pickup (red, in keeping with the family's preferred automobile color). He slung his bag of clubs into the trunk of Sal's gold Nissan and headed to a public course a few miles away. The weather was close to perfect for a day on the links if not for the humidity. Both boys' shirts were soaked with sweat by the third tee.

As they rounded the turn for the twelfth hole, the boys thought they heard a distant siren.

"Is that a fire truck running down the road?" Sal asked.

The long, winding howl echoed again.

Nathan recognized the difference.

"They're hitting the horn for bad weather. What the heck? The sky is blue."

The friends looked around for a moment, shrugged their shoulders, and continued to play.

As they approached the cup at thirteen, a man in a golf cart headed straight for them.

"You boys not hear the siren?"

"What's going on?" Nathan asked.

"Tornado warning. You guys need to get inside now."

"There's not a cloud in the sky," Nathan argued under his breath, not wanting to be disrespectful of the marshal.

"Talk about a good walk spoiled," Sal whispered back. Begrudgingly, the young men did as they were told.

Back in Sal's car, the sky began to darken overhead.

"Your house or mine?" Nathan asked. They chose Sal's.

Watching the weather coverage on the TV at Sal's

cleared up the situation. Multiple tornadoes were twisting across the state, for real this time. Nathan picked up the house phone and called his mom. Carolyn was relieved to hear from her son, and agreed he should stay at Sal's house. Just like when he was a little kid—if you get lost, stay where you are. But Nathan looked around the room. Sal came from a tight-knit Hispanic family of about a dozen or so people, with one tiny closet in the front hallway. He and Sal talked it over, and decided they had time to drive three miles to their old high school, the city's main shelter.

Never in his life had Nathan gone to a public shelter. It seemed pretty extreme to him. But on the ride there he saw cars parked all over the streets, their drivers taking shelter in nearby businesses—even under their trucks. Everyone seemed to take this one seriously. He saw the storm brewing just to his south—its blackness spilling like ink across the sky.

The school was a zoo. Muffled announcements blared over the loudspeakers, competing with the televisions on full volume and family members and friends yelling to each other. Sal and Nathan inched their way around, trying to find some breathing room. The locker rooms were full, the gym was full, the hallway was full. The longer they searched for space, the tighter it got. Shoulder to shoulder, Nathan and Sal shrugged their shoulders and decided to stay put in the hallway outside the gym. Nathan noticed glass doors all around them.

If this thing hits, we're as good as dead in here.

A few police officers and firemen stood on chairs

above the crowd, shouting instructions and updates, trying to keep order. People moved noisily in their small spaces. Fathers and mothers held their children close; young girls huddled together. Nathan kept his arms crossed and stood on his tiptoes, trying to get a better view outside.

A nearby firefighter yelled out, "Settle down. Find your family. Stay with your family now. If you don't have family, make a friend. It's going to be here any minute."

Nathan thought about his mother and wished he were home. Through the west glass doors they all watched the darkness descend outside; then the school lost power inside. At first there were shrieks of surprise and concern. But the crowd fell quiet in the dark; only the sound of hail pounded the gym's metal roof. They knew the freight train—a sound claimed by every tornado survivor—could scream by at any moment. Just down the road, Nathan thought he saw debris swirling menacingly. The gym was hot with fear. Suddenly, darkness receded. The tornado's funnel shifted south, away from the school. In less than an hour, it was over.

"Are we in the clear?" Sal whispered to Nathan.

"Let's get the heck out of here," Nathan replied, as he edged his way toward the doors.

Before they left, they heard announcements about where the tornado had hit. But in their rush to leave, they misunderstood them. By the boys' accounting Nathan's house was fine but Sal's neighborhood might have been hit.

When they arrived at Sal's, his house was intact, but it was splattered with thick mud as if the churning of the earth happened close by. Nathan and Sal got out of the car to marvel at the sight. Nathan walked to Sal's backyard, from which normally he could see the Del Aire addition. But it was not there. Instead, he had a direct line of sight to Tinker Air Force Base.

I'm seeing things.

Nathan grabbed Sal's shoulders and turned him around.

"Oh my God," Sal said.

The boys jumped back in the car and raced up Sooner Road, the street between the base and home. As they neared the turnoff into Nathan's mom's subdivision, Nathan saw a crowd of people, some lying on the ground, some kneeling, and some wandering aimlessly.

He yelled to Sal, "Pull over! Pull over!"

The Nissan was still rolling when Nathan jumped out. Sal drove up on the curb, parked, and left the engine idling. He walked over to close Nathan's door and watched his friend sprint toward an unimaginable scene. Nathan's neighborhood was flattened.

Up ahead, a group of women and men, some in uniform, were carrying a board with a woman on top. She was clearly pregnant and very possibly dead. What looked like a large quilt covered most of her body. The rescuers were out of breath, having transported their patient two long blocks. Nathan was too far away to know if it was Christi.

Steve ran up to the only ambulance in sight.

"My daughter. My daughter-in-law is pregnant—she needs to get to the hospital now."

"I'm going to tell you right now," the medic answered, "There are no more ambulances in the whole city." He shut the back doors and made his way toward the front cab.

Steve caught his arm.

"Don't tell me there are no more ambulances in this state."

"There are no more. Not a one left in the city."

"How is that possible?" Steve yelled as the medic hopped in his truck. "They can't lay here and die!"

"Get them to the hospital, man, any way you can."

Steve muttered under his breath.

"This is just great. I've got twelve here close to death and you guys are taking off. Wonderful."

A woman in a blue t-shirt spoke up.

"I have a pickup."

Steve looked at her for a moment and almost hugged her.

"That's just brilliant! Yes! I need a caravan! Anyone with a pickup! Get me fourteen trucks lined up right here. We're running hot!"

"Hospital or Tinker?" the lady with the pickup asked.

"Whatever," Roman said, crouched down next to Christi. "Just get us there."

Steve asked, "What do you want me to do with the tires?"

The woman's flatbed was full of four brand new tires.

"Just throw them out!" she yelled from the driver's seat, thinking she would have a chance to retrieve them later. "Put her in!"

Still on her plywood gurney, now wrapped snugly in the blood-stained handmade quilt, Christi was placed in the back of the truck. Roman hopped in and sat down next to his wife.

Steve ran up to the driver's side window.

"Put on your emergency flashers, don't lay off of the horn, and don't stop until you get there."

Nathan got there a second behind, and pointed at the truck in the distance.

"Is that Sissy? Is that Christi?"

"Yeah, that's your sister," Steve said. "But you need to be worried about your mom."

"Is she alive? Is my mom still alive?"

"She's back there."

Steve gestured in a westerly direction over his shoulder and Nathan started running. He gulped the air, practically tasting the pungent mercaptan, the additive mixed with odorless natural gas so you *can* smell it. Nathan's mind spun, his hands poured sweat, and tunnel vision kept him from seeing a man blocking his path.

"You can't go in there. They're not letting anyone in."

He had not noticed it until now, but as far as he could see, yellow tape stretched from north to south, just as you would expect at a massive crime scene.

"My house is in there! My mom is in there!"

Nathan ducked under the tape and kept running. The man yelled after him, but did not physically try to stop him.

"Nathan! Nathan!"

Nathan stopped, spun around, and refocused. His friend, Andy, jogged up to him. He stared at Nathan as if he were looking at a ghost.

"Nathan, you're okay? You're not beat up? Not a scratch?"

"I wasn't here. I was at the high school. Have you seen my mom?"

"Your mom? No. Your truck? It's smashed flat, man. Like someone beat it with a baseball bat, then crushed the cab. Doors popped off. Whole thing looks like a flatbed. Cables wrapped tight around it. I thought you were in it."

"Are *you* okay?" Nathan asked.

"Our hot water tank tore through the roof. A big freaking hole in the roof where it got sucked out. But anybody down that way is in bad shape. It's all scrap lumber and sheet metal. Anyone that survives is a miracle."

Andy pointed southwest, where Nathan supposed his house used to be. It looked like a giant machete had shredded everything in its path. The scene that met him was daunting. Dead dogs and cats. Shoes that might still have body parts inside them. A lady's slipper pierced a tire. A two-by-four driven through a driver's side head rest. The paint stripped off one side of a fire hydrant. Nathan looked down and saw holes in the ground where hail had driven down so hard.

Nathan ran, breathing quickly, dodging debris scattered everywhere, uncertain if he was in the right place. He got turned around and, if he had continued, he would have ended up back on Sooner Road and barred from his neighborhood. He stopped and whipped his head in every direction, trying to recognize something: a house, a street, a car. Nothing. His heartbeat pulsed in his ears.

He ran for one more block and suddenly noticed his shoes and socks were soaked with water. That's when he found the creek. The tiny creek trickled in the backyards of the neighbors across the street; as a child, it was his favorite spot for adventure. He sprinted along its edge, following it until the old bridge markings where he knew to exit. Then he looked up.

Only the foundation remained. Nearby, in the pale blue light of evening, he made out a hot water tank—*that could be anybody's*—an axe—*that might be mine*—and a red jeep, battered, muddied, and molded around a tree. *That's my sister's.*

The adrenaline rushed faster now, as Nathan felt closer to finding his mom. Never before had he been able to see Tinker from his house. Now he realized how close the base had always been. Without two rows of houses in the way, he might be able to hit it with a football. He began to walk directly toward it, imagining the path his mother might have taken before him if she had survived.

He passed so many people who were injured. A

child laying under a blanket being tended to by a woman he did not know. A middle-aged man searching frantically for his wife despite what would turn out to be his own broken neck. Two elderly women peeking their heads out from a cavern under their home as if they had a basement, asking if it were safe to come out; above them, an avalanche of debris.

Within a few yards, he spotted another group of men carrying a small, deathly pale woman whose head was covered. She was lying motionless on a door. He almost kept going, as he did not recognize the victim, but he could not help but wonder, *Is that lady dead?* As Nathan moved closer, he saw the blood running down her leg and her face. It looked fluorescent red next to her bluish-white skin. The t-shirt wrapped around her head had slipped off, and Nathan thought he saw her skull. Nathan felt sick to his stomach.

Now I know I'm seeing things.

Suddenly, Nathan's body froze. He swallowed hard, then opened his mouth and let out that terrified scream, the one that pulled Carolyn back to life.

"Mom? Mom!"

Two Hospitals

> Consider it pure joy, my brothers, whenever you face trials of many kinds, because you know that the testing of your faith develops perseverance.
> James 1:2–3 (NIV)

"Oh my God! Mom!!"

"Calm down, Nathan. Calm down." Mydonna tried to put her arm around Nathan, but he spun out from her grasp.

"My mom! My sis! My baby niece! Nothing is left!"

Mydonna tried again to hush Nathan.

"Your mom is alive. So is Sis. Freaking out is not going to help them. Sis left on a truck to the hospital. Now you go to Carolyn. Talk to her. But don't mention her head, okay?"

In her dream, Carolyn heard Nathan's voice calling out to her. He wasn't lost, but he was scared, terrified. She wanted to comfort him, but she could not move.

"Mom, it's Nathan. Can you hear me?"

His words were too clear to be imagined. Slowly, Carolyn drifted back to the surface and raised her eyelids. Nathan was indeed standing over her. He was still wearing his golf cap, and his handsome teenaged face contorted with a concern too deep for his years. A wave of sadness poured over her and threatened to drown her. She didn't want him to see her as she was.

"Nay-nay." Carolyn mouthed the words. Tears filled up Nathan's eyes as he grabbed her hand and walked alongside her.

"We're going to get you help, Mom."

I know, baby, I know.

Carolyn hoped her eyes showed appreciation to her son before she closed them again. Although she wished he had not seen her this way, she was relieved to know he was okay. Carolyn had always said that her kids were the air that she breathed. She didn't know how she could be closer to either one of them. They were a family that easily expressed their love with words, but their unspoken bond held them together now.

The men gently laid Carolyn down in the grass bordering the main road across from the Tinker gate, which had been set up for triage. The air was thick with the near-deafening sounds of rumbling diesel engines on fire trucks, thumping helicopters overhead, and periodic sirens or bull-horn announcements.

"If you need shelter, please move to the gym on base. Triage, stay put. Everyone else, move to the gym on base."

People were everywhere; the rescuers running to and fro with basic medical equipment, the survivors walking dazed, their bodies wrapped in blankets. It looked like the end of an outdoor show, when hundreds of people take their time walking back to their cars; except here, no one had a clear direction about where to go, and every face showed a measure of concern. Tinker personnel seemed to be in charge as they tried to bring order to the chaos, but they had to rely on good Samaritans who were well-meaning but not always the best informed. The street was jammed with vehicles as drivers tried to find their neighborhoods and their loved ones. As the injured were loaded into backs of pickups and SUVs, Nathan heard questions shouted out loud again and again:

"Who's driving this one?"

"Do you know where to go?"

"Can I get an ambulance?"

That last question was Nathan's, crying out to anyone who would listen.

The line of headlights that extended north and south for miles lit up the sky. People were driving to find their loved ones, their friends, their neighbors, their homes—but they also drove to offer help to strangers who had lost everything.

"Nate," Carolyn whispered. "Not DCH. Baptist. I want Baptist."

"Mom, don't you worry about that. I'll take care of it."

Del City Hospital was the place where Carolyn's father had gone in with a heart condition and never came out. For her, going there was tantamount to going to the funeral home. But Integris Baptist Hospital was in Oklahoma City on the northwest side of town, and where her internist, Dr. Mary Ann Bauman, practiced. Nathan was doubtful they would have the luxury of getting to choose where his mother would go.

From the triage area, Nathan surveyed the destruction on base. The softball field was ripped up, a row of barracks had collapsed, and a stable lay in rubble. Nathan thought he saw a few dead horses scattered around the old barn.

A female officer rushed over, quickly outfitting Carolyn with oxygen, re-dressing her hip wound, and inspecting her head. Carolyn groaned faintly.

"Think she's priority enough to get an ambulance?" Nathan asked.

"Maybe," the officer said.

She instructed Nathan to kneel down on the other side of his mother, hold the oxygen mask over her nose and mouth with one hand, and apply pressure to the bandage on her hip.

The officer reached into her box of supplies and pulled out some gauze. She was going to wrap Carolyn's head. Nathan looked away, not quite able to put out of his mind what he had seen underneath the shirt.

He busied his mind looking around for an ambulance, but below the sea of wandering survivors and rushing rescuers, he realized that his mother had been placed along an orderly and discouraging line of flesh. *Corpses, body parts, and then Mom.* Airmen, firefighters, and medics moved among them, directing traffic, recruiting drivers, corralling crowds, and supplying oxygen, bandages, blankets, and body bags.

Nathan overheard two men in uniform talking about their supplies.

"How many bags did you order?"

"Three hundred."

"You're going need a freezer the size of Texas."

They were clearly well-trained for the trauma of war.

Nathan could not escape the horror around him, the terror inside of him, but he fought back against the frightening prospect that his mother may not live to see a hospital bed. Knowing her head was freshly bandaged, he looked back at her face. He had never watched his mother sleep before. While she appeared peaceful, he feared that the oxygen mask was doing most of the breathing for her. Then he noticed that the blood pooling on the door—her gurney—was fresh. In it, he saw the reflection of blinking lights.

Turning back around, the flashes of blue and red made Nathan's heart race. He wanted to scoop up his mother and jump into the back of the ambulance, but he feared the mask would slip or the compress on her leg would fall off. He worried about moving her at all. The ambulance rolled to a group of dead bodies and stopped.

Oh no. No, no, no. Please come for my mom. Please come for her.

The female officer ran up to the driver and pointed to the end of the line. Nathan did not have a free hand to wave them over, but he did not need one. As it neared, the growl of the ambulance's engine sounded more like a purr. Two medics jumped out. The driver was tall and lean; a shorter stocky one popped opened the back doors.

The tall one talked to Nathan while he glanced over Carolyn.

"I hear she's got head trauma. Got room for one more. St. Anthony okay?"

Nathan nodded.

"Anything but DCH." He pointed to Carolyn, who had slipped out of consciousness. "She thinks it's a deathtrap. She did mention Baptist."

The medic shook his head.

"Not taking head injuries."

"Saints it is," Nathan said.

Nathan stepped back as the men loaded Carolyn and her oxygen onto a gurney. As they pushed her into the back of the ambulance, Nathan noticed what a tight fit it was going to be. There were already two patients inside, morphine drips in place.

The shorter medic looked up at Nathan as he closed the doors.

"You can't ride in here. We're the last ambulance out, so we've got to stack them."

"That's my mom. I'm not leaving her."

Nathan felt a huge lump in his throat.

"I'll strap myself to the hood if I have to."

"I understand you're worried, man," the medic said. "But you can take your vehicle and meet us at the hospital."

"Dude, my truck's about a foot tall and wrapped up in power lines."

By this time the driver was anxious to get moving. He rolled down his window and stuck out his head.

"Just get in up here!"

The driver agreed to buck protocol and let Nathan take the front passenger seat. The short medic shrugged and hopped in back. He sandwiched himself into the only space left among the three patients, knowing full well he would not be in a position to treat them. The ambulance pulled out into traffic outside the gate at Tinker, ran the siren, and headed north on the slowest ride Nathan had ever taken.

On a normal evening with moderate traffic, the 9.44-mile drive to St. Anthony Hospital in downtown Oklahoma City would've taken less than fifteen minutes.

But traffic was unlike anything any of them had seen before. Drivers swerved around power lines; the traffic lights were out; yellow lines were irrelevant. Even with the siren sounding, and the tall medic pressing on the horn and screaming out his open window, "Get out of the way!" the other drivers in the road could not budge, even if they had wanted to. Likely, they did not want to, because nearly everyone behind the wheel had a personal emergency: children they couldn't find, a wife who called for help, or a home that no longer existed.

Much of the gauze wrapped around Carolyn's head was soaked in fresh blood.

The short medic was closest to Carolyn, so he pushed an IV into her arm. The prick of the needle brought her back to semi-consciousness long enough to hear the ruckus: the siren, the honking, and the chatter. She sensed that the ambulance was parked.

The medic sat back down in an awkward pose with a sigh. He and the driver struck up a conversation through the interior window, complaining about the movie they had been about to see when this tornado episode seriously inconvenienced them.

Peace. Peace and quiet, Carolyn thought.

Nathan looked at the medics impatiently, then out the front windshield. Up ahead, he could see that traffic was moving slowly—but it was moving—on the shoulder of the interstate.

"I'm getting out," he announced.

His sudden exit quieted the medics as they watched Nathan run out into the intersection, bang on the windows of cars, and begin to direct traffic. Within minutes, he had parted the way. He jumped back in the front seat of the ambulance. The drive on the interstate was quicker and not quite as maddening. Drivers darted in and out of the shoulder, many of them ignoring the ambulance. The trip took forty minutes.

In the driveway of the hospital, the medics pulled Carolyn's gurney out first. They rushed her past the open doors of the ER. Nathan ran in behind her.

"That's as far as you go." A nurse held out her arm, stopping Nathan from following his mom. "You need to get her registered."

Nathan watched his mother disappear behind the swinging doors. Then the words "*Patient Registration*" caught his eye, and he stood amazed at the long line of people behind it. For the last hour, Nathan had felt as though nothing mattered more than getting *his* mother to the hospital—saving *her* life. Now he realized how many people were exactly like him. The ER was flooded with them.

A hospital chaplain worked his way down the line and gently touched Nathan's elbow.

"Who are you here for, son?"

"My mother."

"Hurt in the tornado?"

Nathan nodded.

"After you're finished here, we have an area for families up on the third floor. There are refreshments. A quiet place to rest. Is there anything I can do for you?"

"My sister, Christi Duren. She's pregnant. She was with my mom. I think she was loaded into someone's pickup. Is she here?"

The chaplain walked behind the registration desk and picked up a clipboard thick with paper. It was a roster. He shook his head as he scanned it. He disappeared into a back room and returned nearly half an hour later. Nathan was still waiting in the registration line.

"I found your sister. She's in stable condition."

"Where is she?"

"DCH."

Nathan's face lost all its color.

Code Black

No testing has overtaken you that is not common to everyone. God is faithful, and he will not let you be tested beyond your strength, but with the testing, he will also provide the way out so that you may be able to endure it.

1 Corinthians 10:13 (NRSV)

Sometime after nine o'clock, Sarah Leona and Russell pulled up as close as they could to the Del Aire neighborhood. The thirty-minute drive had taken nearly two hours. They had never traveled so slowly in all their lives. Power lines blocked the usual route, forcing them to drive miles out of the way. Traffic jammed up every highway, side-street, and shoulder. But instead of reacting impatiently with each other as people typically do in rush hour traffic, nearly everyone drove with their windows down, talking about where they were going, whom they were looking for, and which areas were rumored to have been hit hardest. They accepted the fact that this was a widespread disaster over which they had little to no control. They simply inched along from their house to where Carolyn's used to be. Russell drove over the curb and turned on his hazard lights.

"I could have walked here faster," Sarah Leona said to him. Of course it was not true, but Sarah Leona had a comment for just about any situation.

Limping along in the darkness with tentative steps, Sarah Leona squinted to see better. Instead of light from front porches and streetlamps, a half-moon illuminated the ground below. The streets were still wet, but now the night sky was cloudless—one of few silver linings of a storm's aftermath. The flutter of flashlights gave Sarah Leona glimpses of the piles of debris, the bare trees, and the total devastation. She could not see the faces of people still searching for survivors; their silhouettes and flashlights appeared and disappeared behind shapes foreign to anything Sarah Leona had ever imagined. The aura of the place reminded her of a graveyard and gave her goose bumps. She stopped walking and turned to Russell.

"Where are we, Pappy?"

"I'm not sure," Russell said, holding on to his wife's arm. With her sixty-three-year-old sore knees, which felt weaker with each step, he didn't want her to fall. And with her hard hearing, he needed to be close enough for her to read his lips.

"I've got the car in sight. Let's not wander too far," he said.

Sarah Leona stopped hobbling along.

"Let's just get out of here. We should've gone straight to DCH."

As they felt their way through the night back to

their car, Sarah Leona spotted some boys about her grandson's age.

"Do you know Nathan Stager?" she asked.

"Yeah, but we can't find him. Found his truck, but not him."

Another wave of fear rushed over Sarah Leona, numbing the pain in her kneecaps, and she picked up the pace back to the car.

Then Russell heard a woman call out Sarah Leona's name. It was Mydonna, her long hair blowing in the breeze and her face and body covered in dirt and blood.

"Oh thank God!" Sarah Leona said. "What a mess you are! Have you seen Christi or Carolyn?"

"They took them—to DCH, I think," Mydonna answered.

"Do you need a ride? Let's go. I don't know why we didn't think to go there first."

Sarah Leona knew why. When her first husband went in complaining of chest pains at age forty-seven and never came out alive, she made a point of avoiding that particular hospital. She did not like to look at it. If she had to drive within a few blocks of it to get somewhere else, she would turn her head or close an eye, treating the building like she would road kill. Sarah Leona did not look at road kill.

Mydonna was right. DCH was only a few miles away, the most likely place to take two people who had been in the tornado's bull's-eye—two people and one unborn baby she prayed had survived, even though their home had not.

Mydonna left her car behind—wherever it was—and rode with Sarah Leona and Russell. Traffic had not improved, so they knew what to expect. But because the cell phone towers were either down or tied up, Sarah Leona had no way of knowing that as they inched down Sooner Road, her youngest daughter, Patty, was thirty minutes ahead of her.

Aunt Patty and Uncle Charlie could see DCH, but the sea of red brake lights in front of them and the line of white headlights in the other lane appeared insurmountable.

"I'm going crazy," Patty told Charlie. They only lived about ten miles from the hospital. A ride that should take them no more than fifteen minutes had lasted an hour already, and the hospital was not yet in sight.

"Why don't you pray some more?" Charlie asked.

"Honey, I've been praying like I've never prayed before. Prayed all day. Heavy-duty prayer. Tears and all. Had no idea why. Now I know. Now I really know."

As they rolled past various cars and trucks, Patty would crane her neck to see who was in them. In front of them at a stop sign, Patty spotted a pickup truck with someone sitting in the back holding up what might be an IV bag in the headlights. Patty could not sit still any longer. She jumped out of the passenger seat and ran to the back of the truck to see if it were Christi or Carolyn. But the patient lying in the flatbed was a man.

"Sorry," she said to the person tending to the patient. "Trying to find my sister and niece."

He nodded as if to say, "I know you are."

Patty looked ahead and decided she was close enough to the hospital to run to it. She waved at her husband, pointed at the distant lights of the building, and weaved her way on foot in between the traffic. Charlie watched her go, knowing he would catch up sooner or later. He was not surprised to see his wife make such a bold move. Patty was the go-getter of the two of them; she had the curiosity, the quick tongue. Charlie was the deliberate one; he had gentleness, the calm. He was the cool water to her hot coals. He would tell everyone, somewhat romantically, that they had been married forever. She would say, frankly, "We're all looking for father figures." Even their looks contrasted with each other's: she with the rosy cheeks and a shock of blonde hair dyed to maintain the golden hue of her childhood; he with the thick black moustache and sympathetic eyes. He could sit at that stop sign for another ten minutes. She could not.

At DCH, Patty ran in through the automatic doors, pushing them faster than they should turn. She shoved her way through the waiting area outside the ER and barged through the swinging doors of the restricted area. She ran straight past the nurses' desk like she knew just what she was doing and where she was going even though she had never been to the newly-renovated ER, much less inside the hospital since Daddy died. No one was going to stop her. She cranked her head into every room, not watching where she was going. She bumped into patients and nurses, stepping over people sitting and lying on the floor.

She circled around again, checking each room twice, when someone grabbed her arm.

"Haven't found the girls?" Charlie asked.

"Not yet," Patty said.

"They may not be here." Charlie held her arm tighter. "Honey, you know they are probably dead."

"You're crazy. I know they're alive. I just know it."

Patty started her search again, weaving in and out of people, when she bumped into Roman.

"Roman! Are they okay? Please tell me they're okay?"

"Christi's right in here."

Patty looked at him incredulously. She had stuck her head in this particular room at least two times.

"No!" Patty said in disbelief. She whispered, "Christi?"

Patty did not recognize the beautiful, curly blond-haired, blue-eyed girl who some people mistook for her own daughter.

The tangled mess that was Christi's hair had fooled her. The mud and blood in her hair had dried black. All kinds of debris were caught in it, like a thousand insects in a spider's web. Various pieces of metal were stuck in her body. She was lying on her side; the gash on the back of her right leg was deep purple and blood red.

Half a dozen doctors surrounded Christi, focused on her pregnant belly, a fetal monitor, and an ultrasound machine. Patty could not get close. She turned around to Charlie and whispered.

"At least she's alive."

"I'll go look for Carolyn," he said.

"She's here too somewhere," Roman said.

Just before midnight, Sarah Leona, Russell, and Mydonna pulled into the parking lot at DCH. The three said little to each other during the two-hour-long trip except for the moment Sarah Leona stopped talking in tongues.

(When asked about her ability to speak in tongues, Sarah Leona simply called it the "Pentecostal holiness in me." She would always say, "It is so awesome. Got to be the Holy Spirit working through you. Just takes over. There is Truth in this. Truly, I tell you, there is Truth in this.")

Raised Baptist, Mydonna had heard some enthusiastic sermons, but she had never heard anyone actually speak this way before in the flesh. Sure, she had read about it and seen it on TV. She thought it was strange and even a little frightening. But at this moment, she felt oddly comforted by it. She begged Sarah Leona to keep going.

"Don't stop. Please, don't stop."

Sarah Leona did not stop again until they reached the hospital. Cars were parked everywhere in every direction—layers upon layers of them, bumper to bumper—with no thought about how any of them would go home.

"We'll never get out of here," Mydonna said.

"No one gets out of DCH, Mydonna," Sarah Leona said darkly. "No one."

They rushed into the waiting room and immediately spotted Charlie.

"Where's Christi? Where's Carolyn?" Sarah Leona asked.

"They're in back. Patty's back there talking with Sissy," Charlie answered.

"Praise Jesus!" Sarah Leona yelled out as she and Mydonna squeezed hands. "I've been feeling so guilty, so guilty. You know I told Christi to go to her mama's house. I need to see them. I really need to see them."

For the first time since she arrived in the ER, Patty took a look around the circular hallway without being in a total frenzy. She was horrified at the chaos. This place was supposed to be their best hope for help. Instead, it was a jungle of flesh, blood, confusion, and torment. Bodies were strewn across the floor. The dead and dying lying among them. The family of a neighbor of Carolyn's was there, writhing and screaming, no one there to comfort them. She heard a nurse scream on the phone, "We're down to our last two units! Where is the blood?"

The doctors quickly filed out of Christi's room. They assumed the woman standing guard at the door was Christi's mother, and Patty assumed the role without flinching.

Patty tugged at one of the doctors' arms.

"Excuse me. How is she? How's the baby?"

"Baby's got a heartbeat. Mom's placenta appears

intact. It's astounding that it wasn't knocked loose," he said.

"How do you know it wasn't?" Patty asked.

"She would've bled to death," he said, "on the spot." And then he was gone.

Christi was still lying on the hard door that was used to carry her out. The patchwork quilt that someone had stitched so lovingly had been cut off of Christi's body. Patty could not believe that the doctors had not tended to Christi's right leg, which was clearly sliced open, with the skin folded back and just hanging there. Patty saw something long, shiny, and white inside. *A tendon? A bone? If they missed that, we're in big trouble.* Patty winced at the open wound and thought she might vomit.

Christi looked up at Patty, tears streaming down her face.

"My baby. Is my baby okay?"

"I don't know yet, sweetie. Those doctors are doing everything they can."

"Where's Mom?"

"Here somewhere. You don't worry about her."

Patty touched Christi's forehead. Only her face and her belly were spared from the lashing. Patty stared dumbfounded at the countless shards of glass and chunks of wood embedded in Christi's long matted hair and skin, as if she had been sprayed by bursting shrapnel.

"Everything hurts so bad," Christi said. "I want my baby to be okay."

"I know, baby."

There was nothing Patty could do for Christi's terrible pain—the pain in her body and the pain in her heart.

"Patty?"

Patty knew the voice without turning around.

"Where's Christi?" asked Sarah Leona as she stepped into the room.

"She's right here, Mother."

Sarah Leona gave Patty a perplexed look, and then stared at the woman on the bed. She covered her gaping mouth with her hands. Her knees buckled, and Russell held her steady. Slowly they approached Christi's bedside.

"Bless your bones, sweet baby doll. Bless you, honey. I'm so happy to see you."

Christi whimpered and gave her granny a sad smile.

"Mother," Patty said. "Let's let her rest."

After a little while, Sarah Leona and Russell rejoined Charlie in the waiting area. Mydonna was not with them.

"Where did she go?" Sarah Leona asked.

Charlie shrugged.

"And where is Carolyn?"

Charlie shook his head.

"And Roman?"

Charlie gave her the only information he had.

"A nurse was in here a minute ago. She said there were people to help us in the cafeteria. Want to go there?"

They looked around, but every chair was taken. Even the floor was packed with people sitting and waiting, talking on cell phones, or holding each other. The family agreed to head to the cafeteria. Shortly after they gathered around a small round table a priest joined them in prayer.

Moments later, Mydonna came running over to their table.

"Carolyn's not here! She's not here. They say she's at St. Anthony."

"What?!" screamed Sarah Leona. She whipped her head around to face Charlie with fire in her eyes.

"You told me she was here! You told me she was okay! Why would you lie to me?"

Charlie put his hand over his heart, partly out of contrition, partly to protect it from eternal damnation.

"I'm sorry, Sarah Leona. That's what Roman said. I didn't know."

"Well, you shouldn't've said somethin' if you didn't know nothin'. We have to get over there," Sarah Leona said, still scowling at Charlie. "You drive."

"Traffic's going to be..." Charlie trailed off as he thought better of what he was saying to his mother-in-law. In his fifteen years of marriage to her youngest daughter, he had never seen her so angry.

Mydonna chose to stay behind with Roman and Patty, wanting to be there for Christi when she came out of surgery. Sarah Leona stomped out ahead of Charlie. As they walked back through the ER waiting room, all but Sarah Leona heard an announcement over the loudspeaker:

"Code Black clear. Code Black clear."

It was two o'clock in the morning.

Code Gray

Rejoice always; pray without ceasing; in everything give thanks; for this is the will of God for you in Christ Jesus.

1 Thessalonians 5:16–18 (NASB)

"Carolyn, would you like a prayer?"

Carolyn opened her eyes, and a priest with silver hair and a kind face was seated by her gurney. Carolyn thought for a long time about his request, waiting for the mist in her mind to clear. She believed in praying without ceasing; she had practiced it most of her life, and never more than in the last few hours. The priest was clearly well-meaning, but he looked ready to read the last rites. She was not ready to hear them.

"Hold on, Father," she answered.

"Are you in terrible pain?" he asked, concerned.

"Sure. Oh sure. But I'm not going to die. Someone else needs you more than I do right now." She added good-naturedly, "Plus, I'm not Catholic."

At this he laughed and gently tapped her shoulder.

"Our Heavenly Father doesn't discriminate, and neither do I," he said. "May God be with you."

Carolyn was grateful that he left. But then she wondered.

If I were going to die, he would have stayed, right?

She did not want to kid herself that she was scot-free, but she refused to believe she needed the Lord's Prayer one last time. Another kind of prayer rang in her inner ear.

"We give him praise ... we give him praise ... "

The choir had belted the hymn from the organ loft. Carolyn had sung along with vigor just Sunday and hummed the tune for the rest of the evening, and now it was back, ringing in her head.

Her head.

She still had no idea what had happened to it.

Dr. Thomas Janssen was not about to be the first to tell her.

He had been smacking golf balls at the driving range when he heard the sirens. The tornado stayed several miles to his south, but the smell of natural gas after it tore through was so potent that it unnerved him.

Someone could blow this place up with one match, he thought.

His pager buzzed at 7:30 p.m.; having done orthopedic surgery for two decades, he was used to that. But he wasn't used to the message on the pager.

911 to ER

It would normally read "*Code Gray*," the term the hospital used when inclement weather—stormy gray skies—caused the emergency. The only other time he had seen the 911 page was four years ago on the morning of the Oklahoma City bombing. The chaotic experience of that catastrophe sensitized him for this one. This time, he felt prepared.

It couldn't possibly be worse.

Dr. Janssen ran into the emergency room of St. Anthony Hospital within ten minutes of the page. A sea of doctors gathered around a roster forty patients long. They divvied up the list according to the physicians' specialties and the patients' needs, keeping in mind that new waves of critically-injured patients could follow. Dr. Janssen knew which one was his.

Room 3, Head & Hip

"I'm ortho—I'll take that one," he said.

Dr. Janssen walked through the door of room three, unaware that the woman lying there would have a profound effect not only on him but also on someone who never got personally involved with his patients—his wife.

Carolyn was resting on her back on a gurney. Even though he knew instinctively that her injured hip would be his focus, his eyes were drawn to her head, which had been bandaged, probably by a medic he guessed. Within the bandages was a lady with a very broad smile. Carolyn was wide awake. There was a brightness in her demeanor that caught Dr. Janssen off-guard. Carolyn could not explain it either. Perhaps it was because she felt comforted to be getting care or simply relieved to be alive.

"Good evening, I'm Dr. Janssen. I see you've hurt your hip. Mind if I take a look?"

"Sure. No problem. I'm really just fine. Are you alright?"

"Well, yes I am. But I wasn't just hit by a tornado. If you weren't wrapped up in a pound of gauze, I might wonder whether you weren't either."

"This headdress is the latest fashion statement in tornado wear." Carolyn giggled, mostly out of self-consciousness.

She was not used to talking to doctors, especially an attractive gentleman of her same age with a slim, athletic build like Dr. Janssen's, or anyone for that matter, looking the way she did. Her hair was disheveled, her lips were unpainted, and her bra and underwear nowhere to be found.

Dr. Janssen laughed out loud while he inspected Carolyn's leg. A deep gash sliced the top of her hip, and he suspected a break. He could have easily stuck his fingers in through the wound to feel the broken bone as he did on cadavers in medical school, but he would order x-rays instead. Carolyn appeared fully capable of waiting for Dr. Janssen to make up his mind about whether she would need surgery. He asked her a few questions about whether she remembered twisting her leg or whether something struck it. She did not recall, although she answered him as lucidly as if she were talking about a toothache.

Wow! This is unusual, Dr Janssen thought. *Must be shock.*

But she did not look like a woman in shock. In Dr.

Janssen's experience, most emergency room patients were dazed, especially after being injured catastrophically. They would moan or whimper, some of them might cry, but rarely did they engage the physician—much less crack jokes.

"Speaking of that headdress, why don't we take a peek?"

"Go for it. Everyone's been fussing over it all night."

Dr. Janssen paused for a moment, looked into Carolyn's eyes, and then scanned the rest of her body. He wanted to make sure he wasn't missing something. The bandage wrapped around Carolyn's head was blood-soaked near the front.

"Where were you when it hit?" Carolyn asked, perfectly willing to carry on a conversation while Dr. Janssen leaned in toward her head.

He expected a deep cut, just like the many deep gashes from glass and metal he saw after the bombing. Slowly, carefully, he lifted her bandage.

"Uh, just north ... the driving range ... " Dr. Janssen's voice trailed off.

He hoped Carolyn was not looking at him, because he felt sure he could not hide the fact that his eyes almost popped out of their sockets.

"You play golf?" Carolyn asked innocently. "So does my son. Today his game was cut short, though. Sorry if yours was too."

Oh my God. She has no idea.

He could not answer her. As clear as day, Dr. Janssen saw bone. Sure, an orthopedic surgeon sees a lot of bone, but not a fully exposed skull, with a patient chatting away as if she had a paper cut. A large section of scalp had been taken clean off as if a surgeon had done it with a knife.

Now Dr. Janssen was truly stunned. After having lost part of her scalp or having a blunt head injury or a combination of the two, Carolyn should have been delusional. To see someone so conversant seemed to Dr. Janssen to be almost supernatural.

Another doctor walked into Carolyn's room and introduced himself as Dr. Paramjit Bajaj, but Carolyn could not have repeated his first name if asked. He stood about a head shorter than Dr. Janssen, and he was a few years his senior. Between his exotic name and his nicely trimmed white beard against his dark skin, Carolyn determined that he was from India—the less common kind of Indian you usually meet in Oklahoma. Her friends in the Clematis Club, after a glass or two of chardonnay, would seek clarification less elegantly. "Feather or dot?"

The doctors exchanged pleasantries and briefly discussed Carolyn's condition. Then Dr. Bajaj finished unwrapping the bandage around Carolyn's head.

Dr. Janssen left the room and returned with more medical staff rolling in portable x-ray machines. Behind them were Don and Sue, the first of Carolyn's family to arrive. Carolyn caught the worried expressions on their faces and gave them a grin. Not wanting to get in the way, they retreated to one free corner in the room. A mass of doctors, nurses, techs, and machines enveloped Carolyn. Don and Sue could no longer see her, but they could hear her recounting the first few minutes of her survival story.

"My daughter and I were in a closet under the hall stairs. Next thing we knew, the house exploded—"

Mid-sentence, Carolyn turned her head and threw up the half of a sandwich she had eaten right before the tornado—bacon, tomato, bread—and a Coke.

"Oh! I'm so sorry," Carolyn cried out. She was mortified. "I'm so sorry. I can't believe I did that."

"I can," Dr. Janssen said. "No need to apologize."

"It's to be expected," Dr. Bajaj said. "Do not worry."

Sue ran over to a sink and wet down a few washcloths. She helped a nurse quickly wipe up the mess. Sue put a clean, cool washcloth on Carolyn's forehead and stepped back again. Carolyn looked up and mouthed, "Thank you," as the doctors held Carolyn steady for the head and body x-rays.

After the machines were pulled back, the medical team packed up and moved out as quickly as they had moved in, likely to go to the next patient, and the next, and the next—forty in all as a result of the tornado. Both doctors stepped out too, leaving Carolyn alone with two people she considered close friends—her ex-husband and his wife. They rushed to her bedside.

"We got here as soon as we could," said Sue.

"Don't worry," Carolyn said reassuringly. She was happy to see them. "You practically beat the doctors. Where's Sissy?"

"We're not sure," said Don. "But we'll find out."

"And Nathan?"

Nathan's father answered.

"He's in the waiting room, poor kid. They won't let him in. It's pretty crowded out there."

"How did you get in?" Carolyn asked.

"Said I was your husband, which is true if you count the *was* part. And this here was your sister, which would be really weird if it were true." That was just like Don, to find a way no matter what.

Sue smiled at Don, then turned to Carolyn.

"What do you need, Carolyn? Can I do anything to make you more comfortable?"

"The washcloth is great. I'm fine. Really. I still can't believe I threw up."

Just then Dr. Bajaj and Dr. Janssen returned with x-rays in hand, still conferring with one another. Carolyn could barely hear them as they whispered.

"Shall I discuss first?" Dr. Bajaj asked out loud. Dr. Janssen nodded.

"We need to operate on your head. We don't have a choice. You have a whole area of skull exposed. This will not heal if I do not fix it."

In his thirty-two years practicing plastic surgery, Dr. Bajaj had only seen one other case similar to Carolyn's. A woman with long hair got it caught in a machine where she worked.

"Did you say skull?" Carolyn made a face of disgust.

"Skull, yes, skull."

"You mean I was scalped? Like how the Indians—I mean, the Native Americans—used to scalp?"

"Precisely."

Dr. Bajaj explained the surgical plan as simply as he could. Carolyn would be given heavy painkillers and potent antibiotics. Nurses would wash her wounds, cut away "traumatized" tissue, and debride the areas. Then Dr. Bajaj would cover the exposed bone with two skin flaps rather than skin grafts. "Because grafts are free pieces of skin with no circulation," he said, "they will not adhere to the bone. Grafts need soft tissue to grow and repair the defect." He planned to lift the back of her scalp and create a skin flap to cover the front of her head. Once he shifted the scalp, he would then take skin grafts from her legs to lay over the soft tissue on the back of her head.

Carolyn listened, trying to imagine how anyone could carve up a head like a puzzle and sew all the pieces back together.

"How do you think it happened?" Carolyn asked.

Dr. Bajaj and Dr. Janssen looked at one another, and shook their heads.

Dr. Janssen spoke first.

"Not anything sharp or anything heavy or you wouldn't have lived through it."

"Even a piece of paper could have become a lethal weapon, Carolyn," Dr. Bajaj said, matter-of-factly.

A piece of paper.

It is one thing to have a paper cut—a tiny slice in your skin, an angry red spot where it happens—and that certainly hurt. But a piece of paper shearing the scalp off a human being? The whole thing seemed too bizarre to be real.

Carolyn decided to let it go for the moment and just feel grateful to be alive.

The surgery would wait until morning. Dr. Bajaj explained that Carolyn was stable enough, the ER would settle down in a few hours, and she would have the full attention of the OR staff. Plus, he wanted her to rest for this surgery because Dr. Janssen was going to operate on her hip at the same time. With this news, Carolyn looked to Dr. Janssen for his assessment while Dr. Bajaj re-wrapped her head.

"I know this is a lot to take in," said Dr. Janssen. "You've got a fractured pelvis. It looks like some kind of blunt injury to the iliac crest, which is the top of your hip. And since I know you'll ask, it looks like a penetrating injury. In other words, something hit your hip like a flying two-by-four, sliced it open, and then cracked through the bone."

"Let's just stick me in a body cast head to toe and I can go home—well, to somebody's house."

Dr. Janssen smiled sympathetically. How she had escaped death was a mystery; how she seemed to be free of a brain injury was beyond him; how she still had a smile on her face was a marvel. As for the fracture, he believed it would heal by itself without his help. But because it was an open fracture, he wanted to clean it out surgically to stave off the risk of infection.

Dr. Bajaj asked if she had any questions and then went to book an operating room. Don and Sue followed him out to get a few more details on the surgery.

Carolyn turned to Dr. Janssen.

"Am I going to be able to handle two surgeries at once?"

"We think so. This is not unusual with trauma, Carolyn. And you'll have less time under anesthesia, which is a good thing."

Carolyn had surgery only once before in her life when she miscarried and needed a D and C procedure. Her biggest fear back then was being put to sleep; she was nervous about anesthesiology because she had heard about people who were put to sleep forever. That and needles. Just the thought of the needle's sharp prick made her queasy. But this time, she was not afraid. She had seen what death would look like and felt what it would feel like, and it was not frightening to her. She was worried, but not about herself. She ached to see Christi and know that her baby was alive and well too.

Carolyn did not ask Dr. Janssen about her head any more, and he was glad for it. Although he was confident there was a surgical solution after the skin flaps, he had no idea what it was. He only knew that he did not do that kind of work; Carolyn was a living miracle; and he did not have the heart to talk about what she would look like once it was over.

"I'm going to let you sleep if you can. I'll see you in a few hours." With that, Dr. Janssen left Carolyn alone in her room.

Dr. Janssen walked over to the physicians' lounge and called his wife to let her know it would be a while before he could come home. Even though he would be working on Carolyn's leg, not her head, he let his wife know he was awestruck.

"Cyndy, I've just met the most remarkable woman. She's clear-headed, bubbly, and downright cheerful. And she was scalped. Scalped!"

Carolyn put the scalping out of her mind. It was too surreal. She focused instead on last Sunday's hymn. But this time it was not her own voice singing. She was being serenaded by angels.

Give him praise...

She closed her eyes, listened, and began to pray: first for Christi and the baby, then her neighbors and other victims, then for her surgeons and nurses. As the hymn had guided her all night, she praised God for bringing her through the storm, for sparing her for some purpose. She praised him for a second chance at life, trusting that no matter what happened in the operating room she could live with it. She felt washed over with peace—weightless enough to join the angels.

"Carolyn?"

Am I dreaming?

"Carolyn, honey, are you awake?"

The dream disappeared as Carolyn felt a thud. Her body awoke, slamming up against reality, and her head throbbed. Knowing Mother must be worried to near-death almost made her cry. But she did not dare. She teased her instead.

"Mother, isn't it past your bedtime?"

"Oh Carolyn—" Sarah Leona could not fight back tears at the sight of her daughter. The bulky white bandage wrapped around her head was clean, but a few clumps of blood-soaked hair were sticking out in back. Normally something of a chatterbox, Sarah Leona contained all but one thought of the many spinning inside her mind and blurted out, "Honey, you look like a red-headed little mummy!"

"That's what I hear." Carolyn did not take offense. On the contrary, she was grateful that Mother could say just what she was thinking. Not that Carolyn was willing to talk about it with her. "Who's with you?"

"Oh, there's Pappy and Charlie. Nathan—he's got your cell phone—it has forty-something messages he says. And Cheryl, she came in with me. Sue and Don are there—look like they seen a ghost. They're all in the hall over here. Do you want everyone to come in? We're all worried to death. You know we've been looking for you forever. Charlie told me wrong. Me and Russell even tried to find you at your house, but we couldn't see a darn thing, thankfully we ran into Mydonna—"

"It's not there, Mother. My house is gone. I never knew I'd see the day when I didn't have as much as a toothbrush to my name."

The thought quieted Sarah Leona. Feeling her knees tremble, she took a seat and a deep breath. Seeing her daughter and granddaughter in back-to-back hospital beds and not knowing about her great-granddaughter was too much to bear. Sarah Leona's physician already had her on stroke-watch, and she wondered if it were time for another pill. Her right arm began to go numb, and her breathing became labored. Not to mention that all of it was awfully hard on the heart. Would it make her feel better to tell Carolyn? She had no choice. Carolyn would want to know.

"Honey, has anyone told you where Christi is?"

Carolyn looked at her mother and shook her head.

"Well, she's okay. They've got machines listening to the baby. Patty and Roman's family are staying with her—so ornery that crew is. Patty even told those doctors—"

"Mother," Carolyn interrupted. "Where is Christi?"

"At DCH. I know what you're thinking, honey, but don't—"

No, no, no, no, no.

"It won't be like last time. It just won't. It just can't."

No, no, no, no, no. Not there.

Carolyn bit her lip to keep from screaming.

"Mother," Carolyn said slowly in an effort to stay calm. "Could you please say a prayer?"

Born Again

Put on the full armor of God, so that you can take your stand against the devil's schemes. For our struggle is not against flesh and blood, but against the rulers, against the authorities, against the powers of this dark world and against the spiritual forces of evil in the heavenly realms. Therefore put on the full armor of God, so that when the day of evil comes, you may be able to stand your ground, and after you have done everything, to stand. Stand firm then, with the belt of truth buckled around your waist, with the breastplate of righteousness in place, and with your feet fitted with the readiness that comes from the gospel of peace. Take up the shield of faith, with which you can extinguish all the flaming arrows of the evil one. Take the helmet of salvation and the sword of the Spirit, which is the word of God.

Ephesians 6:11–18 (NIV)

After picking up his daughter, Jayme, at the Tulsa airport and dropping her right off, J.R. gunned his Suburban to the turnpike. He ran about ninety miles per hour, and a still a few drivers passed him, likely rushing to their own crises. About thirty miles from

Oklahoma City, he hit the worst traffic imaginable and literally sat parked for the next two and a half hours. When he got into the city, he saw first-hand the downed power lines and overturned semis clogging the roads. J.R. pulled into the parking lot of St. Anthony Hospital at four in the morning.

He poked his head into Carolyn's room where she was sleeping.

"Get in here," Cheryl said to him. "How was it getting here?"

"Brutal," he whispered. "First, she and Christi are screaming on the phone. Then she hangs up on me. I nearly lost it. All I'm thinking is, I could have a darn airplane, and still I couldn't get to her. I've never been so frustrated in my life." J.R. looked over at Carolyn and the bandages around her head. She was lying so still—too still. J.R. felt his stomach turn. "Is she going to make it?"

Cheryl nodded yes.

"Poor thing was scalped."

"What?!" J.R. did all he could not to scream it. "My God, does she have brain damage?"

"Doesn't seem like it. She's a miracle."

Looking at Carolyn, two thoughts passed through J.R.'s mind.

She's alive; everything else is insignificant.

He told himself this over and over to compensate for his second thought.

I can't make this any better. Just like before, I can't fix this.

When J.R.'s wife Patti became bedridden from

cancer, his closest physician friends told him that his wife would die, and that all he could do was to "make things pleasant" for her. He did not want to think about making things pleasant for Carolyn just so she could go and leave him.

She's alive. She's alive.

J.R. did not want to get emotional about Carolyn. The hurt was too deep.

"Of course she's going to survive," J.R. said to Cheryl. "She's meaner than snot."

Cheryl rolled her eyes, knowing full well that Carolyn did not have a mean bone in her body. Even though J.R. Richards had only been in Carolyn's life a short time, they fought like old lovers. J.R. liked to be crass because it made Carolyn feisty. He would tell her friends who would ask how they met that the first time he saw Carolyn; she was bent over in the parking lot at the state capitol. She forever insisted that J.R. had fabricated the whole scene.

"And I was like, wooo-eee!" J.R. would shout without a shred of shame.

At this point, Carolyn would roll her eyes. She would not even blush because she knew J.R. Richards, which is just what she always called him, was full of it.

"Senator Hendrick's secretary, what's that girl's name?" J.R. would ask every time, even though he knew her better than Carolyn did at first.

"Cheryl Willie, one of my best girlfriends and business partners, could sell ice to an Eskimo."

"Right, well, that's how she sold me on you. So Sharon—"

"Cheryl."

"Okay, Cheryl asked me if I was married, and I said, 'That's just what I need—a woman in my life.' And who happened to be there but the same chick that had her little skirt hiked up in the parking lot—"

"J.R.! This isn't even true! I was moving a cone! You're making that up!"

"And so here I am, this little fat bald boy, grinning from ear to ear. I made up some harebrained excuse like I wanted to be a lobbyist and needed to feel her out. You know, give me a piece of that—"

"J.R. Richards!"

"...that *brain*, I was going to say. What do you think I am, some pervert?"

In spite of her protests and their age difference—he was a decade older—J.R. did make Carolyn laugh. He had been married twice. Number two was a six-month disaster. Number one, Patti, lasted twenty-seven years until breast cancer took her. J.R. spent the last five years of their marriage by her bedside. Carolyn admired his loyalty. She knew his humor was armor around his heart.

The chairs in the waiting area outside the Critical Care Unit were filled, many of them by Carolyn's family and friends. Besides Cheryl and J.R., Bobbie Brown and Guy Robison—two Clematis Club ladies—wanted to stay through at least the first surgery, and all of them planned to be there the moment Carolyn awoke.

Just as they had described, Dr. Bajaj and Dr. Janssen worked simultaneously on Carolyn, and both operations went smoothly. There would be a future complication, however. Carolyn and her doctors did not know it at the time, but over the next three years, she would have to undergo nearly one hundred out-patient and in-patient medical and surgical procedures. Fortunately for Carolyn, for now, she took each hour one at a time, because reality—Christi, baby Abby, her home, her head—taken as a whole was beyond overwhelming.

It was late Tuesday afternoon, nearly twenty-four hours after the storm, when Carolyn awoke from surgery. As she came to, the voices of some of her favorite people were swirling around her room—Cheryl, her Clematis Club girlfriends, as well as Nancy (*we were supposed to be in Cancun, not a hospital*), fellow lobbyist, Susan Hillman, and several colleagues from work. Carolyn looked at the crowd through a prescription drug-induced haze. They watched her, not knowing if she were going to fall asleep again or start chattering as her family had described. A touch of pale pink had returned to Carolyn's cheeks, but with her head bandage, her hospital gown, and the bed sheets, she was white from top to toe.

"You look so peaceful," said Diane.

"A newborn baby," Carolyn said.

The women were not sure what she meant. Maybe the drugs were still working over her brain. Maybe she was thinking of Abby, Christi's unborn baby. Maybe she was talking in her sleep.

"I'm just like a newborn baby. I have nothing."

Then they understood.

"But Christi and I are alive, right? So what does it matter?"

"Have you talked to her?" Cheryl asked.

"They say I have, but these meds are good at erasing your memory of anything. You know she's at DCH? I hate being in different hospitals. It's hard to be away from her. All I want to do is wrap my arms around her."

The women offered to pay a visit to Christi on Carolyn's behalf. They offered to go out and buy toiletries for a start. They tried to think of every possible way to be useful.

Carolyn's colleague, KD, mentioned that she could help get the FEMA disaster assistance process underway even though Carolyn had none of the required identification. Her driver's license was in her wallet, and only God knew where that was. KD, being former military, knew the systems of government well, and said she would find a way around this one too, probably using tax forms at the office.

"Carolyn, I have to tell you," said Cheryl, "when I called you fifteen times on your cell phone and you didn't answer, I knew you were hurt. I just knew it."

Cheryl did not want to traumatize her friend, but she needed to uncork the bottle of worry that had bubbled up inside her for the last dozen or so hours. Diane and KD both nodded like overprotective sisters.

"I keep thinking about how I saw you working on your emails and talking on your phone, and I didn't want to bug you," Diane said. "I keep wondering, if I'd warned you better about the storm, would you have had time to get to a shelter."

"Naw. You know I'm an Okie girl, not afraid of a little tornado. Never dreamed I'd be scalped—"

Jamie winced and interrupted, hoping to avoid the gory details.

"We heard. Just a miracle you survived."

"I thought I must've died," Carolyn said with an embellished accent, as she tugged on her hospital gown, "because they put me in this." Her friends had no trouble recognizing her old humor and laughed out loud.

"What, did you think they were going to give you a leopard-print teddy and some red lipstick?" KD shot back. Now they were in hysterics.

"Well, ya-ah!" Carolyn exclaimed. "At least I'd have a fighting chance with some of the cute doctors around here."

"Come on now, what man wouldn't want a mummy for a girlfriend?" Cheryl teased.

The women were relieved to laugh together. If they had closed their eyes, they could have imagined having the same loose conversation at the office or over lunch. Carolyn refused to let her—or any of them—dwell on what had happened to her and her family or on what they had lost.

She would never say it, but Carolyn was exhausted. She closed her eyes and took a deep breath. Her friends let her have a moment to herself. Diane and Sue Ann said silent prayers to themselves. They had just come from a Catholic service where they lit candles for Carolyn's healing.

Jamie turned out the overhead fluorescent lights.

"Carolyn," Cheryl said quietly, "You don't have to greet everybody who comes in the door. You know every other person in the universe. They all want to come see you."

"It's okay," Carolyn said, her eyes still closed. "They can come."

"Then I'm setting up shifts," KD said, in drill sergeant fashion. "If you're going to turn on the sparkle for every Tom, Dick, and Harry, then we're going to man the door. You don't understand—everybody and their brother want to wish you well. It's a little ridiculous."

Just then, as if on cue, an attractive woman in a bright blue track suit popped her head in the door. The ladies almost scowled at her.

"I—I'm sorry. I just have something to … I'll … I'll come back later." And she was gone.

Jamie closed the door behind the stranger.

"Who was that?" Carolyn asked.

Jamie turned around to face her.

"You mean, you don't know?"

"See what we mean?" Cheryl said.

"Well, what if she wanted to give me a new house or something?"

Cheryl rolled her eyes in mock exaggeration. Diane and KD walked over to a table and picked up a few x-rays of Carolyn's hip.

"Mind if we look?" KD asked.

Carolyn shook her head no.

"Just don't go telling everyone I need a hip replacement. Sounds geriatric."

"Your vanity is award-winning," Cheryl said.

All of them laughed. Even half-asleep, Carolyn made her clever jokes as if nothing had changed. But the x-rays told a different story. KD's jaw nearly dropped. She was surprised to see that the pelvic bone had shattered in numerous places, and she worried about Carolyn's chances of walking again. For all the years she had known Carolyn, she knew her to go at one pace: high speed.

"You are one seriously tough cookie," said KD.

"Doctors have their work cut out for them," said Sue Ann.

"They're good," Carolyn said. "They'll get me through this."

"No, Carolyn," Cheryl said. "With God at the helm, *you* will get you through this."

A nurse walked in to the room, flipped on the lights, and checked Carolyn's vital signs.

"Do you need us to leave?" asked Jamie.

"Actually, no," said the nurse. "I need you to help. We're a little short-handed."

KD stepped forward.

"No problem. We take orders."

The nurse put KD to work swabbing Carolyn's hip wound and donor site for the skin grafts with medicated q-tips. Then the nurse wanted to wash Carolyn's head and explained that she needed two people to hold it steady. Many of the women cleared the room for practicality's sake. Cheryl, Diane, and

Jamie stayed behind, however, and flanked her bed. It was by accident that Jamie ended up on the bad side, the side where Carolyn was clearly scalped, not to mention the patchwork of grafting Dr. Bajaj had just done. As the nurse unwrapped the gauze and revealed what was underneath, KD noticed Jamie's face start to lose color.

"Jamie, just look at me," KD said. She got a good look at the skin grafts on Carolyn's head. They looked like raw meat stapled on top of bone.

"Yeah, but what you've got in your hands isn't very pretty either!" said Jamie, clearly feeling queasy.

"Hey, now," said Carolyn, as if she were offended.

"Hold still, sister. Your head is heavy!" Cheryl said.

Lesser friends could not have done what Carolyn's army had done—dropped everything to rally at her side in a moment's notice. KD understood it this way: that just like a mother who surprises herself when she is not disgusted by her own baby's spit-up—and KD would say it as bluntly as that—the women wanted instinctively to take care of Carolyn. They knew she was the kind of person who never asked for help. She had always given the impression she could do it all; and mostly, she did. Besides working full-time, she made time for her friends' children and grandchildren. She was known for dropping in on recitals, bringing cinnamon rolls over for the holidays, and leaving trendy gifts in funky bags on doorsteps just because. She rarely turned down an invitation to a charity luncheon, a birthday party, or a chance to chat over a glass of wine.

Carolyn's friends could not build her a new house, they could not heal Christi, and they could not ensure the safety of her grandchild. Cleaning out her wounds seemed a small offering by comparison, although they knew they could not do it every day.

"We're going to see if Senator Snyder wants to come up here and pitch in," KD joked. Carolyn and Senator Mark Snyder had often gone head-to-head—so to speak—over a number of issues throughout the years.

"If he sees me like this, he'll take advantage," Carolyn said.

"Are you kidding? You've got the sympathy vote hands down," Cheryl said.

"Thank God the session is nearly over," Carolyn said, her speech slurring some. "I should be in Cancun right now." She closed her eyes again, and this time, she fell asleep.

"We wore her baby butt out," KD said.

The women tidied up the room, turned down the lights again, and closed Carolyn's door.

Waiting outside was the woman who had dropped in earlier.

"Is it alright to go in?" she asked timidly.

"She's sleeping," KD answered directly.

"Do you mind if I ask who you are?" asked Cheryl.

"I'm Cyndy, Dr. Janssen's wife."

Angels

Keep on loving each other as brothers. Do not forget to entertain strangers, for by so doing some people have entertained angels, without knowing it.
Hebrews 13:2 (NIV)

For he shall give his angels charge over you, to keep you in all your ways.
Psalms 91:11 (KJV)

Cyndy walked tentatively down the hallway to Carolyn's room, not knowing what to expect. Her stomach was tied in knots. Her hands felt slippery from sweat. Her ears burned bright pink. She did not want to intrude.

"I'll just leave this with the nurses out front," Cyndy Janssen said, lifting up three shopping bags.

"You can give them to her yourself, Cyndy," said Rhonda, a nurse who had worked with Dr. Janssen, as she pushed open Carolyn's door.

Cyndy was certain she had been called upon to do this. However, now that she was close by, she worried. She did not want to be given credit for the gifts she brought. That was her first excuse. Her second was that she really did not want to find out what this patient would think of her. Life would just be easier if she walked away. But something led her steps forward.

The sight of Carolyn took her breath away.

"She looks like an angel lying there," Cyndy whispered to Rhonda.

"Some angel was looking out for her, that's for sure," Rhonda said.

"Look at that." Cyndy waved her hand in a circle around Carolyn's bed. She was lying propped up on her back with a tiny smile on her lips.

"Yes," said Rhonda.

As the setting sun cast its golden glow on the world, there was an aura of light around Carolyn—a beautiful light that made Cyndy forget about the broken bones and the torn scalp, the shattered lives and the shredded earth. It made her realize that what she had brought, whether it was right or not, did not matter. To her, Carolyn was bathed in God's love just as she was in sunshine, and their presence together gave her comfort. Cyndy knew her footsteps had been guided for a purpose. She was where she belonged.

My God, Cyndy thought, *the world's going to be okay because of you.*

Carolyn blinked a few times, clearing the sleep from her shining blue eyes.

"Hello," Carolyn said brightly, as though she had been expecting her.

Cyndy sat down in a chair and scooted it close to the bed.

"My husband came home and told me about you."

Cyndy went on to explain who she was and the depth of her desire to help. That afternoon, when she had taken water to her son's baseball practice, several fathers agreed to transport the drinks down to the devastated neighborhoods. They had willingly traded their passion for watching their sons play their favorite sport with a passion for giving not only outside of their own gene pool, but outside of themselves to perfect strangers.

"I was giving, but it felt so empty," Cyndy said. "I felt helpless. I needed to see a face. I wanted to reach out to someone in particular. But I didn't know who."

She described how her husband had called her from the ER, and then could not stop talking about Carolyn once he got home. Even though her case, from an orthopedic perspective, was not particularly interesting, Dr. Janssen was fascinated by the devastating yet limited scope of Carolyn's head injury, and, in spite of having lost all her possessions, her indomitable spirit. When it dawned on Cyndy what she needed to do, she was unstoppable and so very happy about it. She raced around town like a woman on a mission.

"From my car, I called Tom on his cell phone and asked him what size you were. He said medium, but you're the tiniest little thing. Ah, men! Anyway, I went shopping. I don't know you, I don't know your tastes, but I put myself in your shoes and went shopping.

"I just prayed to the Lord, 'Let me know what she needs.' I felt led to every purchase."

Cyndy had a lot of good reasons over the years for going on a shopping spree, but being God-driven had never before been one of them. Considering her mission, the purchases were not extravagant. It was not as though Cyndy could ask, "What would Jesus buy?" and expect a practical answer. So she focused on putting herself in Carolyn's place. *What would I want?* she asked herself.

Out of the first bag she pulled out an ultra soft cotton nightgown, white with blue flowers, and a robe to match. In the second bag was a set of Bobbi Brown makeup, red lipstick included. The third bag contained a pair of black rip-away wind pants and a matching fluorescent green jacket, plus a few sets of matching bras and underwear.

"I hope you don't think this is weird," Cyndy said with a smile.

Cyndy knew it was not, even though she had never reached out to one of her husband's patients like this before. She would often ask him how she could help, but every idea felt too intrusive. Cookies left in the waiting room, yes. Cards sent to their homes, sure. But in their twenty-five years of marriage, of all the patients Tom had talked about from his second year of medical school until today, Cyndy had not experienced such a powerful urging to help. She decided to quiet her doubting mind and listen, to be open to this urging.

So overwhelmed, Carolyn was rendered speechless. She could almost imagine herself in Cyndy's shoes, wanting to help and walking into a hospital with three shopping bags. She was certain she would have done the very same thing for any of her friends. But for a stranger? Now that was awe-inspiring.

The robe reminded Carolyn what a luxury a long, hot shower would be, especially once she wrapped herself in cozy cotton and refreshed her lips with color. The jacket and rip-away pants with buttons down the side would be easy to get on and off, and they would see a lot of time on her treadmill once this ordeal was over. She did not have much use for the bra and underwear at the moment, but they were the only ones she owned and would need them soon enough.

Who was this woman?

More important, she marveled that a perfect stranger knew exactly what to do. It was as if she knew what Carolyn wanted more than Carolyn knew herself.

"Cyndy, everything is beautiful. You *do* know me. Down to the fact that I didn't even come to the hospital in underwear."

"I swear Tom did not give me that information!"

Carolyn and Cyndy smiled at each other, each grateful for what the other had done—grateful for the way God had made them friends.

A quick knock turned their attention to the door. Nathan, covered in dried dirt and sweat and still wearing his golf clothes from the day before, had a Cheshire cat grin on his face.

"Hi," he said to Cyndy with a little wave. Then he turned to his mom, not even noticing the lingerie on her bed, which would have embarrassed him slightly. "Sorry to interrupt. But you're not going to believe what we found."

Found

Do not store up for yourselves treasures on earth, where moth and rust destroy, and where thieves break in and steal. But store up for yourselves treasures in heaven, where moth and rust do not destroy, and where thieves do not break in and steal. For where your treasure is, there your heart will be also.

Matthew 6:19–21 (NAS)

Nathan, Don, Sue, and Pappy planned to spend the entire day going through the rubble in the Del Aire addition.

"Hey, Dad, Mom wants to know if you're going to borrow a trailer to get all her stuff," Nathan said with a smile.

"A trailer?" Don asked in disbelief. "Does she not know there's nothing left but a hot water heater and a concrete slab?"

"Dad," Nathan said with a laugh as he shook his head, "She doesn't have a clue. I guess it's hard to imagine that there is no washer and dryer left. There's nothing left. What we find we'll fit in a trash bag and toss it under my feet."

Sue moved over so Nathan could hop in. The windows in the truck were down, and Nathan could feel the blazing sun and the strong wind. From a distance, his old neighborhood looked like piles of dirt with busy ants crawling on top and through them.

"The turn's here, right?" Nathan guessed.

"Well, I never," was all Don could think to say. Sue's hands covered her gaping mouth. Even though they had seen it the day before, the shock in the bright sunlight had not worn off.

Much about the scene looked like a war zone, except for one enormous distinction. People had already posted signs showing that their sense of humor remained intact. One sign read, "Free lumber"; another, "Fixer upper"; and yet another in front of a pile of debris, "Home for sale. Cheap."

Someone had partially bulldozed the streets earlier in the day so that families could drive in and start looking for lost valuables. Don was able to pull up right in front of the pile they thought belonged to Carolyn. Christi's Jeep and Nathan's truck were their most obvious clues as to where the house might have stood.

"There she was," Nathan said, as his father slowly put on the brakes.

Roman was already on-site, nailing a board to the only tree trunk that still stood on Carolyn's property. He shook a can of spray paint and wrote,

Stager
3324 Del Aire Place

"Good thinking, young man!" Don called out to his son-in-law as he unloaded gloves, trash bags, and a half-dozen picks, shovels, and rakes from the truck.

Thirty-three twenty-four Del Aire Place had all but disappeared.

The makeshift sign would serve a purpose for the insurance inspectors, due out in the coming days, to assess the damage. It did not take an expert to see that nothing of value remained. Almost nothing.

Nathan looked around; it was too overwhelming to just jump right in. Piles of debris stood as high as the homes used to be. The mangled metal of carports, car parts, and gutters were still wrapped around lampposts, tree trunks, and any vertical structure that survived. Sidewalks remained invisible, cluttered with junk. To find anything that mattered, Nathan decided he could not look at the forest as a whole, so to speak. He would have to focus on each and every tree.

Just then, something caught his attention. Off to his right, he noticed a dog lying motionless on the ground. He grabbed a blanket from his dad's truck and walked over to the animal. Don, Sue, and Roman watched him.

Nathan knelt by the dog and placed a hand just under his rib cage where he hoped to feel the dog's torso rise and fall. But the pup was still. There was no tag around the dog's neck. Nathan covered him up with the blanket, made a cross out of two sticks, and laid it on top.

When Nathan returned, Roman asked, "Not one of ours, I hope."

Nathan shook his head.

Earlier in the morning, Roman had called the local shelter and every veterinarian in Del City and Midwest City. Jake and Little Miss Muffin were still missing, and Roman assumed they were gone forever.

A few of Nathan's buddies pulled up in a pickup truck and jumped out. Nathan gathered the group around a battered water heater, found a few feet away from Carolyn and Christi when they were rescued.

"We think this was the back yard. That's the new water heater. That's mom's treadmill."

Roman pulled out his video camera and started taping.

"There's Nathan, who's in pretty good spirits all things considered. Wave to Sis, man," Roman said as he narrated the scene for the camera. It was a lie, but an understandable one; anything to cheer Christi. Nathan complied and wondered when his sister would be stable enough—physically and mentally—to watch a tape of the spot where she nearly lost her life and the life growing inside her.

Roman turned around with the video camera still pressed against his right eye.

"Your mom's house is probably the worst of them all. There's Sissy's car," he said as he zoomed in to a crumpled jeep with its hood popped open and its body bent around a tree.

"The Jeep's demolished. Of course, everything is."

Roman zoomed back out and faced the house pile again.

"There's Nathan's truck. It landed on the staircase. Sissy and Carolyn started out under there in the closet. Good thing they didn't stay there."

Roman climbed to the top of a ten-foot-high pile of debris and shot the landscape while turning 360 degrees.

"I want to show you how lucky you are."

"Did you see Carolyn's car down there, Roman?" Don yelled up to him.

Roman looked around. There seemed to be more trashed cars and trucks than anything else. At least, you could make out what they used to be as compared to the loads of broken lumber that gave no indication they had ever been part of a house. Roman walked down to Carolyn's car about five properties away. Being red, it was easy enough to find, but comprehending how a wind could be strong enough to flip it like a matchbox car and crush it like cardboard would take time.

"Unbelievable. There it is. Can't even tell it's Carolyn's car."

Roman turned and shot back toward his in-laws and their friends.

"Look at this. Just nothing. For miles and miles it's like this." As Roman zoomed in to a tree stripped bare, he turned quiet. The shot had gone out of focus, but he did not notice.

"Everybody's been asking about Sissy and the baby. My baby's a miracle."

Even though the tape was for her, Roman had stopped talking to his wife who lay in critical condition while carrying their first child in a hospital's emergency room. It was as if he were talking to someone who was there with him, even though he stood alone.

"There's no way they should have lived. It's unbelievable."

Roman shut off the camera and walked back to the crew, which had grown in the last half hour. Nine men stood shoulder to shoulder, lifting Nathan's flattened pickup tangled in cables to see what was buried underneath.

Baby pictures.

Soaked in mud were photographs of Nathan and Christi when they were newborns. Carolyn must have left them inside the closet where she and Christi had hidden. The pictures were not salvageable, but at least they knew they were looking in the right places. Nathan picked up one of Christi holding her baby brother, brushed off as much dirt as he could, and tucked it in his pocket.

Before the men lowered the truck to the ground, Nathan reached into the glove compartment. He fished around for the one thing he remembered leaving in there—his Oakley sunglasses. He found them, unscratched.

"Now that's quality!" he said as he held them up in the air.

The group gave out a half-hearted cheer. Once the truck was righted, Nathan placed the glasses on the battered hood and admired the triumphant hood ornament that, to him, symbolized survival.

"Look," Nathan said, "we can spend all day looking for crap. But let's focus on three things Mom cares about—her Bible, her wallet, and her blue sock."

Even Nathan knew how unlikely finding any of them would be. A Bible? Possibly, if the wind had not ripped it open. A brown leather wallet? Everything was dirt brown. A sock? A sock could have been blown to Kansas.

"A blue sock?" Roman asked. "You're joking, right?"

"She kept all her good jewelry in a little blue sock," Nathan explained. "I know it's like finding a needle in a haystack, but at least that gives us something to work toward."

Carolyn had mentioned the blue ladies' sports sock to Nathan, Don, and Sue back in the hospital, not because she was desperate to have it, but because it was possible in her mind that the contents would still be in it: the gold watch, the matching diamond, and sapphire ring and bracelet. Nathan understood their monetary value, but did not know the stories behind them.

A long-time friend had given Carolyn the watch for her birthday. It was the most expensive gift she had ever received. And a generous former boyfriend gave the jewelry to Carolyn years before. She had gone down to Houston to attend a national meeting with a board member named Pat Ringrose and happened to meet John in a country and western dance hall and restaurant called The Rose. Carolyn was uninterested in two-stepping, so she watched her friends. John sidled up next to her and, once the dancing was over, invited her and Pat to his hotel for a nightcap. Before Pat could open her mouth, Carolyn shot him down, saying they needed to get back to their own hotel. John worked for an off-shore drilling company but he was from New York City, and Carolyn assumed all those Northern city slickers were full of bull. They exchanged business cards, and she politely agreed to a dinner if he wanted to meet her in Oklahoma City sometime. She doubted he ever would.

The next day, a vase of one dozen fat yellow roses arrived at Carolyn's office with an invitation to dine in Oklahoma City the following weekend. The whole rose theme was lost on her; she found herself suspicious and untrusting. She told herself, *I will never be alone in a vehicle with him; I'll be home by 9:30; I'll tell all my girlfriends and my children what I'm doing, where I'm dining, and everything I know about this man who calls himself John Norrad.*

John turned out to be the most interesting man Carolyn had ever known. He had lived in Bahrain, traveled the world over, and for the next two years, he took her and the kids with him everywhere: Key West, Disney World, Hilton Head Island, he even sent Nathan to Space Camp. He would have wine from Napa Valley, fish from New Orleans, and lobster from Maine delivered to her door. The ring and bracelet were gifts to Carolyn when she received her college diploma after years of night school.

As lavish as their life had been with John, Carolyn saw the signs of failure along the way. He drank too much. He was twice-divorced. She had no intention of uprooting the children. When they parted ways, he was gracious about it. Carolyn had enjoyed the ride, and certainly appreciated the spoils. Had her heart become attached to the man who had given them so much, God only knows where on earth they would have been on May 3, 1999. But it did not, and so she had stayed.

The spoils might as well have been buried treasures on Del Aire Place now. Nathan and the crew spread out with their heads down and began the search for something worth saving.

Sue was intent on finding Carolyn's sock. When Carolyn mentioned it, these thoughts were second nature to her—that biblical teachings say the eyes of the Lord run to and fro over all the earth. In Carolyn's heart, she knew that the Lord could find the needle in the haystack—the sock in the rubble. But she had her doubts that any man, woman, or child could actually find it.

Some boys came by, asking if the baseball cards belonged to any kids in the neighborhood. Don knew Nathan would like to have his signed Johnny Bench card returned to him, even thought its frame was likely destroyed.

"Where did you find those?" Don asked.

"Over there." The kids pointed to a pile across the street.

Nathan and few friends followed them there. Within minutes, they had discovered some of the contents of Nathan's bedroom.

"Look!" Andy yelled, as he held up a photograph that used to stand in Nate's room.

"A picture with the glass still in it!"

In the picture, Nathan was holding a large bass he had caught one summer on Lake Thunderbird. That the glass remained intact was a mystery, but getting the photograph back was a gift.

I'd like about a thousand more of those, he thought.

They found Nathan's wrestling and football letter jacket, stained so dark with mud that only someone who had seen it before would have known it was three colors: khaki, green, and white. Roman grabbed a brown cardboard box from his truck and shook the spray paint again. He wrote:

Lost and Found

Roman put the jacket and frame inside the box.

When they also recovered a rug and a fishing pole snapped in pieces, both from Nathan's room, they were certain they had pinpointed Carolyn's home's second story. Most of the day, they had been searching the remains of the downstairs structure without success. The TV, coin collection, pots and pans, and furniture all from downstairs were nowhere in sight. They came to understand that the top floor had moved across the street and the bottom had blown away.

Next to the lost and found box, they started a junk pile of recognizable items. Even though they planned to throw most of them away, it gave them a small sense of accomplishment to see a few items unbroken.

Unbroken, but not untouched. Anything that had

even a crack was filled with mulch, shingles, leaves from tree limbs, and dirt. The muck was stuck in between every page of every book. The grime packed every crevice, no matter how small. The grit did not miss a hole. With no way to get it clean, most of the stuff was worthless.

The search was getting depressing. No sign of Carolyn's Bible, her wallet, or her blue sock. No sign of anything that mattered much to any of them. They began to wonder what, if they could find anything, would truly matter.

Don and Sue had some luck finding coins. Carolyn used to own a couple of vending machines and kept untold numbers of coins in her bedroom on the second floor. Sue filled up two coffee cans with coins.

They dug for several hours. They found a certificate from a technical school. It belonged to the neighbor across the street that had died. Like Christi and Carolyn, he and his girlfriend had hidden in a closet under the stairwell (the floor plans of both homes were similar), but they were the ones found under a car.

The work was drudgery. Nathan rubbed the back of his neck, sore from looking down. He came across a few of his mom's ceramic angels, tiny inspirations to keep him looking for more.

Suddenly, they heard a loud noise like a lawnmower chugging down the street. They all looked up to see what was making the racket.

Nathan squinted to get a better look.

"Who—is that LD?"

The first smile of the day crept to his face.

LD's grandmother lived around the corner, and Nathan had known him since kindergarten. LD was the scrappy friend you did not want to underestimate, weighing only 103 pounds in high school but on the wrestling team nonetheless. He had left his maroon Ford Ranger pickup at his grandmother's house just before the storm hit. Ever since, his truck had been MIA, and he had been pretty upset about not being able to find it. But there was LD, with safety glasses still on his head, driving some banged-up piece of metal straight out of a junkyard. The windshield wipers were torn down to stubs, and the windshield itself was covered in dirt, so LD drove with his head out of the driver's side window.

"Woo! Yeah!" LD screamed as he pulled up to the site. "I found it about a hundred yards that way."

"I can't believe it runs. It's trashed, LD," Nathan said through chuckles.

"All I've got is liability," LD said. "I'm going to keep her!"

All of them doubled over with laughter. LD's exuberance was a welcome distraction. And in an unexpected way, it gave everyone working on Carolyn's property a glimpse of hope, and a wide stroke of good fortune.

Bessie and Cecil, Carolyn's elderly neighbors from across the street, came to investigate the racket. They had survived the storm, hiding in their bathroom, the only part of their house left standing.

Cecil put his arm on Don's shoulder.

"If you find my billfold, I'll give you twenty bucks."

Don smiled and said he would do his best.

His best was good enough. Within an hour, Don found that billfold. Cecil was so happy, he tried to stuff a twenty in Don's pocket, but he would not take it.

Over the afternoon, more friends and neighbors stopped by, all sharing their remarkable stories of recovery. Motorcycles found in swimming pools. Beds on top of telephone poles.

A man from a neighborhood half a mile to the south asked if they'd seen a brown van. He searched on foot, walking directly north, and found it on top of another car.

A high school friend of Nathan's named Leigh Ann said the roof was knocked off her house, but the glass bowl of hot tamales that always sat on the living room coffee table did not move. All tamales were accounted for.

A man driving a black SUV pulled up to the site. He held a small piece of paper in his hand.

"I'm looking for Christi Dawn Stager," he said. "The phone book said 'C Stager' lives here." He estimated his home was about six miles away, but finding this address on this day took quite some time.

"Christi's my daughter," Don said, stepping forward. "Can I help you?"

The man handed Don the piece of paper. It was her high school graduation announcement.

"That little card impaled the roof of my wife's car. But I thought she would want it. And I kind of wanted to know who she was."

Don looked down at the card, and felt a lump in

his throat. *Christi Dawn, Abby Dawn* ... both named after him. Sue saw that her husband was struggling.

"Christi's in the hospital right now," Sue said, "but she'll be glad to have this. Thank you for making such an effort to find her."

"I'll keep her in my prayers," he said, and that was the last time they ever saw him.

Don wiped the tears from his eyes before they could fall.

A Salvation Army truck pulled up the street. Volunteers handed out cheeseburgers from the local Sonic drive-in: chips, soda, water, even strawberry-flavored Pop Tarts. Everyone shed their gloves, found an empty bumper for a seat, and took a break.

Just as Roman was taking a bite of his burger, his cell phone rang. It was his mother, Mydonna, who had stopped by his and Christi's house, which was not damaged in any way. On their answering machine, someone was looking for the owner of a dog. A local veterinarian had given her a phone list. Roman would not let his hopes get too high, however—the caller had described the puppy as a *black* Lab, not yellow.

The pile of rubble was growing. Sue and Don planned to focus on it again, as they had some luck discovering coins and a few of Carolyn's belongings. But they did not anticipate finding any buried treasures there. Cecil and Bessie had hired a crew to sift through their ruins as well. The stuff that was deemed worthless was dumped onto the remains of Carolyn's second floor, and so the pile of trash grew.

Within the pile was a cave, small enough to be

a child's cubby. Sue squinted and refocused her eyes on something dangling in the wind, hanging from the top of the cave.

"Don," Sue asked, "What's that? It's blue."

She pointed at it.

"That dingy, nasty-looking thing?" Don asked.

"I think that could be Carolyn's sock."

The sock hung long and heavy, as if something were inside of it. Don reached in and yanked it out. He brought it over to Sue, who pulled out a ring, bracelet, and watch, all caked in mud.

"I don't believe it," Sue said.

Don shook his head.

"Only a woman could find another woman's jewelry."

"I didn't find it," she said. "God showed me where it was."

They searched until sundown, but no treasure matched that of the blue sock.

Nathan nearly forgot to grab his sunglasses on the hood of his truck. But when he went back to retrieve them, they were gone.

"Are you kidding me?" Nathan said out loud, but no one was there to hear him.

Unbelievable.

Someone had taken them.

Fine, Nathan thought, *lost forever, like everything else.*

Before getting back on the interstate, they passed a church whose marquee read, "Treasure-Seekers: Free Tetanus Shots Inside." The threesome agreed they would get them tomorrow. Farther up the road, about one mile from the old neighborhood, they stopped at a convenience store. Nathan hopped out and his dad handed him his wallet to buy drinks and snacks for everyone. At the register, the clerk took a long look at the credit card.

"Everything okay?" Nathan asked. He did not mind the idea of explaining that the card belonged to his dad, and that dad was idling in the parking lot.

"Stager? Is that how you say it?" she asked.

"Yes."

"Any relation to Carolyn?"

"That's my mom."

"These were scattered around the gas pumps." The clerk pulled out a small stack of cards. "I think I have one of your mom's credit cards."

For the second time in the last hour, Nathan found himself uttering, "Are you kidding me?"

Sure enough, the card belonged to Carolyn.

I guess not everything is meant to be lost.

Nathan thanked her and ran out waving the card.

"We can stop looking so hard for Mom's things," he said. "Looks like they just might find us."

Hellhole

Therefore Jesus said again, "I tell you the truth, I am the gate for the sheep. All who ever came before me were thieves and robbers, but the sheep did not listen to them. I am the gate; whoever enters through me will be saved. He will come in and go out, and find pasture. The thief comes only to steal and kill and destroy; I have come that they may have life, and have it to the full.

"I am the good shepherd. The good shepherd lays down his life for the sheep. The hired hand is not the shepherd who owns the sheep. So when he sees the wolf coming, he abandons the sheep and runs away. Then the wolf attacks the flock and scatters it. The man runs away because he is a hired hand and cares nothing for the sheep."

John 10: 7–13 (NIV)

Christi could not fight for herself. And while she relied on her mother-in-law, Mydonna, her aunt Patty, her friends, and the rest of her family, she was not aware of what everyone did on her behalf at every turn. Someone was there to bathe her. Someone made sure her hair was combed. Someone followed through on her medications.

Mydonna and Patty both noticed that Christi could not lie on the back of her head. They presumed it was the pregnancy keeping her from an uncomfortable sleeping position. But Christi had been complaining about it for days. Patty and Mydonna finally took a look themselves. It was tedious work trying to part Christi's matted hair, but they discovered the cause of her pain. It was worse than any of them had imagined. There was a deep gash in Christi's head, with shards of glass and what appeared to be a thick piece of wood lodged within.

"My God! How did they miss this?" Patty said with disgust.

"I don't want a nurse this time, I want the guy who runs this place," Mydonna said.

Short of storming into the CEO's office, Patty dragged a nurse to Christi's bedside, while Mydonna shamed an ER physician into surgically removing the chunk of wood on the spot.

For the next several days, both Christi and Carolyn were confined to their beds. Mother and daughter spoke to each other in brief exchanges over the phone, but with both of them in and out of surgeries and consciousness neither one remembered any of their conversations. Plus, both of them were sedated; Christi more heavily than Carolyn. While each new morning meant Carolyn was one step closer to healing, Christi's condition was worsening. The ER at Del City Hospital was still overwhelmed.

A constant stream of visitors flowed in and out of both hospital rooms, and it seemed that no one came without a bouquet of flowers in hand. Within days, the once-dainty fragrances began to clash with each other. KD was the first to tell Carolyn, in no uncertain terms, that the explosion of flora needed to be dispersed. She farmed out the bouquets, sending fresh ones home with various family members, friends, and colleagues, and throwing the rotten ones into an outdoor trash bin.

Christi's room, too, smelled downright rancid. Patty, who only left the hospital to shower or eat ever since Christi had gone in, assumed the flowers were the culprit as well. But after she removed them, the odor intensified.

Patty bought cleaning supplies to scrub down Christi's room. She wiped the counters, the table tops, even the floors. She emptied the trash can. Nothing worked. The stench was so overpowering, Patty thought she might throw up.

It smelled like death.

"Christi, honey, have you seen a nurse today?" Patty asked.

Christi shook her head.

"When was the doctor last here to check on you?"

"Don't know."

Roman said, "I don't think we've seen the first doctor since her surgery when she came in. The janitor could've operated on her head."

Patty started sniffing the cabinets in Christi's room, desperate to find the source. When she got a whiff of the sheets, she nearly fainted. Patty rolled

Christi on to her side and looked at the back of her leg—the leg that had already been operated on. It was festering.

"Oh God, Christi, it's you. It's your leg."

Patty ran out of Christi's room in a rage. She grabbed the first nurse she saw and demanded that a specialist come immediately. To her surprise, a surgeon arrived within the hour. A brief look at Christi's leg was all he needed.

"There's better than a fifty percent chance she's going to lose this leg," the doctor told Patty, who was on the verge of exploding.

As calmly as she could, Patty said, "Let's continue this conversation in the hallway, shall we?" It was not a request. Roman shut the door behind them.

"First off, I want her moved out of this death ward. Everyone around her is dying." Patty spat out the words, aware that she was basically channeling the wrath of Sarah Leona. But she felt death hovering in every corner of the ER, and knowing Carolyn could not be there, she felt a deep maternal urge to protect Christi.

"Second, if she loses her leg, it's on your hands. If she loses that baby, you'll have someone upstairs to answer to. You people have let her lie here without a shred of concern. You've ignored her. It's despicable."

"Listen," he pleaded, "I only just heard about her case."

"So you wouldn't have any clue about whether her baby needs to come out now, because I think she does." Patty felt her hands tremble.

"I don't know," the doctor admitted. "She may not be stable enough yet. That's not my specialty. I'll have to get someone else to assess—"

"What about her first surgeon, the one who screwed her up in the first place?" She had seen him, but in her fury, she could not be sure of his name. She was too angry to pay attention to this doctor's name.

The doctor looked down at Christi's chart.

"We can't find him."

Patty was not sure she heard him correctly.

"You—you, what?"

"Ever since the first night, we haven't seen that Dr. Eye—Dr. Eisenburg. But I give you my word, I'll do everything I can to…"

"You are right you are going to do everything you can. My daddy died here! My friends died here! And I'll be damned if you're going to let my sister's baby and grandbaby die here too!"

Patty crumpled to the floor and sobbed into her hands.

Two hours later, Christi was wheeled into her third surgery.

Two hours after that, she was asleep in a new room in the intensive care unit of DCH, with a portable hyperbaric chamber secured around her leg. It was something of an experiment to limit the treatment to Christi's leg. Because of her pregnancy, the medical staff could not pursue the conventional course of putting Christi's whole body in the chamber. The impact on the baby was too uncertain.

Surprise

Ask and it will be given to you; seek and you will find; knock and the door will be opened to you. For everyone who asks receives; he who seeks finds; and to him who knocks, the door will be opened.

Matthew 7:7–8 (NIV)

Days had passed, and still Roman could not find Jake. He returned the call to the woman who left a message on his answering machine, and left a message of his own explaining that his missing puppy was blond, not black.

Roman returned to where the old house used to stand and looked around at the devastation. He called out Jake's name, but knew in his heart that the dog could not have survived.

On his way home, Roman was overwhelmed. How would he tell his hospital-ridden wife that her dog was dead? Not wanting her to give up hope, he decided he would not mention it until she was well enough to handle it, although he could not picture when that day would come. He would not lie; he would simply say the truth as he knew it—that Jake had not been found.

Seven days after the storm, the woman called back. "Hello," said the voice. "Is your puppy named Jake?"

Roman started to cry so hard he could not give a proper answer.

She asked him again.

"Yes, ma'am," he answered through tears. "Is he dead?"

"No, honey, I found him under my car—and he's still there—so covered in mud I don't know what color he is anymore. Been feeding him. Finally got close enough to read his tag. But he won't come out for me. Think he's hurt, but he's alive."

It took a few minutes for Roman to stop sobbing enough for him to get directions to the woman's car, just a few blocks from the old house.

Roman ran up to the car and lay down on his belly.

"Come on, boy," he called.

Encrusted in blackened mud and bone-thin from a week without food and water, Jake limped out from under the car on three legs.

Still shaking from the emotion, Roman drove Jake to their veterinarian, Dr. Ohman, at the Oakwood Veterinary Clinic near their house. Roman explained frenetically that his pregnant wife was hospitalized. He needed this dog to be alive, he told them. He begged them to save his life.

"This little guy's going to need surgery on his hind leg if I can save it at all," Dr. Ohman said.

Streams of tears rolled down Roman's cheeks.

The vet looked confused.

"Don't worry, son. Just a broken leg. He's going to be fine. He is."

"It's just," Roman said, "his mother loves him so much, and they were in the tornado together, and he protected her pregnant belly from getting hit, and we don't know if her leg's going to heal either."

Roman drove straight to the hospital to tell Christi the good news, and she cried tears of relief just as Roman had.

Another five days passed, and Jake had recovered enough from surgery to go home. The Del City vet had sent Jake up to a surgeon in Edmond, who saved his leg. When Roman picked up Jake, the pup hopped into his arms and licked his face as though nothing had ever happened.

Roman feared getting the bill from not just one vet, but two. But neither of them charged him a penny.

He knew he was bending the rules. But he did not care. Roman was desperate to lift his wife's spirits. He could barely stand to see her so wounded from the outside in.

Roman waited anxiously outside the lobby of DCH. When he saw Christi coming, her eyes squinting from the first sunlight she had seen since the tornado, he could not keep from smiling ear to ear. Nor could he control the puppy squirming in his arms.

"Surprise," Roman said.

Roman pulled back the blanket and revealed a wet-nosed puppy with a small cast on a hind leg. He wiggled out of Roman's arms and threw his front paws onto Christi's wheelchair.

"No, Jake!" Roman pulled him back.

Christi smiled. She actually smiled.

"Oh my gosh. He looks so big. And he's got all four legs. Lucky little dog." She bent over gingerly, scratched Jake's ears, and let him lick her face.

"You should have seen him when I got him out from under that car. He was covered in mud. Looked like a black dog, not yellow."

"Then it *was* him," Christi said.

"Yes, honey, it was him all along." Roman feared Christi was still out of it. But seeing Jake actually had the opposite effect on her. Knowing that he lived gave her a moment of clarity.

"No, I saw him right afterward, right after the tornado," Christi explained. "I thought I was dreaming. I called out to him even though he was the wrong color, but he just looked at me and limped away. What about Little Miss Muffin?"

Roman shook his head.

"Someone else found her, but she was all but gone. They put her down the same day."

"Oh no."

Tears slipped out of Christi's eyes. She had always loved every dog she had ever known. She even had a tender heart for dogs she did not know, often stopping her car to check on strays, to shoo them away from traffic, or to call their owners.

"What a miracle mutt," Christi said, sniffling, as Jake sniffed around her wheelchair.

"We need a few more of those. Miracles, I mean, not puppies," Roman said. He handed her a Kleenex.

"Don't you worry, Ro'," Christi assured him. It was the first time she had done so since coming to the hospital. "I'm going to make it through this. I've got to—"

"Yeah, you've gotta come home and take care of Mr. Jake-a-roo."

"I love this dog," Christi said as she looked at him—a cast on his hind leg and curled up by her feet. "But I've got to make it through to be Abby's mom."

Home

"Therefore I tell you, do not worry about your life, what you will eat or drink; or about your body, what you will wear. Is not life more important than food, and the body more important than clothes? Look at the birds of the air; they do not sow or reap or store away in barns, and yet your heavenly Father feeds them. Are you not much more valuable than they? Who of you by worrying can add a single hour to his life? And why do you worry about clothes? See how the lilies of the field grow. They do not labor or spin. Yet I tell you not even Solomon in all his splendor was dressed like one of these. If that is how much God clothes the grass of the field, which is here today and tomorrow is thrown into the fire, will not he much more clothe you, O you of little faith?

Matthew 6:25–30 (NIV)

Carolyn was ready to go home. Except that she did not have one.

Carolyn thought about where she could live for the next few months, a place where she would gather enough strength to face the multiple surgeries ahead and perhaps start looking for a new house.

She did not want to impose on Roman, so Christi's house was out of the question. Plus, they would soon have their hands full with a newborn baby.

Many of Carolyn's friends offered up their places. Cheryl insisted on giving up her master bedroom for an indefinite period of time. But as much as she hated to admit it, Carolyn would need help on a daily basis, from getting around to washing what hair she had left.

Nathan had been bouncing between Andy's house and his dad's, and that arrangement was working out well. As for Christi, there was no telling as to when she would be released from the hospital. One short week ago, Carolyn saw her kids on a near-daily basis. Now they were splintered all over the city, each one in a foreign place.

Thanks to KD, her other colleagues, and her friends, who were more organized that she ever imagined, Carolyn's mail and insurance checks were arriving swiftly. Cheryl filled out the mail forwarding address forms at the post office the day after the tornado. The first check, for two thousand dollars, went to Nathan to start rebuilding his wardrobe from scratch. He had been living in his golf clothes for nearly a week, and was in desperate need of everything from a toothbrush and deodorant to underwear and socks—literally, from head to toe.

Nathan had taken the cash to Old Navy. With the wad in his pocket, and looking fairly ragged in his dirty shirt, shorts and red baseball hat, he rushed through the store, piling up layers of shorts, khakis, jeans, golf shirts, t-shirts, hats, and flip flops. One by one, he felt the suspicious eyes of the salespeople, busy whispering in their headsets. They started to trail him through the store. Nathan chuckled to himself, knowing he not only looked and smelled like a man without a home, he *was* homeless, and he understood why they undoubtedly thought he was robbing the place.

If only they knew what I've been through.

Any other homeless man might have had the very same thought.

Nathan filled two shopping carts. But as much as he tried, he found he could not spend all the money. When he returned the remainder, his mother noted that his sister likely would not have had the same problem.

One of the menial tasks ahead that Carolyn dreaded most was getting a new driver's license. She did not like having her picture taken in general, but now she could hardly imagine getting wheeled into the DMV, her hair standing in clumps on her head, and taking a photograph she would be willing to let anyone see.

The day before she was to be discharged from the hospital, Nathan brought Carolyn a white envelope that had arrived in her new P.O. Box. The return address was "Choctaw, OK," a town about fifteen miles away from Del City. Inside was a Post-It note that read, *Look what the wind blew in.*

Carolyn smiled, and then squealed. Under that note was her old driver's license, mailed to the home address which no longer existed. That small, laminated card had been sucked out of a wallet that was inside a purse that was inside a house and carried fifteen or so miles until the wind flung it back on the ground. And someone in a fairly rural part of the county happened to stumble across it and care enough to mail it back. Carolyn stared at the photograph of herself with a thick head of blonde hair, having never before wondered what her life would be like without it. She was surprised by her own joy at having it.

It would be a few months before Carolyn would get the chance to use it. With the tenderness in her head and the broken bones in her hip, she would not be able to drive for a while. The hospital arranged a walker to go home with her, wherever home would be.

On May tenth, her eighth day in St. Anthony hospital, Carolyn awoke to another surprise, an even greater gift. Lying on her bed, enclosed in a plastic bag, was a tattered and dirty book. She did not recognize it from the head of her bed. But when she pulled it close, however, she knew it right away: her burgundy leather Bible. She ran her fingers over the gold-print letters that spelled her name.

Attached to the bag was a note from the woman who had found it.

Dear Carolyn,

You may not remember who I am, but our paths have crossed a time or two in the capitol. Now I suppose we both know the reason we've met before, so that I would know how to return this to you.

May God continue to bless you.

Sharon Veazey

Sharon Veazey! Carolyn knew just who she was. She worked in state representative Gary Bastin's office and lived only a few blocks away in the Del Aire addition. She had an overwhelming feeling that Sharon had been chosen to hand-deliver the book that Carolyn could not live without.

Even though she was shaky on her feet, Carolyn was anxious to leave. She went in to the hospital with nothing; she was going out with her Bible, her driver's license, and her blue sock of jewels. Her faith, her identity, and her treasure.

She would need to see one more thing before making up her mind about where to stay.

Carolyn's family arrived just after noon on the discharge day. Sarah Leona and Pappy collected the remaining balloons, Carolyn's cousin, Pam, and her husband, Bobby Newman, had the most recent bouquets of flowers, Cheryl manned the walker and a new Kate Spade purse she had bought for Carolyn, and J.R. lugged a small suitcase of mostly robes and pajamas. Nathan helped Rhonda lift his mother out of her bed and into a wheelchair. Her head was still wrapped in thick white gauze.

"I don't need this silly wheelchair. I can walk," Carolyn said.

"It's not that we don't believe you. Except that we don't believe you," Rhonda said. "Plus, hospital policy."

They wheeled Carolyn past the glass doors into the bright sunlight. Of all the large and expensive items she lost, all she wanted at that moment was an old pair of black Jackie O-style sunglasses. As her eyes adjusted to daylight, she thought she saw Nathan opening the rear door of a white stretch limousine.

"What on earth?" Carolyn's jaw dropped.

"Your chariot awaits, Mom. All J.R.'s idea."

Slowly, Carolyn pressed herself up out of the wheelchair and accepted help crawling into the limo.

"This is too much!" she said. But, in truth, she was enjoying the extravagance immensely. She felt as though she should have been wearing a sequin dress, a fur, and high heels rather than a fresh head-wrapping and the preppy plaid dress her colleagues had given her to wear home.

One by one, they found their seats around her. Carolyn heard a *pop* and before she knew it, J.R. was handing her a glass flute filled with Dom Perignon champagne.

"Are you sure this goes well with painkillers?" Carolyn asked.

"Never been surer of anything in my life, lady," J.R. said.

Sarah Leona frowned at J.R.

"Come on now, Sarah Leona!" J.R. defended himself. "Carolyn's been in prison with her head chewed up and her hip run over for the better part of a week."

Sarah Leona winced. J.R. continued, mostly for effect.

"Look at her! Your daughter looks like a Holocaust survivor. We've got to celebrate her escape from prison!"

"J.R. Richards!" Carolyn yelled feebly.

Sarah Leona let out a *harrumph*.

"And you ought to know a thing or two about that place."

"Mother!" Carolyn had to stop them, or who knew where they would both go.

Sarah Leona softened, turned toward Carolyn, and patted her knee. Her eyes welled up with tears. It was amazing to Carolyn how quickly Mother could turn off one emotional switch and flip on another. At least she never stayed mad for long.

"Seems like I've been waiting for this day for so long, Carolyn."

"Me too, Mother."

Carolyn looked at her mother, her fair smooth skin, and her smiling eyes. She could not imagine the world without Sarah Leona. Even though mother and daughter had switched parenting roles after Daddy died, Carolyn still regarded her as the family matriarch, the one with all the answers.

Carolyn placed her free hand on her mother's.

"Mom, could I come stay with you for a while?"

"Oh, honey, I would love nothing more." Sarah Leona's cheeks were wet now.

"I'll probably gain fifty pounds, living with you."

"You can stay forever."

"Wait a minute, now," Pappy chimed in. Everyone laughed.

Carolyn knew she would not stay forever, but finally she could picture her life for the coming year. She would likely sleep on the living room couch—it would be easier to get in and out of. There was also the bonus of her mom's home cooking, the best in the world: a chicken fried steak that made you want to lick the pan; mashed potatoes and gravy; homemade apple pie that none of them could duplicate; and cinnamon rolls which, when they lost the state fair contest the year before, made the entire family indignant.

Carolyn tipped her flute, letting the liquid touch her lips, just enough for the bubbles to tickle her nose.

"Mmmmmm," she said, as she closed her eyes and swallowed. She anticipated the moment that would come, sooner than ever before, when she felt light-headed and carefree.

The driver ducked his head through the open interior window. Carolyn beamed when she saw him—it was Jay Burns, the husband of her dear friend, Betty. He worked for J.R.'s cousin, who owned the limo service. She blew him a kiss.

"Everybody set? Next stop: Del City Hospital."

Carolyn held out her glass to J.R.

"Fill her to the top, please."

Together

The Spirit himself testifies with our spirit that we are God's children. Now if we are children, then we are heirs—heirs of God and co-heirs with Christ, if indeed we share in his sufferings in order that we may also share in his glory. I consider that our present sufferings are not worth comparing with the glory that will be revealed in us.

Romans 8:16–18 (NIV)

Carolyn closed her eyes as J.R. wheeled her into DCH. She tried to push away the painful emotions that she associated with that hospital. They rode up the elevator in silence. As Carolyn entered through the doorway of Christi's private room, she wanted to leap out and run to her daughter, just as her heart had already done.

"BoPeep?"

Christi was lying on her side in her bed.

"Mom?"

J.R. pushed Carolyn as close to the bed as he could. Carolyn pulled up on the bedrail and gently clasped Christi's right hand. In a way that reminded them of the time they were last together, they looked each other in the eyes and cried. But these were not tears of fear and farewell. These were tears of relief.

Carolyn whispered, "It's so good to see you, baby. So good."

Christi whispered back, "I can't believe it's been so long."

"That was the hardest part," Carolyn said. "Not knowing how you were."

"I didn't know if this day would come, Mom. I think being cooped up and bedridden in the hospital has been worse than the tornado. It's been pretty rough. But we made it, right?"

"God has blessed us both," Carolyn said. "All three of us." Carolyn patted Christi's belly.

"I'm so sorry about Little Miss Muffin," Christi said.

"Me too," Carolyn said, sitting back down in her wheelchair. "It breaks my heart. But she was old and had a good life. I hear Jake paid you a visit."

"Mom, you know how we held the dogs tight, right before the tornado? I wonder if Jake is the reason my tummy doesn't have a scratch. I wonder if he took the brunt of the beating, protecting Abby from the worst."

"It is possible, Sissy. That dog would do anything for you."

"Before they found him, Aunt Linda brought me that Beanie Baby dog." Christi pointed to a small red stuffed dog on a shelf, surrounded by various get-well gifts. "She thought it would cheer me up, but I just bawled. She felt so bad. But it wasn't just Jake. I was crying over everything."

Even though Carolyn and Christi had spoken over the phone, neither remembered doing it, so they spent the next hour talking about thoughts they had stored up for the last eight days. While Christi was worried about Abby, Carolyn was relieved that her own daughter was alive and well enough to worry. Christi showed Carolyn her bruised body, the staples in her head, the dozens of places where doctors had stitched her up like a "rag doll," and still dozens more where glass shards and long splinters would have to work their way out. She told Carolyn the saga of almost losing her leg, her doctor who went MIA, and the wood block found in her head. While Carolyn's skin grafts were a week into the healing process, Christi's infection would have to improve before getting grafted. But not a single one of her bones was broken, and her belly was round, beautiful, and unmarked.

Christi explained how she had been bedridden nearly twenty-four-seven for the past eight days, except for skin debridement, which had just begun. She sat in a whirlpool bath and endured excruciating procedures to clean and remove infected and dead skin. She had tried to limit her intake of painkillers because of Abby. Nurses explained what would be expected of her in physical therapy, but as it was, Christi was so swollen that she could not move her arms and legs.

"Mom, I had to lie on a table, just like for surgery, but I wasn't under. And I just screamed through it, knowing I had to do it."

"I can't stand it that you've been in here, of all places. I'm so sorry I haven't been here for you," Carolyn told Christi.

"I'm sorry I haven't been there for you, Mom."

Carolyn downplayed her own wounds, saying the scalping was not as bad as it sounded.

"The doctors think something as harmless as a piece of paper could've done it."

"Mom, a leaf could've knocked our heads off if it had hit just right. How did we survive?"

Carolyn almost forgot to mention her broken hip.

They marveled at how two people could start in the same place and end up with such widely different injuries. They had both seen images of the Del Aire addition on the news and wondered how they had survived. They likened it to a horrific car accident where it doesn't seem possible for anyone to have walked out alive, and then someone does, without a scratch. Then there are fender benders where someone dies of a heart attack. Who can say who will live and who will not? There is a time to tear down, a time to build; a time to be born, a time to die. There is a time for everything and a season for every purpose, and we are not the ones who set the calendar or wind the clock.

Carolyn clasped Christi's hand once more. They closed their eyes and prayed together.

"Dear Lord," Christi began, "Thank you for bringing my mom here and for healing her so she can go home. Thank you for keeping Abby alive. Please help us get through this trying time. The staff of this hospital needs your help, too, Lord. We love you, Lord. Amen."

Carolyn continued.

"Lord, thank you for sparing us for some purpose. We promise to find out what that purpose is and fulfill it. Please continue to protect my child. We are powerless without you. With you, we know all things are possible. From this day forward, let Christi, little Abby, and me always be a testimony to your power to perform untold miracles. We put all our trust in your hands. Amen."

Mother and daughter had exhausted themselves, physically and emotionally, but neither of them wanted to let go.

"I love you so much, Mom."

"More than ever, baby. More than ever."

"Where are you going now? I mean, where are you going to live?" Christi asked.

"I thought maybe Granny's and Pappy's house."

"Well, Roman has to go back to work, so... when I get out of here; can I stay there too, with you?"

"You can stay with me forever, BoPeep."

The Durens: Paul, Steve, Roman, Christi & Mydonna

Christi: National Cheerleading Champion/Kerr Jr. High

Christi, Roman & Bo at Bo's Pre-K graduation

Nathan with his wife Marci, the love of his life

Del City Mayor Brian Linley, State Representative Scott Inman, Carolyn, Christi & Bo attending the memorial dedication to those Del Aire residents who lost their lives in the tornado

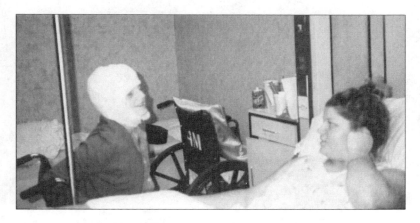

Mother & Daughter Reunited: Together

Bo & Momo (Carolyn) after her successful reconstructive surgeries

Manning (Mimi) Stager & Sloane Suiters

The Clematis Club: End Times

The American Spirit on Del Aire Place after May 3

*Carolyn & Christi were found near
the hot water tank: Found*

TWIST OF FAITH

Cable wrapped around Nathan's truck; he and his friends trying to turn upright

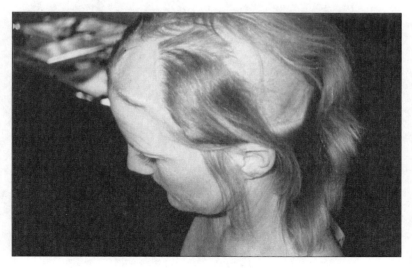

Carolyn scalped with skin grafts

A visit from Rep Laura Boyd

Nancy Nichols taking Carolyn for a doctor's visit

Jane Bown (one of the many friends who took turns staying with Carolyn)

Sarah Leona & Russell Morgan (mother & pappy)

Christi's jeep

Pappy & Don Stager searching through debris

Bo with Pa (Fireman Steve Duren)

Mimi's first birthday (with wig & crown)

Bo modeling one of Momo's hats

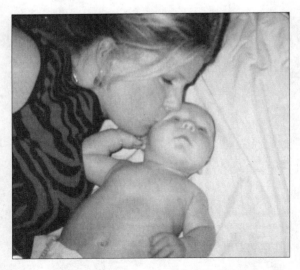

Beautiful Baby Bo & Mom (Christi): Beautiful

Baby Abby's grave: One by One

Baby Abby's grave: One by One

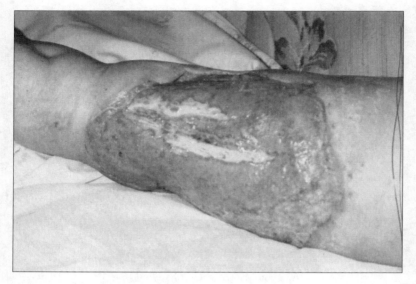

Christi's injured leg

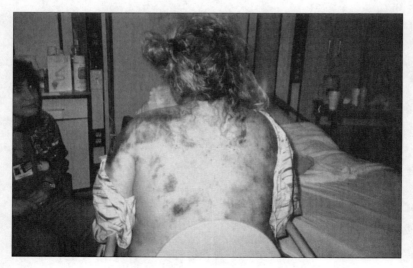

Christi's back

*Carolyn with her children, Christi &
Nathan: the air she breathes*

Pappy searching through debris

Miracle Pillow, taken 2 nights before the storm: Miracles

Miracles

You are the God who performs miracles; you display your power among the people.

Psalm 77:14 (NIV)

Carolyn lived at her mother's house for nearly a year. It was not exactly her childhood home, but she had close to two decades of memories in it already. Her mother and father had bought it together back in the late seventies only one year before his untimely death, and the family spent many holidays and weekends gathered there. As far as a place to recuperate, it turned out to be the right choice. She needed the steadiness of familiarity and the comfort of her own mother to get through the most turbulent and trying twelve months of her life.

The constant rotation of friends and family members carried over well from the hospital to home. KD scheduled two-dozen people to take turns sleeping in a recliner next to the sofa where Carolyn spent her nights. J.R.'s sister Sharon, friends like Saundra Naifeh, Susan Hillman, Charlotte Edwards, and Jane Bown, a former colleague, volunteered to care for Carolyn overnight, lifting the load off of Sarah Leona and

Pappy. The group took turns transporting Carolyn to the hospital for continuing care of her scalp and for physical therapy to help teach her body to walk again.

As grateful as Carolyn was for the time her friends and family took to serve her needs, all their help in the face of all her helplessness made her uncomfortable. She did not want to rely on them, and yet, she had no choice. The process of physical therapy was so slow and tedious that she did not talk about it much. She certainly did not like to complain lest she burden those she loved with what she considered her own problems. There are some people who will share their intimate struggles, but over the years, Carolyn had witnessed those depressing details weighed people down. She always believed in the power of positive thinking, and liked to watch the way it lifted people up. Often, Sarah Leona would be left guessing how terrible the day might be, or how much she must miss Christi, but Carolyn tried to downplay the uphill struggle. She was not trying to play the super hero and pretend that nothing hurt, but Carolyn felt guided by a supernatural power that ultimately gave her a sense of calm and serenity throughout her recovery.

At her lowest points, when Carolyn wanted to disappear from view, she would curl up on the couch and close her eyes. When her family and friends would wash her hair and apply medicated ointment to her surgical scars, she hid her deep embarrassment by making jokes about her appearance. She knew it was wrong to be vain—she had her life after all—but she had lost control over the way she liked to present herself to the world, and she felt terribly vulnerable.

It had never been her way to open the floodgates of emotion to anyone, except to God. Too tired to write in her journal, she prayed about the things too painful to speak of—Christi's continued hospitalization, the life of her unborn baby, and the unsightly condition of her own scalp. Her head and her heart were both exposed, try as she might to shield them.

The easiest gift in the world to give Carolyn was a scarf. She wore one around her head every day. They were soft, light, and even stylish. She did not have to worry about them blowing off, exposing her patchy scalp underneath. Better yet, they did not make her want to scratch her head, as a wig would. She even bought some ultra soft material, and her friends Wilma and Chris offered to sew a few bandanas. By summer's end, she had one scarf for every outfit she owned.

A more difficult gift to give Carolyn, but one she needed badly, was clothing. Her entire wardrobe had been wiped out. Carolyn's stylish and form-fitting outfits would not be practical in her fragile condition anyway. She was reliant upon her friends who did their best picking out colorful frocks and house-dresses.

Carolyn did not gain fifty pounds, partly because Sarah Leona did not cook nearly as much as Carolyn had expected. She did not blame her mother, however. Sarah Leona had done more than her share of cooking over the years. Plus, Carolyn's appetite had diminished after the hospital stay, affected by the amount of painkillers in her system. Some nights she would skip supper altogether, and indulge in her favorite treat-being Toffee Nut Chocolate ice cream from Braum's, the local dairy shop up the street. More often than she would like to admit, she would chop up a Heath bar and sprinkle it on top to give it more crunch. She did not care if the habit gave it more fat too. Normally, she would care, but she believed her evenings on the treadmill would resume one day.

As she had pictured, Carolyn camped out on the living room couch. Friends had a place to sit and visit, and Carolyn did not have to get out of "bed" to see them. Keeping her head elevated was easier on a couch. She could not lie on her left side because of the skin grafts or on her right because of her broken hip. She would have been tempted to lie down in a bed despite the terrible pressure on her head. Because Sarah Leona was concerned about infection; every single day she washed Carolyn's sheets and the cases of ten pillows that surrounded her. The bi-weekly visits from physical therapists also happened in that same space. A phone, a TV remote, a CD player, books, magazines, a food tray, and her walker were all within reach. The bed in the guest room sat untouched, awaiting Christi's arrival.

Christi stayed at DCH for a full month. She nearly went stir crazy. Like Carolyn, there was no comfortable sleeping position. Christi's leg had to be elevated, so she could not lie in the fetal position. Being pregnant, she could not lie on her stomach. She had no choice but to lie on her back, which made breathing difficult, and, as Christi learned later, was not the optimal position for her unborn baby. No one in the family was satisfied with her care, especially when they discovered that Christi remained mostly bedridden for the duration of her stay. At least the hospital staff had kept a fetal monitor running without interruption. At night, Christi would lie awake listening for the blip-blip-blip on the screen, hoping it was the sound of her daughter's heartbeat and not just the machine running its course.

Learning to walk again proved more challenging for Christi, because she could not put pressure on her right leg. The therapist at DCH told her to use one crutch. It made Sarah Leona cringe to see her granddaughter, heavy with child, wince in pain as she hopped on her good leg.

After one of Christi's many surgeries—this particular one happened to be for her leg again—she began contracting. The doctors were frantic, believing her body was not strong enough to endure labor. A c-section was out of the question as well because of the risk of infection and her immune system's compromised ability to fight back. Her obstetrician, plastic surgeon, kidney specialist, and nurses all agreed that the baby should not be delivered yet. Birth would be too risky for Christi, they said. Fortunately, her contractions subsided, and Christi remained mostly bedridden.

Carolyn was eager to be mobile, but the doctors did not want her driving for a minimum of eight weeks. A manicurist named Carolyn Page offered to set up shop at Sarah Leona's to continue their long-standing friendship over nail files and polish. After a few home sessions, Carolyn's work friends were happy to play chauffeur. KD's husband, Steve, even volunteered to take Carolyn out for appointments, and Carolyn wondered whether KD had suggested the kindness or enforced it.

Every beautician, mailman, and visitor wanted to hear the story of how Carolyn and Christi survived. Carolyn told it twice a day every day for many weeks. But Carolyn liked to turn the question around too because it seemed everyone had a near-miss story of their own. One of her favorites came from Phil Ostrander, a state representative from Owasso, a respectably-sized suburb of Tulsa with a population of 18,502, who was kind enough to visit Carolyn throughout her convalescence.

"We knew the storm was coming," he told her, "but nobody could get home in time, so we charged out of the capitol but only got as far as the Stomp, and you know how fancy that deal is…"

The Buffalo Stomp, as they called it, was an annual event for lawmakers and lobbyists to break up the monotony of long legislative sessions. It was held in an infamously inelegant place—a dive, to be sure—but everyone looked forward to the camaraderie, free food, and ample drink. With so many frightening stories about May 3, Carolyn could tell already that Phil's was going to make her laugh.

"One of the guys got into his car and tried to leave, but police waved him off the road. So he sees this overpass—I know, real smart, right? He hides out with all these people under an overpass, and one of the ladies there was real cute. Here they all think they're going to get blown to bits, and he up and says to the pretty one, 'I'll just hold on to you, honey!'"

Carolyn knew every single person in Phil's story, and they truly were characters. As she laughed harder, she was surprised at how much she missed the good ole boys' club culture at the capitol. Maybe it was because they had never made her feel like an outsider, even though she fell into the lobbying profession by accident.

A decade earlier, Carolyn had been working part-time for an attorney whose office was in the same building as the Municipal League. The league took to the legislature issues that mattered to cities and towns, like water, roads, and taxes. The head of the league, Don Rider, stuck his head in Carolyn's office.

"I'm not being nosey. Just wanted to see if my interviewee is hiding out here."

Partly kidding, Carolyn answered, "If he doesn't show up, I'll interview."

In ten minutes, Carolyn combed her hair, put on lipstick, and filled out an application.

"They're ready for you," Don announced.

The "they" stuck with Carolyn for years afterward, because she had not anticipated that she would have to defend her credentials before a panel of directors. Carolyn told them that she had worked for the federal government (at Tinker), that she had run her own business (children's clothing), and that she was a quick study.

A short while later, a board member whom Carolyn did not know well came into her office to borrow the phone.

"I'm not sure if you'll get the job, Miss Carolyn," he said, "but you were very impressive."

Carolyn was up against some stiff competition, including a former speaker of the state house. She knew this because someone accidentally left the resumes in the copy machine. But fortune was on her side, and so was Don. He convinced the board that he could bring in someone fresh and teach his way. Carolyn was hired. She was just thirty-four years old, had two kids at home, and had never stepped foot inside the state capitol building.

Her first session started in January, and Don died suddenly in April. Without her mentor, Carolyn was lost. She called herself the Green Machine, literally dropping paper clips around the capitol so she could find her way out.

Listening to Phil reminded her of those days, when his funny stories put her at ease.

"Then Bob Plunk—you know Bob, of course..."

Carolyn nodded. Representative Plunk came from a tiny town called Allen, population 951, southeast of the city. He and Representative Ostrander had always given Carolyn their time, their unbridled opinions, and their respect.

"I'm in the room next to Bob at the Stomp. I hear all this noise. Old Bob is pulling the mattress off his bed, knocking darn near everything off the walls trying to shove it through the bathroom door. I swear to you that the Stomp was spared except for one room—

Room 15. Bob's room. It took a direct hit. I think Bob got nothing but a bump on his head when he hit the tub."

Carolyn laughed so hard she thought she might have pulled a muscle in her stomach. She wiped the tears from her eyes and told Phil he was good medicine. Even after he left, the laughter stayed with her. She could not wait to get back to work.

In one of her first forays out of the house, J.R. took Carolyn back to the old neighborhood. In a way he was the right one to do it; he was neither prone to sentimentality nor nostalgia. While she was eager to see it, she dreaded it too. But with J.R., she knew she would be expected to hold it together. He had already shown her the photographs, but she found that they were indeed snapshots, incapable of telling the whole story.

The Del Aire addition was still secured by police tape and the National Guard. Only homeowners and their family and close friends were allowed to go in. As J.R. and Carolyn sat parked in front of her property, her eyes welled up with tears, because the home she had loved for twenty-two years looked like it had been hit by a bomb. From the guardsmen to the decimated landscape, she was the closest she had ever been to understanding the look and feel of a war zone.

Carolyn had already thought about relocating and weighed the benefits of rebuilding. There would be a bond with her neighbors unlike any she had experienced before, but that prospect was not enough. Seeing the destruction with her own eyes sealed it for her. She accepted that her time on Del Aire Place had served its reasons and its seasons. The home where she raised her family no longer existed. The kids and grandkids would never get the chance to see the place where they grew up. Their old address was literally wiped off the map, and she had no desire to put it back. Thirty-three twenty-four Del Aire Place had disappeared forever.

Knowing she could stay with her parents as long as she pleased gave her a good measure of comfort. The last place she wanted to pour her energy into was negotiating with architects, builders, and painters, or sifting through fixtures, tiles, and toilets. Besides, she had a family to keep intact and a head to rebuild. Those two things were more than enough.

Carolyn began to investigate how to get her hair back. She imagined it would be an easy fix and made an appointment to discuss the options with Dr. Bajaj. He told her that reconstruction might be possible, but that she would have to wait at least a year for her head to heal completely from the skin grafts. After their consultation, Dr. Bajaj inspected his work and discovered that one of the grafts applied in the hospital had not taken well. It would have to be redone. Dr. Bajaj had already harvested two skin strips off of the left hip; this time, he would have to harvest from the right, below her broken bones. Going back to St. Anthony's for the surgery felt surreal to Carolyn. Here she thought she was not only home, but one step closer to returning to normal, not one giant step backward. She kept reminding herself that she was in a far better place this round than the last one. But in the back of her mind, she began to glimpse the fact that she had barely started on the road to recovery.

Carolyn returned to her mother's house after two days, faster than she should have. But she could not force herself to spend any more time in a hospital anywhere. The sudden move back home shocked her system, and this time she reacted to the painkillers with violent shaking and vomiting. Dr. Bajaj changed her prescription, but she cut back on her dosage, preferring the reality of suffering to the drug-induced haze.

As her head and hips began to heal, Carolyn thought it wise to seek a second surgical opinion. Through several friends, she had heard about Dr. Timothy Walker, a skilled plastic surgeon at Mercy Hospital in Oklahoma City. Something stuck with her when she thought about this doctor whom she had not yet met—a touching story about his reconstruction of a little boy's ear after it was torn off by a Pit Bull. She was also intrigued to know that he was artistically-inclined—a gifted pianist. When she called his office, she thought she would have an answer from him within a few weeks. However, she would have to wait months before Dr. Walker had an opening for a new patient.

But all of that would happen after Christi finally came home from the hospital.

Every day away from Christi was a painful one. Carolyn spent many evenings praying with her mother that God would, first and foremost, heal her daughter and watch over her unborn granddaughter. She also asked God to forgive her for not staying with them in the hospital. And she prayed that God would release her guilt over having asked Christi to come to her house before the tornado struck.

"Here she comes, bouncing like a bunny up the driveway!" Sarah Leona yelled out as Christi and Roman slowly made their way to the front door.

Roman carried a few of Christi's belongings—a suitcase full of maternity clothes, the red Beanie Baby puppy, and a thick pillow from their bed at home. The decision to have Christi stay at her grandmother's came easily for both of them. Roman needed to return to work full-time, and Christi needed someone to take her to the hospital twice a day. But even before the storm on May 3, they had a stormy marriage younger than a full-term baby. They fought frequently and injured each other with harsh words, as young lovers tend to do with reckless abandon. They would make up partially, but with each argument, they shook the foundation under them, deepened the cuts that hurt them, and eroded the love they believed they once felt. Christi did not know how to articulate it, as they had not learned the art of gentle communication, but all she wanted was a husband who would take care of her, especially at this time. Although he knew she was not physically capable of it, Roman wanted his wife to take care of him as well; at the very least, to recognize that he had open wounds from the tornado too, however invisible to her. Living apart at such a tender time gave them both relief. Roman's mother Mydonna would look after his needs, and Granny Sarah Leona would look after Christi's.

"I still don't think that's right, just one crutch. Look at her! Why didn't they give my Christi a wheelchair? That's got to be hard on the baby, don't you think?" Sarah Leona asked Carolyn.

"Let's just get her in here, Mother, and we'll take care of her."

"You won't do a thing. She's my baby now."

Sarah Leona rushed outside to give Christi a hand. Carolyn managed to push herself up onto her walker, and as Christi hopped through the front door, she shuffled toward her daughter. They were both bandaged and damaged, but they were home. They stood, holding each other for longer than they had ever done before, ignoring the pain in their bodies because of the pleasure it gave them in their hearts. Just to be upright was special. Sarah Leona watched her daughter and granddaughter disappear behind a waterfall of tears.

"Oh my land!" Sarah Leona interrupted. "If you two don't stop, I will cry until I die!"

Christi moved into the guest bedroom, and Sarah Leona took to the daily cleaning and changing of her sheets as well. She cooked simple meals most of the time, but one night she whipped up a chicken fried steak, mashed potatoes, cream gravy, and her famous apple pie to celebrate the homecoming. Many of Christi's and Carolyn's caregivers showed up to enjoy the meal, and they stayed until the bright stars called them home.

One morning, a few days later, Sarah Leona had an announcement.

"I can't take it anymore."

Carolyn and Christi looked at each other, wondering what she meant. Surely she did not intend to kick her daughter and grandchild out on the streets, although the women might have understood if she had.

"We have got to do something about that rat's nest on Christi's head."

Christi's hair, still tangled with debris, had become one of Sarah Leona's projects, if not an obsession. Each day she would try to run a brush through a matted area without luck. It was incomprehensible to Sarah Leona that so many bits of glass, dirt, and wood could be anywhere much less in her granddaughter's hair, and more than a month after the tornado. Patty warned her mother that she had done the same thing for the last four weeks in the hospital, but that the knots would not budge. Sarah Leona had bought every kind of brush, from soft ones with wide spaces to fine toothed combs, determined as ever to bring back her granddaughter's long, lush locks.

After several days of struggle, Sarah Leona invited Christi to join her at the beauty shop. Getting her hair styled and set was a weekly indulgence for Sarah Leona; never would you see a lily white curl out of place. Christi agreed, but only if they would not cut her hair, as Sarah Leona had suggested in frustration a few too many times. Four girls worked on Christi, massaging her head with fistfuls of high-powered conditioner and using their fingers to unbind every twist and turn. After three hours, they had done it. Sarah Leona declared it a miracle. They would not accept a penny for their labor or time. It was difficult to know who was giddier over the return of Christi's lovely curls—Christi herself or Sarah Leona.

When grandmother and granddaughter returned to the house, they found Maxine, a cousin of Sarah Leona's, visiting with Carolyn. After they fussed over how much Christi resembled her former self, Maxine handed Carolyn an envelope.

"What is this?" Carolyn asked. She opened the envelope and pulled out a small square of white material, no more than three by three inches. It looked like a piece of an old pillow case cover.

"It's a prayer cloth," Maxine explained. "In Matthew's Gospel, he says people were healed when they touched the hem of Jesus' garment. Wish I could get you some of that, but this will have to do. You'll be amazed by the power of this soft little square."

Maxine described how she took the square of material to a prayer service and had it anointed with oil, just like she had read about in James where the sick are anointed. Her minister led a prayer of healing over the cloth, she said, as Paul might have done. A friend had given Maxine her first prayer cloth when she was diagnosed with cancer, and she wore it still, removing it only at bedtime.

By luck, or by grace according to Maxine, her dentist had discovered a lump on the floor of her mouth. It turned out to be follicular non-Hodgkins lymphoma.

The doctors had told Maxine that after chemotherapy, radiation would burn her throat and destroy her saliva glands and her teeth. She would have all of her teeth pulled, as the bone structure would be too weak to support them. Her gums would shrink and mouth sores would be slow to heal. Dentures would not be possible.

"Those were my dark ages. They lasted three months."

Maxine was terribly anxious about the ordeal and lost sleep as she imagined the worst-case scenarios.

Then a friend brought her the cloth. It had been prayed over by people Maxine did not know. When it was hard to pray for herself, she felt the prayers of others lift her up. To her it symbolized a way to pray without ceasing, something she did not always have the strength to do.

Her prayer cloth was a spiritual IV, a pain patch, a constant continuation of prayers every second of the day. She often placed her hand over it and felt the flow of comfort. A point of contact that calmed her down. Eventually, the doctor said she would not need radiation after all.

"'Thank you, God!' I shouted," Maxine said with a smile on her face, her hands in the air. Sarah Leona had joined her, arms waving over her head.

"Carolyn, I'm telling you, the power of prayer cannot be underestimated."

"No, it can't," Sarah Leona added. "Amen, Maxine. No it can't."

Carolyn did not mind their animated expressions in word and action. Growing up in a Pentecostal household, she was accustomed to the boldness of their faith.

Maxine continued.

"So, first it healed my mind, my emotions, and my spirit. And then, I believe, it healed my body. I pray for the same for you."

"Maxine, I don't know how to thank you," Carolyn said. She fingered the cloth, already sensing the power within. "What a thoughtful gift."

"Oh! I'm not finished!" she said, and turned to Christi.

Maxine picked up a photograph out of a stack that she had brought and handed it to Christi. It was a picture of Carolyn and Christi smiling serenely, leaning in toward each other while sitting on Sarah Leona's living room couch (the one that was now Carolyn's bed) two nights before the tornado. Carolyn helped her mother prepare the big meal that night, just as she would even if she had a long day at the office, an hour on the treadmill, and two different spring parties. No one had noticed at the time, not even Maxine (who had taken the photograph), that lying next to mother and daughter was a pillow that read:

Miracles Happen To Those Who Believe

Yes, they do, Carolyn thought.
But sometimes they do not.

One by One

For you created my inmost being;
you knit me together in my mother's womb.
I praise you because I am fearfully and wonderfully made;
your works are wonderful,
I know that full well.
My frame was not hidden from you
when I was made in the secret place.
When I was woven together in the depths of the earth,
your eyes saw my unformed body.
All the days ordained for me
were written in your book
before one of them came to be.
Psalm 139:13–16 (NIV)

Christi arrived at her grandmother's house very upset. She hopped angrily into the guest bathroom. One by one, Carolyn heard bottles of prescription medicine crash at the bottom of the plastic trash can.

"What happened, Sis?" Carolyn asked.

"Why didn't anyone at that God-forsaken place tell me pain meds would hurt my baby?"

Roman was unusually quiet.

She and Roman had just come back from their first appointment with her regular obstetrician since being released from the hospital a week earlier. Dr. Perry had explained that her baby could arrive addicted to painkillers and might suffer from withdrawals.

"I don't want to do that to her, Mom."

From that point on Christi refused to take a pill, not even an aspirin. Her leg and head still throbbed, and movement in her arms was limited, but she was determined to give her baby a fighting chance. They had made it through the tornado, the hospital, and only had one more month to go before her pregnancy would be full-term.

Six days later, Christi awoke to a wet bed. She wondered if her water had broken, but she was certain she was not having contractions.

She brought it up to her grandmother and Roman, who had come over for breakfast. Carolyn happened to be visiting J.R. in Tulsa.

"You know, Sis, I haven't heard you talk about Abby moving much," Roman said. "When's the last time you felt her kick?"

Physically, Christi had felt surprisingly good this morning, the best day yet since the tornado. But now she was alarmed.

Christi picked up the phone and called Dr. Perry. She could not remember when Abby last moved.

"She's probably just pressing on your bladder," Dr. Perry said.

"Go on down to Presby, and they'll hook you up and listen in so you can see that everything is okay," he reassured her. "And if it's time to deliver, I think you're strong enough."

I am strong enough, thought Christi.

Dr. Perry planned to deliver the baby at Presbyterian Hospital in Oklahoma City, a few blocks south of the capitol, which suited Christi as she never intended to voluntarily return to DCH.

On the trip to the hospital, Christi kept telling herself that nothing was wrong. Neither she nor Roman said a word.

The nurse began the ultrasound, and the room was silent. Roman stood in the doorway, feeling tenser with each passing second. Then, without a word, she walked out.

A second nurse walked into the room. She looked at the monitor and readjusted the ultrasound position.

"We need to bring a specialist in."

"Why?" Christi asked.

"We're going to have to work on this, because we can't find a heartbeat."

"Well," Christi pleaded, "keep trying. Beause I know she's okay. I know she is."

But her words were empty. Christi wanted to believe with every fiber in her body that her baby was okay. But in her heart, Christi knew that Abby was gone.

Roman took a long look at the ultrasound. Usually, Abby's hands would be pointed up, her tiny fingers spread wide. The second he saw that her hands lay limply, he knew too.

Roman lost it. He kicked a chair and punched a

hole in the wall. He could not say what he was thinking. *What else can possibly go wrong? What else? And for what, God? I'm just married, having a baby, supposed to be the happiest time of my life. And it's the worst. The worst. You're not supposed to lay on me any more than I can handle. Well, I can't handle this.*

Roman punched the wall again. The knuckles of his right hand were bleeding.

He waited until his chest stopped heaving to call his mother and then Christi's.

Carolyn listened to his words, but all she could hear was another voice in her head saying, "The thief in the night is back, and he's taken Abby with him."

The specialist confirmed in dry, medical terms that the fetus was non-responsive. Dr. Perry, the same doctor who delivered Christi twenty-five years earlier, pulled up a chair and took hold of her hand. She could not look at him. She stared at the ceiling while she sobbed.

He gently explained that a c-section was not an option for her because of the trauma her body had already sustained and the infection risk. She had two options: to carry the baby until the body naturally aborted or to deliver.

Christi chose to deliver Abby. She could not stand the thought of carrying a lifeless baby for another second.

Roman called the family and close friends, and they rushed to the hospital. But all fifty of them, except for Roman and Carolyn, waited outside the delivery room.

The Pitocin worked its way through Christi's body, bringing on contractions fast, hard, and strong. Her labor pains were great, unbearable by any measure, exacerbating the pain in her broken heart. Christi bawled through all of it. Carolyn stood at the foot of her daughter's bed, powerless and numb.

"I see her...here she is," Dr. Perry said calmly, although he felt his heart seize up. First the tornado, then this; the worst double-jeopardy he had ever seen. It was painfully unfair. He swallowed the lump in his throat and said, "Christi, this is just what I expected."

The umbilical cord was wrapped around her neck.

Dr. Perry handed the tiny baby to a nurse for weighing, measuring, and documenting her prints.

Then he asked, "Do you want to see her?"

"No," Christi answered. "I can't."

Christi did not notice the nurse, whose name she did not know, and whose face she would not remember, leave the room and return with a stuffed white bear. On its back were two golden wings. She gave it to Christi, who held the bear to her chest.

"Christi," she said in a soft voice, as if she were an angel whispering a secret in her ear, "you need to reconsider. Moms who don't see their babies have a harder time later, and then it's too late. If you have anything left inside of you, do this. You will not regret it. I promise that one day you will be thankful that you saw the beauty God created through you."

Christi hugged the bear harder, burying her face in its head. The nurse waited patiently by her bed.

Christi looked up at her, handed her the bear, and nodded.

Once Christi saw her daughter, she did not want to let her go.

Abby Dawn was wrapped in a white hospital blanket with pink and blue stripes and a pink knit cap, the same as if she had been alive. She weighed only three pounds.

Christi cradled Abby in her arms and let her tears fall onto the blanket.

This could be a dream. At any moment she could wake up. Any moment.

These were Christi's thoughts, but just like her husband in anger, she could not express them in false hope. All Dr. Perry and the nurses saw was a woman drowning in sorrow.

Oh, Abby, the whole time I was pregnant, I couldn't wait to see what you looked like. Now I know. You look like me, when I was a baby.

I pray that you did not suffer because of me. You don't look like you did. You're the most beautiful being I've ever seen.

Christi raised her daughter up to her lips and placed a kiss on her forehead.

I don't understand why God took you, but I see the peace he's given you.

Roman stared at the floor and did not move his back from the wall. His feet would not move.

"Take all the time you need, Roman," said Dr. Perry.

But he could not move from the wall.

Slowly, each of the family members streamed into the room. Everyone was crying.

"Look," Christi said.

She lifted Abby's pink cap, revealing the most unusual head of newborn hair any of them had ever seen. Thick and shiny, it looked like platinum.

"My sweet little angel."

One by one, each of them took a turn holding Abby. One by one, they unleashed their grief.

Christi watched them and prayed in a way she had never done so before.

I don't understand you today, Lord. Pregnancy made my recovery that much harder. And then you took her anyway. After everything, you took her anyway! I just don't understand that. I never will.

The nurses allowed the family and Christi to have as much time as they needed with Abby. Once she was back in her mother's arms, a nurse told Christi, as tenderly as she could, "Let us take her now, to another room."

And she took Abby away.

Afterward, Dr. Perry explained that Christi had preeclampsia and no fluid in her placenta. During her stay at DCH, Christi thought the nurses and doctors had paid close attention to her unborn baby. Had she not been listening to Abby's heartbeat all along? But all of it had gone undiagnosed. The family was horrified. Their worst fears about the hospital were confirmed, and they knew Christi was living and breathing only because her family had fought for her.

Exhausted both physically and emotionally, Christi

took a long nap. Carolyn went home, but Sarah Leona stayed. It was dark outside when Christi awoke. She looked at her grandmother, who gave a sympathetic smile in return.

"Granny," Christi told her, "it's going to say June 13 on her death certificate."

"I know, baby," Sarah Leona said. "It's okay."

"I'm so sorry. It's your birthday."

"Christi, it took a lot of heart and soul to have that baby. I won't think of this as the day she died. It's the day she was born. It's touching to me to know she went to the Lord on my birthday."

Because of the preeclampsia, Christi's blood pressure was too high to safely release her from the hospital. She would stay at least two nights. Everyone else would handle the funeral arrangements.

Christi did help Roman write the obituary. He took out a long yellow legal pad and started writing. For a tiny baby who never lived on earth, they had a lot to say about her.

> Abby Dawn, our little angel, was born and went to be with Jesus on June 13, 1999. Abby will join in heaven her great-grandparents, Nathan Crump, Fran Duren, and George and Marie Stager; great-great grandparents, Ada Crump and Emmett Paul Papin, Sr., Edna and Art Mitcham, and Dorothy Wilcoxson. She is survived by her parents, Roman and Christi Duren, Del City; grandparents, Don & Carolyn Stager, Steve & Mydonna Duren; great-grandparents, Emmett & Margaret Papin, Don Duren, Leona & Russell Morgan; uncles, Paul Duren & Nathan Stager and aunt, Angie Hunter

and a host of other relatives and friends. Abby: Even though God's perfect will did not allow you to enjoy a long life in this world as we were planning, we know you are safe in heaven with your Heavenly Father. We love you, baby, more than words can even say. You will be in our hearts and lives forever, and we will look forward to the day when we are re-united with you and God in heaven as a family. Love, Mommy.

Baby girl: We know you are in a better place. I know your great-gram will take care of you till me and your mommy finally come to see you. Love, Daddy. Services will be at 2:00 p.m. Wednesday, June 16, 1999, Bill Eisenhour Southeast Chapel with burial at Sunny Lane Cemetery. In lieu of flowers, a fund has been set up in the name of Abby Duren at Arvest Bank in Del City to help defray medical expenses due to the May 3 tornado.

"We can't afford to print all this," Roman said.

But every word was printed. Their aunts and uncles covered the cost.

Carolyn chose the dress which came with a matching cap and blanket. It was a dress for a preemie, for a child weighing less than four pounds. Lace, tiny pearls, and a bow of ribbon framed the neckline. The body was made of white crushed cotton—dainty yet fancy enough to be a gown for a baptism. Christi told her that it was perfect, and that she would like to keep it after the worst of the nightmare had passed.

Mydonna took care of the rest, right down to the smallest casket, the size of a doll's cradle, lined with plush pink satin. She told Christi not to worry about a single detail. Christi was grateful to have two mothers helping her through the aftermath.

Roman's minister from his childhood, Rev. J. Harold Thompson, and the preacher who married Roman and Christi, Rev. Kent Pierce, performed the service. Christi's friend, Stephanie, would sing "Amazing Grace." A sweet song about dancing in heaven's courtyard, "Serenaded by Angels," also would be played. Carolyn's friend Barbara Smith had heard it before and made the suggestion. Christi and Carolyn would remember very little of any of it, except for one important detail. Abby would have an open casket.

While that arrangement might sound strange to outsiders, everyone wanted to see her, and Christi wanted her to be seen. Lying in perfect peace in her casket, Abby looked like a porcelain doll with pink lips and shiny hair. Christi wanted all to bear witness to this beautiful and precious child; to the truth that, even in death, she was a miraculous creation.

A few hundred people poured into the funeral home, spilling out into the hallway. A few hundred people came to say goodbye, not to a baby they had never met, but to a baby they had all hoped for. Abby was supposed to be the silver lining in one family's terrible tragedy. One by one, they walked up to her small casket. They walked slowly and lingered long, needing to bond with her or to admire her flawless skin and platinum hair. Everyone was allowed whatever time they needed to mourn the baby. Their sadness and pity deepened when they saw Christi, far too young to be sitting in a wheelchair and too innocent to be burying a child. Under a gray scarf and leaning on a walker, Carolyn looked older than her years as well. They had both been battered from the outside in, and their punishment seemed cruel and unjust. They had survived only to experience a living death. The first storm tested their physical strength, but Abby's death was the storm that tested their faith.

Everyone could not help but wonder, *how can one family possibly endure so much loss?*

When the viewing was over, Roman and Nathan carried out the coffin, which appeared even tinier in their hands. Carolyn met them in a private room and asked the funeral director if she could remove the gown to save it for Christi. She pulled a pink doll-sized dress out of her purse to use instead. But the director looked at Abby and shook his head. He could not do it. The baby's skin was too fragile, and the white gown needed to stay on. Carolyn understood, and she tucked away the pink dress.

In the infant section of the cemetery around Abby's plot lay dozens of teddy bears, clusters of balloons, and thousands of flowers. Even the high school football team had given a floral arrangement in the shape of a jersey.

The pink stone of the grave marker featured an etching of a little girl looking up, her hands clasped in prayer. It read:

Abby Dawn Duren
June 13, 1999
"Our Little Angel"

Christi and Roman could not bear the grief and did not find comfort in each other's arms. Abby had been evidence of their affection. While their baby lived in heaven, they were sure it was their love that felt dead and buried.

"I know what you are going through, Roman," Dave Remudo, a friend of the family's, whispered in Roman's ear. "Margie and I had a stillborn baby, and we cried for a long time. It was a pain like nothing else. One of these days, you'll have another one, and it'll make it all better. I promise."

Roman shook his head and watched his tears water the ground.

A dark cloud lingered in Sarah Leona's house for a long time. Carolyn and Christi's bodies were healing despite their hearts. Spiritually, they wrestled. Before Abby's death, they had prayed easily and fluidly, out loud and mostly joyously with each other. Now Christi questioned some of their prayers, as they suddenly sounded cliché to her. Most evenings, Christi preferred to wrestle with God by herself in her room.

One night, a week or so after the funeral, Christi was lying on the bed in her room, re-reading cards sent to her since Abby's death. A woman she knew peripherally who had lost twins sent her a poem that she wanted to keep. There was no title, and no author, but of all the offers of consolation, this one spoke to her.

> Tread gently near the tender souls who've lost a child,
> whose hearts are bruised and bleeding,
> for the healing comes slowly,

with pain in every forward step, tears
in every backward look.
So much life still flows for that special one
Arms reach out to hold and back to cling
But reach forward only numbly,
fearful of forgetting or being disloyal by going on.
There is guilt in laughing, feel-
ing pleasure, even being alive.
There are questions, longings, heartaches.
But slowly, surely, strength and healing come,
In God's own time—
Not as answer, nor as forgetting, but as acceptance
that this pain, this loss is ours to live with
and somehow, by God's grace, to use to bless.

"You okay, baby Christi?" Sarah Leona asked as she walked into the room and sat down on the bed.

Christi nodded unconvincingly. Then she picked up a card with an angel on the front—a winged, blond toddler, her eyes looking dreamily upward, her chin resting on two chubby hands propped up by clouds. The printed inscription read, "May you be touched by the sweet thoughts of angels." A handwritten note from Carolyn to Christi and Roman said, "May these next few months be blessed with sweet angelic thoughts of God's blessing on your life. I love you and can't wait to have grandbaby number two. Love always, Mom"

Carolyn walked in and recognized the card immediately.

"I love this card, Mom. I want Abby's grave marker to have this baby's face on it. The baby is angelic, just the way I picture Abby," Christi said.

Christi looked at the drawing again.

"The devil puts all these things in motion, doesn't he? God wouldn't do this."

Sarah Leona nodded, but Carolyn spoke up—softly.

"God is all-powerful, Sissy. He has plans for each of us, and we have to trust that plan."

Christi felt anger well up inside of her.

"He *planned* for Abby to die? That was the plan? That's a little hard to take right now."

"*Because* I've watched you suffer, and that pain has been nearly unbearable for me as your mother," Carolyn explained, "I *have* to believe and trust that God has the perfect plan. But sometimes the reasons are never revealed to us. Sometimes they come later in life. My first instinct, with the tornado and now this, was to see evil forces at work, like a thief stealing from us. But we have to look for the blessings, for what we're given. With time, we'll understand all of this better."

"Carolyn's right, Christi. We are not capable of understanding why. But we know God is always good, so very good. We know he spared your mother. We know he spared you."

"As sad as it is and as hard as it is for all of us to understand," Carolyn said, "it must not have been God's will for Abby to live."

"But I still think the hospital killed that baby," Sarah Leona blurted out, uncooperatively. "Your uncle Charlie says you should sue."

"Mother!" Carolyn shot back. It was not the time to talk about such things.

But Sarah Leona was relentless.

"What with her on one crutch, I blame the doctors and the therapy. After being rolled in that tornado, she had to hop so hard. I'm so mad at myself. I should've spoken out. I blame myself."

"We do not control these things, Mother," Carolyn said intensely. "We don't get to say who lives and who dies."

Christi was no longer listening to her mother and grandmother spar back and forth.

"I want to try again," Christi said to no one in particular. "I'm going to try again."

This quieted Carolyn and Sarah Leona. They both raised their eyebrows, and looked at each other, hoping the other would speak up first. Knowing that saying anything was risky, Carolyn tread cautiously.

"Don't you think it's a little too soon, Sis? What about your recovery?"

"Which one? My physical recovery? Dr. Perry says a couple months. My emotional recovery? That'll take forever. You yourself said you can't wait for grandbaby number two."

"Don't feel like you need to replace Abby Dawn, honey," Sarah Leona said.

There was a new determination in Christi. As Carolyn watched her daughter, she realized that her will was—much like her grandmother's—unstoppable. Christi was no longer a child who had lost a child. In the last two months, she had grown up. She had become an amazing woman overnight. Although Christi had been struggling with her faith, Carolyn could see it was temporary. A woman of strength and resolve was breaking through.

"I thought I was supposed to be Abby's mom," Christi said. "I thought that was the plan. I am Abby's mom, but she's not here. So I'm telling you what's in my heart. I'm ready to be a mother again."

"Is Roman ready to be a father?" Carolyn asked.

"I guess he is," Christi answered. "We haven't talked about it. We didn't even plan on Abby. But we got used to the idea of being parents. It's a want we both have—an unspoken one."

"Before you think about the next child," Carolyn said, "I believe you wanted this."

Carolyn handed Christi a white box wrapped with a pale pink satin ribbon. Christi pulled the ribbon slowly, so soft on her fingertips, knowing that the gift had something to do with Abby. None of them made a sound; only the rustle of tissue paper being pushed away. It was the dress—the dress that the baby wore the day she was born, the day she died. At least, that was the white lie that Carolyn let her daughter believe.

In actuality, Carolyn had gone back to the boutique where she first found it and bought a replica. She had removed the tags and decided that Christi did not need to know that Abby's body had been too delicate to be undressed.

Just when she thought she could not possibly produce another tear, Christi cried harder than she had in all her life, as if she needed to drown the past in order to be born again. She lay the dress down on the bed and curled up in the fetal position next to it. Carolyn sat down beside her, weeping silently, stroking her daughter's untangled hair with one hand, and clutching her prayer cloth in another. Sarah Leona wiped her own eyes with a handkerchief. She found space in-between their feet, forming a maternal trinity on the bed, and patted them both tenderly, whispering, "Hush. Hush now, babies."

One by one, they dried their tears and fell into dreamless slumber.

Pieces

"For I know the plans I have for you," declares the Lord, "plans to prosper you and not harm you, plans to give you hope and a future."

Jeremiah 29:11 (NIV)

The ladies at the office had gathered around the reception desk, looking at photographs from Cheryl's recent mission trip. KD happened to glance up first.

"I don't believe it," she said.

"What?" asked Cheryl, thinking she was referring to a surprise in one of the pictures.

"It's June," KD said.

"Yes?" Cheryl responded.

"What in the world are you doing in here? Are you even allowed to drive?" KD asked. Cheryl opened her mouth to answer, but someone else spoke first.

"You have M.S. and you show up for work," Carolyn said.

At the sound of her voice, all of them looked at her, their faces filled with a mixture of surprise and shock.

"I haven't had a near-death experience," KD answered.

"It's boring living out of a couch. Think they'll let me in the capitol looking like this?" Carolyn said.

Wearing a black cotton dress, a red scarf, and lipstick to match, Carolyn pushed her walker toward the group. Now that she was out of bed and out of loose-fitting hospital gowns, she looked smaller to her colleagues than they imagined she would. Cheryl and KD ran around the desk to help out, but Carolyn waved them off. She leaned heavily on her walker, and they could tell that, physically, she probably would not last two hours at work. The contrast to her former self—the heel-clicking, cell-phone chirping, power-lobbying woman she was two months earlier—was a stark one. But her friends shared the same impression: Carolyn had never looked stronger in all her life.

Carolyn turned her back to the front desk, placed her hands behind her, and hoisted herself up.

Jamie gasped.

"How's everybody doing?" Carolyn asked brightly.

"*Now* you're showing off," Cheryl said.

"You want to give *me* that walker?" KD teased. "Wait a second, are you trying to finagle a handicapped parking pass?"

"Didn't you just break a million bones in the biggest tornado ever?" Diane reminded her.

"I've realized, through hours of contemplation on my mother's couch, that we can't control circumstances, we can only control our *response* to circumstances," Carolyn said, sounding like a seasoned psychologist. "You're looking at me like I'm crazy. Maybe I need counseling, because I don't think I do."

The issue of counseling was on her mind because, for the first time, someone advised her to seek it. During her most recent appointment with Dr. Bajaj, he scribbled on her chart:

> Patient has now realized the extent of injury. Head itches all the time due to graft breakdown in front. Suggested psychological counseling. Patient not ready for counseling at this time.

Carolyn's head was healing well, although she understood her hair would not come back on its own, and wondered whether the bumps behind her ears would fade with time. Dr. Bajaj called them "dog-ear folds," a kind of deformity that happens as a result of shifting skin tissues. Carolyn began to picture the scope of her physical recovery. There would be much more cutting and pasting of her head before she would feel whole again.

Dr. Bajaj had seen it before. With such focus on the physical repairs, the emotional fissures would be felt later. Carolyn knew he was the pro, but she had no intention of calling a shrink and setting aside hours each week for internal examination. It was more a matter of time economy than anything else. For her, as she gained more strength every day, there was no looking back. It was nothing but full steam ahead; the way she had always lived her life.

As she watched her friends, she hoped in her heart that they did not share the doctor's opinion.

"Seriously. You're all staring at a cuckoo bird, right?"

"We're staring at you because you are an amazement, my friend," KD said.

"Or you're in deep, deep denial," Cheryl teased.

Carolyn sat before them like a bright star against a dark sky, especially considering the backdrop of her life. Her home was gone. She and her daughter were survivors. Her grandchild was not. This surprise office visit was the first time Diane and Jamie had seen Carolyn since Abby's funeral, and that loss was very much on all of their minds. No one dared to bring it up, of course. They had expressed their love and concern, but their hearts remained soaked with sympathy. They wanted Carolyn to know they supported her implicitly, without having to say the words, *I'm so sorry about your grandbaby.*

Just thinking about it made each of them want to fall apart for different reasons—whether it be guilt because as grandmothers some of them were what she was not, or a painful sense of injustice, feeling that their friend did not deserve the cards she had been dealt. They expected Carolyn had to be shattered inside. And she was. But she was not beyond repair. Her faith supplied the glue as she put her pieces back in place. Getting to the office was one of those pieces.

As for the ladies, if they held themselves together half as well as she did, they knew they could provide Carolyn a safe place to work through her grief if she needed one. But at this moment, she did not seem to need one. In fact, there was a brightness to Carolyn's spirit that made them feel—unexpectedly—happy.

Jamie broached the easier topic.

"How's that head of yours?"

"It's good; God is good," Carolyn said. "Some spots where they operated are numb, which is kind of annoying. Like a constant tickle. But then when they're not numb, they kind of hurt."

"Wait a minute," KD said dramatically, "are you admitting to pain?"

Carolyn protested.

"No, it's just—"

"Thought she could do it, but no!" Cheryl chimed in.

They all smiled at Carolyn's tough-girl exterior and watched the wonder woman she had become with admiring eyes. KD, in particular, had seen how the tornado could break a woman down. Another friend of hers escaped injury but lost her home. Her family had been put up in a hotel. One afternoon she had gone to Target to buy a coffee pot, but she could not bring herself to do it. She was paralyzed. There were ten coffee pots from which to choose. She literally stood there, in the store aisle, and called KD to come get her. Her friend had come to the realization that she had to choose one, and then after that, she had about ten-thousand more decisions to make. The math was overwhelming. She simply broke down staring at those ten pots. Soon after, like dominoes, other facets of her life fell to ruin too, including her marriage.

But Carolyn—Carolyn sat like a diva on a piano. She seemed to have everything together. Her friends wanted to reach out and help her, but it was her resilience that helped them. They wondered whether they would have the courage to push a walker into work without a full head of hair, and whether they would still be praising God for the follicles they were allowed to keep.

"What can we do for you, Carolyn?" Jamie asked.

"Just don't pity me. I'm fine. Your prayers worked. Now send them out to someone else," Carolyn said.

"But we want to do something," Diane said. "Everyone's been calling the office, asking what you need."

"Probably some toilet paper," Carolyn joked.

"That's a start," said Jamie.

"Actually, I need a house first," Carolyn said.

"I heard about moving, but this is a pretty unconventional way of doing it," Cheryl said.

"Look, even if I found a place, I don't even have a towel to wash my face," Carolyn said.

"That settles it," said Diane. "When you find a house, we'll give you a shower."

Carolyn thought about it for a second.

"You mean, it'll be like getting married, without a husband?"

Cheryl said through laughter, "Precisely. Any excuse for a party, really."

Carolyn agreed. She registered for everything from face towels to a ten-cup coffee pot.

One Sunday after church, Carolyn felt well enough to go house-shopping. Looking at her insurance check for one hundred thousand dollars, she wondered whether she could afford a house in an addition where she had long dreamed of living. Lakehurst was well-established neighborhood situated in Oklahoma City, just east of Lake Hefner, twenty or so miles from the Del Aire addition. The trees were older; so were the homes. But because of their age, they had more character, charm, and longevity. In other words, had it ever been hard-hit by a storm, you could not tell. In Lakehurst, she would not be reminded of the nightmare she survived every time she pulled into her driveway.

As she drove up and down the oak-lined streets and well-groomed properties, Carolyn felt at peace. When she stopped in front of the ranch-style red brick house with a white fence out front, she knew she was home.

J.R.'s voice rang out in her head.

"Ah, for cryin' out loud, Carolyn Crump. Don't even think about it."

"And why not?" Carolyn imagined asking defiantly.

"You going to rob a bank?" J.R. would fire back. "It's gotta be three thousand square feet."

It was smaller than that, but not by much. The living room flowed into the dining room, which lead to the kitchen, which opened to the family room. Charming wide window panes let sunlight into every room. The old green shag carpet and outdated floral wallpaper on the walls and ceiling would have to go, but she easily pictured her yet-to-be-bought new furniture in each space, right down to a treadmill for the back porch. There was a bedroom for her and each of her kids, and ample space if Carolyn were ever to marry again.

"I want it," she said to herself.

Carolyn was surprised to learn the price, evidence to her that it was meant to be. When she called about it, she learned that the homeowner had died, leaving four children to squabble over it. It turned out, they were eager to unload it. She expected them to ask for one-hundred thousand dollars more, but they did not. It was almost as if she had been handed another insurance check. Her monthly mortgage payment would be about the same as it was before the tornado.

In her mind, Carolyn had already moved in.

Sarah Leona was skeptical.

"It doesn't even have a tornado shelter? Are you trying to kill me?"

"Mother, it's beautiful. You'll love it."

"But Oklahoma City? It's so far away."

"Puh-lease. It'll take you fifteen minutes more."

"And I'll have to drive up that parkway where everybody dies…"

"Mother! I'm making an offer on it tomorrow."

Carolyn realized right away that Sarah Leona's dramatic resistance meant she did not want her to move out. She liked having her daughter and granddaughter where she could watch over them. But Carolyn was ready to glue another piece of her life's puzzle.

The moment the work ladies heard about Carolyn's find, they made good on their promise to host a shower. Her friend, Nancy, booked the fancy clubhouse at her condo in Edmond, a northern suburb of the city. Hundreds of people showed up with gifts from Carolyn's registry.

Although she was ready to work in the office with her closest colleagues, she was not ready to play host to throngs of well-meaning acquaintances who wanted to help her build back her life. As courageous as she had been about many things, she could not bear the thought of three hundred questions about her grandchild, three hundred sympathetic smiles, and three hundred pairs of eyes staring at her wig. Worse than that, she was not comfortable with the idea that people would be giving her things. She nearly felt compelled to make all the guests gift bags to thank them for their love and support. She would rather be the giver. But she reminded herself that God would want her to be a gracious receiver too. And so she went, and as it turned out, she loved every minute of it.

Back at her mother's house, Carolyn folded up her many scarves and put them on sabbatical. Uncertain about the surgeries ahead, she was not so naïve as to think she would not need them again. For now, though, she started a new collection of hats. Just like the scarves, she wanted a hat to fit not just every occasion, but every outfit.

The hats were a hit at the capitol. They were an easy conversation piece for people who felt uneasy talking about her injuries. The half-year session had not yet resumed, but staff members were there, allowing Carolyn to ease back into a comfort zone. She was thankful to have a few months to prepare for the start of session in January and the return of the bulk of the political players.

To gear up for session, Carolyn's boss gave the

lobbyists at the office a Palm Pilot and a mandate to use it. Carolyn regarded it as a nuisance, one more thing to lose at the bottom of her purse.

"I'll carry mine when you get one that matches my bag, my shoes, and my hat," Carolyn said in mock defiance.

The ladies at the office only needed to hear the challenge once. They divvied up patterns—leopard print, zebra stripe, polka dot, crimson and cream (the colors of the University of Oklahoma), pink toile, black lace, brown satin—and sewed a series of Palm Pilot covers. Carolyn thought the effort was hilarious, and was proud to swap them out in accordance with her outfit each day.

The only hitch with the hats was the wind. It blew constantly, in every direction. You cannot count on the Oklahoma wind to blow in a hat's favor. One moment the force would push the front brim down over Carolyn's eyes, and then without warning, a gust would pop it off her head. Carolyn's co-workers developed a talent for catching them. A handful were nearly lost forever. The hats would have to be a temporary statement. Carolyn was too frustrated to let them last.

So she did something she never imagined she would—she bought a wig from a woman she trusted. Ann Patton had several ties to the Crump family. She had grown up in Wewoka across from Carolyn's grandparents' farm. Ann's sister was married to a third cousin. Carolyn knew she catered to professional women who suffered from cancer. She wanted to be fitted privately in an intimate environment, and that is just what Ann did for Carolyn.

Carolyn walked out of the hair design shop with a lightness to her step and a sporty blonde bob on her head. She felt dramatically different. How invisible she had been! As a gaunt waif, she had hidden below scarves and do-rags, behind a walker, underneath her self-consciousness. The moment she had a full head of thick blonde hair again, she noticed something she had forgotten—that men gave her a second look, and that it felt very good.

In September, when she swept into Dr. Walker's office wearing her wig and carrying a new feather and sequin purse with high heels and a palm pilot to match, the nurse behind the reception window nearly fell off her chair.

"You're Carolyn Stager?" asked a pretty, red-headed nurse with green eyes, although with her New York accent it sounded more like Cahrolyn Stayguh. She looked Carolyn straight in the eye, gave a firm handshake, and introduced herself.

"I'm Rosemary."

Carolyn liked her bold style immediately. She could tell that this woman would give her opinion and would not give an inch. She wondered if Rosemary's parents had been inspired to name their child after her rose-tinted locks or whether the girl had grown into a spirited woman who liked the idea of coordinating her personality with her hair.

"Good to meet you," Carolyn said in a chipper voice.

Rosemary stared at Carolyn for a moment, surprised that her appearance contradicted every detail she had imagined. Carolyn was far more pleasant and far less damaged than Rosemary pictured.

Rosemary swung her red bob around and marched Carolyn back to Dr. Walker's office rather than a treatment room. Carolyn noticed that Rosemary's stride was intentional, her long legs muscular. She imagined that Dr. Walker did not mess around with Rosemary.

"Will Dr. Walker examine my head right away? I can take off this wig."

"No need for that," Rosemary stated, matter-of-factly. "He's not going to take you as a patient."

Carolyn thought she had misheard. She did not want to be rude, but surely Rosemary was mistaken. Suddenly, Rosemary's directness lost its appeal.

Carolyn struggled to understand.

"Not going to—I've just waited—why?"

Rosemary flipped through a new chart, although Carolyn wondered why, since apparently she would not be returning.

"It's weird for us to say no. In my fifteen years as his right-hand gal, I've rarely seen him do it. But Dr. Walker doesn't do your kind of scalp reconstruction."

Carolyn sat dumbfounded. *Could you not have told me this on the phone three months ago?* she thought.

"So, why did he have me come in? I hate to be a bother," Carolyn asked as politely as she could through gritted teeth.

Rosemary organized Dr. Walker's desk as if she were prepping him for surgery. She answered without looking up.

"A patient convinced us."

Carolyn assumed the patient was Farrah, a regular at Dr. Walker's. She happened to give facials in a salon where Carolyn was a customer. She knew Carolyn well, even before the tornado, and had always liked her. After the storm, Farrah's gentle facials were an indulgence Carolyn enjoyed every few months.

Convinced them to take me so they could kick me to the curb? The feeling was irrational, she knew, but Carolyn took the rejection personally.

Carolyn's eyes welled up with tears. Rosemary noticed the strain on her face, and handed her a tissue. She dabbed the corners of her eyes, pretending to loosen a clump of mascara.

"I'm sorry," Carolyn apologized, "but this is somewhat distressing. I thought he was the best in town."

"He is," Rosemary said. She sat down next to Carolyn and held her eyes again. "He has a plan for you."

Carolyn sat up straight. Her tears vanished, and suddenly she understood that she was, indeed, in the right place. In her mind's eye, she finished the rest of Rosemary's sentence.

"... plans to prosper you and not harm you, plans to give you hope and a future."

Or, as Rosemary might put it, a fyoochuh.

Broken Hearts

"Naked I came from my mother's womb,
and naked I will depart.
The Lord gave and the Lord has taken away;
may the name of the Lord be praised."
In all this, Job did not sin by charging God with wrongdoing.

Job 1:21–22 (NIV)

THE IMPACT OF GRIEF ON A MARRIAGE

The reaction to the death of a baby is as individual as the person experiencing it. Spouses often grieve in different ways, frequently misunderstanding each other's reactions or needs.

Crying is an area where partners may differ. It is an acceptable and healthy expression of grief but many fathers may find it difficult to allow themselves to release built-up tension through crying. Fathers often feel the need and are encouraged by others to be strong, but crying is a normal and healthy reaction.

Grieving is emotionally, physically, and mentally exhausting and does not leave much energy for anything else. Communication may be difficult but is essential so that misunderstandings and intense emotions do not lead to problems in the marriage. Grief, however, is stressful and couples need to be aware that grief does not always bring partners closer together.

(From the brochure entitled *Stillbirth, Miscarriage, and Infant Death*)

The article was printed for parents suffering through an infant death experience, given to Christi by a friend. The woman invited Christi to a support group, but she never went. She could not face other mothers and fathers who were grieving over their dead babies. She imagined it would only multiply her own sadness. Still, she held on to the information and intended to read it. But as she scanned the titles within—"A Letter to Our Precious Little Boy," "When Hello Means Goodbye," and "A Letter to Our Sweet Little Girl"—she put it aside, and missed the message about the impact of grief on a marriage.

This, however, was an article from the local paper that she and Roman did not miss:

WORST IN OK WEATHER HISTORY
May Tornado Most Powerful
675 Regional Deaths and Injuries

September 3, 1999—Oklahoma City—Four months after an F-5 tornado and a series of multiple supercell thunderstorms produced as many as seventy tornadoes devastating hundreds of Oklahomans, Texans, and Kansans, the Oklahoma Department of Health released new statistics today, confirming the magnitude of the storm now known as The Great Plains Tornado Outbreak of May 3, 1999.

"Tornadoes are among the most violent and lethal of all natural disasters, but May 3 topped them all," said Jeb Johnson, acting secretary at the state health department.

F-5 is the highest rank for a tornado on the Fujita scale, meaning the tornado produced wind speeds capable of reducing houses to rubble, anywhere from two-hundred-sixty-one to three-hundred-eighteen miles per hour. On May 3, the fastest wind speed recorded was 318 miles per hour. The largest hail size indicated was 4.5 inches, the width of a softball.

In one instance, a freight car weighing approximately eighteen tons was picked up and blown nearly one mile across an open field. The car left gouge marks in the field every fifty to one hundred yards along the way.

Six-hundred-seventy-five people in the path of the deadly tornadoes sustained injuries. Twenty-three percent of them were hospitalized. Seventy-seven percent were treated in a hospital emergency room and released. Ninety-six people died, and more than half of those fatalities were in Oklahoma. At least one unborn child was lost as a result of the tornado.

"These numbers show the human toll, what our radars can't tell us," said Tom Scales, director of the National Weather Service in Norman.

Other relevant statistics in Oklahoma County:

1,780 homes destroyed
6,550 homes damaged
$1.2 billion total damage estimate

The damage estimate makes the outbreak the costliest in the country.

"When we saw it coming, we knew it was a monster. As of today, May 3 is, unquestionably, the most powerful tornado on record in the history of Oklahoma," Scales said.

On that fateful day, multiple tornadoes tore through Oklahoma, Texas, and Kansas. The most lethal among them, an F-5 twister, which at times grew to one mile wide, carved a path through Bridge Creek, Newcastle, South Oklahoma City, Moore, Del City, and Midwest City. The town of Mulhull and the Tanger Outlet Center in Stroud were destroyed.

Of the people who did not survive the storms on May 3, forty died as a direct result of injuries, three died of heart attacks, one died preparing for the tornado, and one died following it as he attempted to free himself from a pile of debris. When the tornado veered off its course parallel to Interstate 44, it struck the 16th Street overpass in Newcastle, blowing a woman out from under the overpass and killing her. Eyewitnesses said the woman had been hovering over her young son.

Injuries such as cuts, bruises, and scrapes were most commonly reported. Fractures and dislocations were the next most numerous injuries. Thirty adults and nine children suffered serious traumatic brain injuries with the potential for long-term disabilities.

A small number of survivors reported other serious complications, such as impalements of the body with two-by-four boards, lacerations filled with dirt debris that required debridement and surgery, and a scalping.

"It was a day of infamy in Oklahoma's tornado alley. The one bright spot in this dark moment in weather history was that the majority of people had ample warning time to take cover," Scales said.

Lead times for tornado warnings issued by the National Weather Service ranged from eighteen to thirty minutes.

Roman put down the newspaper.

"Eighteen to thirty minutes," he announced in disgust.

"What?" Christi asked.

Christi had just moved back home after spending the summer at Sarah Leona's. Already, she and Roman, both of whom people used to describe as "happy-go-lucky" when they dated in high school, let the heaviness of their hearts rule their language.

"Paper says people had as much as half an hour to find a safe place." He hit the newsprint hard with his finger. "You could have been in Texas if you wanted."

"Don't start with this," Christi said. "No one could've predicted where it would go. It could've hit your uncle's place. Or the high school."

"But it didn't, did it? And if you'd—"

Christi slammed the bathroom door before he could finish. She needed to throw up.

The first trimester was like that for her.

Instead of clinging to the toilet in misery, Christi washed out her mouth and looked at her sad face in the mirror. She turned to the side and felt her tummy. Christi knew right away that she was pregnant. She whispered a prayer of thanks and decided it was not the time to break the news to Roman. She picked up the keys off the kitchen counter and walked out the front door.

"Where are you going?" Roman yelled after her.

She did not answer back as she drove to the drugstore to buy a pregnancy test.

After Christi's car was destroyed, Metro Church in Edmond, where she and her mom had been attending services, surprised Christi and generously donated a very well-kept green Ford Expedition. It was the perfect size to carry Roman's golf clubs too, and sometimes she would drop him off at the course on his days off before heading into work. (Roman's uncle Paul and aunt Wendy later loaned them their Lincoln Town Car.) She had recently started back part-time at the health department, a few doors down from where records of birth and death were kept. She had not summoned the courage to walk past the elevators and ask for a copy of Abby's death record, although she thought about it every time she saw the sign.

One afternoon, Christi picked up Roman at the golf course where he had been working a few additional hours each week. When he opened the door, he saw a few sets of clothes for newborns lying on the passenger seat.

"What's this?" he asked.

"You're going to be a dad again," Christi said, grinning. Roman had forgotten how pretty his wife was when she did that.

"No way," he said and leaned over to kiss her.

"I took a test. I've already been sick a few times. But I don't mind."

"Yeah! WOO!" Roman yelled out the window as Christi started the car. "I'm going to be a dad!"

Christi let out a giggle as she drove to Roman's parents' house to share the good news.

Roman's dad was where he had been for the last thirty years, working at the fire station a few miles away. But they could not wait to tell their family, so Mydonna was the first to hear. She acted excited. She jumped up and down, clapped her hands, and hugged them both.

After they left, she broke down into hysterics.

Carolyn felt the same way, although she responded more evenly, and chose not to talk about it very much.

Everyone in the family feared another heartbreak before their hearts had time to heal. They worried about what would happen to Christi and Roman, not as wife and husband, but as people who function in society, who work, love, and laugh, if this pregnancy were unsuccessful. If they did not make it to the end.

There was one parent the young couple had not called, and it was Roman's suggestion to tell him.

"Want to call your dad?" Roman asked.

"I already talked to Dad. He and Sue are worried sick, just like all of them," Christi said.

"No, I mean Charlie," Roman said.

"Who? My uncle Charlie?" she asked, surprised.

"No, Christi. Charlie Allen."

Charlie Allen was Christi's biological father whom Carolyn never wed, and he virtually disappeared during her childhood. When Don Stager married Carolyn, Christi was just a baby, and he was more than happy to adopt her, give her his name, and raise her as his flesh and blood forever, which he had. Don was Dad to Christi, and as far as she knew, she had not laid eyes on Charlie for years.

"Sis, you just saw him—in the hospital." Roman also had a personal connection to Charlie, unrelated to Christi. He was Roman's Little League baseball coach years ago.

"What in the world are you talking about?"

Roman could not believe that Christi had such little memory of her days at DCH, although for the most part, he was glad for it.

"Right after the tornado," Roman explained, "when I was not at all sure you were going to make it, I called him. Thought he would want to know. He showed up at DCH within minutes, and stayed with you every day for the entire time you were there. He did all the stuff I couldn't. Even helped you while they did the debridement on your leg and stuff. Cleaned up your puke. Slept in your room night and day. Far as

I'm concerned, he just about made up for all the years he wasn't there when you were a kid."

Christi let the information sink in, sorting memories from dreams.

"I didn't realize he was there all that time."

Roman pulled out his cell phone, dialed Charlie's number, and handed Christi the phone. "Charlie," Christi started off, "you're going to be a—well, Roman and I are having another baby."

On the ride home, Roman yelled out the window again.

"I can't remember the last time I felt so damn happy!" Roman yelled again on the ride home. Instead of dividing them, this time, their fear brought them together.

"Me, too," Christi said. "Not that I'm not scared."

"Oh, I'm scared to death!" Roman said. "But what are the chances?"

Christi and Roman were joined in another way on that day. Silently, and unbeknownst to each other, they sent up the very same prayer, which they repeated in their minds over and over, *Please don't let it happen again. Please don't let it happen again. Please don't let it happen again.*

Dr. Walker's Rejection

As I was with Moses, so I will be with you; I will never leave you nor forsake you.

Joshua 1:5 (NIV)

"Ms. Carolyn Stager." The voice was calm, almost soothing. An elegant-looking man, dressed in black, sauntered into the office.

"Dr. Walker," Carolyn answered brightly, trying to mask her discontent.

Dr. Timothy Walker, the fabulous surgeon, so fabulous he made me wait months and months to get an appointment, only so he could announce ceremoniously that I could not be helped.

Dr. Walker was shorter than Carolyn expected, with longish salt-and-pepper hair cut in layers the way a teenage heartthrob might choose so that he could run his hands through it and feel it fall perfectly in place. Ever since she lost part of hers, Carolyn instinctively assessed everyone's head of hair. Dr. Walker's was set off stylishly by his black designer shirt and pants. He looked more like a famous architect or even an actor than a plastic surgeon in Oklahoma City. His face was pleasant to look at; his cheeks flush with energy.

Carolyn could not tell whether he had had any surgery done on himself, and she imagined he preferred it that way. He lowered his stylish spectacles, picked up Carolyn's folder that was already filled with a chart and records from Dr. Bajaj and Dr. Jansen, and gave an appreciative nod toward Rosemary.

"Thanks, Rose."

Rosemary smiled, but did not leave the room, as Carolyn expected. *Clearly, they're a team,* she thought.

Dr. Walker leaned against his desk, set down the folder, pushed his glasses to the top of his head, and faced Carolyn.

"I've heard many accounts of what happened to you and your family. First, I want to say that I'm sorry for your losses. I want to do whatever I can to restore what you lost physically."

"Thank you," Carolyn said. "I hear you are the best."

He smiled.

"We'll get to that in a minute. If you don't mind, let's start with your memory of what happened on May 3."

Carolyn told her survival story, as she had dozens of times since May. But this recounting felt like an opportunity to plead her case, to convince Dr. Walker that he wanted to take part in her recovery effort.

Dr. Walker listened to Carolyn's every word—the fact that she chose home over a shelter, that her daughter left her wood house to stay with her, that they felt sure they'd be protected in the closet, that instead they found themselves tossed about as if they were in a churning washing machine with nails and two-by-fours, that after they thought the worst was over, they lost a baby. Rosemary brushed a tear or two from her own cheeks.

"Look, I want to help you. I want—" He paused for a moment. "Rose, I changed my mind. Let's see something before we do this."

Do what? Carolyn wondered. Still, hope welled up inside her. Perhaps he would take her after all after he'd seen the injury first-hand. Carolyn removed her wig and held it in her lap.

Rosemary joined Dr. Walker, their heads nearly touching as they inspected Carolyn's missing scalp. She felt terribly vulnerable, almost as if she were back in elementary school, standing, and shivering in her underwear, getting the annual scoliosis check by the town doctor and school nurse.

Dr. Walker and Rosemary made all kinds of assessments as they circled like archeologists inspecting a fossil that they wanted to evaluate and document before touching. Their words overlapped in phrases as if they were dancing in and out of a dream.

"Tremendous loss of scalp..."

"Extensive damage, amazing there was no brain damage..."

"Or facial damage; I'd say we're looking at forty to fifty percent..."

"What did you say one of your doctors thought did it?" Rosemary said in her northeastern drawl.

It took Carolyn a moment before she realized that Rosemary was talking to her.

"A piece of paper."

"Oh my," Rosemary said, unable to hold back her surprise.

"No, no, a board at the right angle could scalp."

"The scalping is not as deep as the Indians would go..."

"It's the soft area where you could practically tear it with your hands..."

Something about the brutality of the last thought made them stop and consider the person attached to the injury. Carolyn did not mind; their fascination over her case from a medical point of view fascinated her.

"Listen," Dr. Walker turned serious as he took a step back. "There are a number of doctors in Oklahoma and Dallas who would attempt to do reconstructive surgery on you. You're a unique case. You'd be interesting to write about. And you seem like a very lovely lady."

Dr. Walker winked at Rosemary, who gave an obligatory smile and quickly turned her head, her shiny red hair hiding her face from him. He continued.

"I am very good at what I do. You need tissue expansion reconstruction, and I've done that. I fixed a baby born without a scalp. Another baby had a brain in her mouth when she was born. I sorted her all out."

Carolyn got the impression that Dr. Walker's list of surgeries was meant to give her confidence, rather than a way to show off. Carolyn almost asked him about the young dog bite victim, the one he was rumored to have repaired and partly the reason Carolyn chose Dr. Walker, but then it occurred to her that he had likely treated a lot of them. All of it was pointless, however. She did not need convincing. She was ready to schedule surgeries and get on with it, no matter the physical or financial cost. She hoped he was talking himself into taking on her case.

He continued.

"So, my point is, I could do this. But I don't do it every day. I have to admit, I've never had a patient who was attacked by nails and boards flying at three hundred miles per hour. You have a huge defect in a tricky place. You've already had some patchwork done. The first shot is the best shot, and I don't want to mess it up."

"I'm sure you would do a fine job," Carolyn said.

As a lobbyist, Carolyn had mastered the art of persuasion, but she was not sure what else she could do to inspire Dr. Walker to take her on. She felt a golden opportunity slipping away. Dr. Walker's mind was made up.

"Look, I always try to decide, am I comfortable in my heart that I can do this as well as anyone in the world? Will the patient say 'I love you' after I take off the bandages? Right, Rose?"

Dr. Walker glanced at Rosemary. She rolled her eyes.

Carolyn laughed at Rosemary's reaction. Their interplay made Carolyn feel as though she were sitting in their kitchen.

"Well, at least he doesn't have a confidence problem," Carolyn said.

"You have to excuse him. He gets carried away," said Rosemary. "Why don't you just tell her your plan?"

"Hold on, Rose. Hold on," Dr. Walker answered calmly, like a professor moderating two sides, although the debate appeared to be between Dr. Walker's mind and his heart. "Carolyn, I just want you to understand my thought process."

"I appreciate that. My concern is, if it's not you, who else is there, Dr. Walker?"

"Please, call me Tim," he said kindly. "And that speaks to my point. I want you to go to the very best. Your reconstruction will be better handled by someone more expert than I. There are two surgeons in the country who have done this kind of thing many times. One's in California. But I want to send you to the other. Dr. Ernie Manders, in Pittsburgh."

"I'm guessing he's not in Pittsburg, Oklahoma," Carolyn said.

"No such luck. As far as bedside manners and pure genius, you need Ernie. He's the best reconstructive surgeon in the world."

"That must've been difficult to admit, Dr. Walker," Rosemary teased.

Dr. Walker pretended to ignore her.

"But Ernie's your guy."

Tim Walker had learned of Ernie Manders' skill after coming across various slide presentations and journal articles on his patients. On a few occasions, Dr. Walker thought he might have treated his own patients differently. So once he called Dr. Manders, who—in-between international travel, a medical supplies business, hundreds of articles, abstracts, chapters, manuals, videos, patents, plastic surgeries, and teaching as a professor of surgery at the University of Pittsburgh—explained painstakingly and enthusiastically why he had chosen one approach over another. Dr. Walker was smitten; professionally speaking, of course.

Carolyn nodded, wondering if Dr. Walker's plan was as well-thought out as he seemed to think it was. She worried that she might have to wait another few months to land an appointment with Dr. Manders, which could mean Christmas and no availability until the new year, and then the start of the legislative session, and then no window to travel to Pittsburgh.

"I promise you, he'll be your best friend by the time it's all over. I've already called him and told him what I knew about your injury. So if you're on board, so is he."

Dr. Walker took his time detailing the rest of the plan. Dr. Manders would be the primary surgeon, but Dr. Walker would serve as the home physician: checking up on Carolyn after surgery, monitoring her comfort level, risk of infection, and progress, and doing any minor maintenance that was necessary. The two doctors would communicate by e-mail and phone calls as needed.

"So you're going to take me as a patient, sort of."

"Yes."

Carolyn was relieved to know she had a place to come back to for medical care and that someone had a surgical plan for her. But how she would get halfway across the country to Pittsburgh, and afford the top surgeon in the world, she could not imagine.

On the way home from the appointment, Carolyn felt deflated. She liked Dr. Walker and Rosemary, the fact that they worked in Oklahoma, and that they had a reputation she could verify. She wanted to trust their assessment of Dr. Ernie Manders.

Ernie.

Carolyn laughed. The only other Ernie she had ever heard of was a puppet with a live-in best friend named Bert, which was her grandfather's name, a name dear to her heart.

Good Gifts

Peace, I leave with you, my peace I give you: not as the world giveth, give I unto you. Let not your heart be troubled, neither let it be afraid.

John 14:27 (KJB)

Leaves of brown, orange, and gold lay thick like a carpet covering the valley. The taxi driver said the trees were past their peak, but Carolyn would not have known the difference, not ever having seen the lush foliage of western Pennsylvania. As she took in their beauty, she tried not to blink.

It was early November when she and J.R. flew to Pittsburgh. With no direct flights from Oklahoma City, they traveled from Tulsa through Chicago, spending the majority of the day in transit. Carolyn was weary from travel, so she let the cab driver do the talking.

"We play the Bears tonight," said the cabbie. "Going to get creamed." He nodded his head left.

Night had begun to fall, and the lights of Heinz Field blazed on the Ohio River, meandering around the city like the moat of a royal castle. Plentiful streetlamps and colorful neon lights reflected off strikingly handsome glass buildings in the city's center.

"PPG Place—one and two. Those are the heart of downtown."

As Carolyn and J.R. neared their hotel, they passed under a majestic building which towered above them and appeared to pierce the stars. The statistics rolled off the driver's tongue as if he had said them a million times just today.

"Cathedral of Learning. Forty-two-story Gothic building, 535 feet tall, second highest educational building in the world. Got no idea which one's first."

Carolyn could not think of a single example of architecture back in Oklahoma that looked anything like the one she was staring at. London, yes, but Oklahoma City? Not even close. *This place evoked history and stature,* Carolyn thought, *even while scraping the sky in a modern-day fashion.*

J.R. tipped the cabbie well and thanked him for the history tour. He nodded in appreciation and handed J.R. a few pamphlets featuring points of interest around town.

The short ride through the city gave Carolyn a confidence that she had arrived in a place where a brilliant surgeon could thrive. She almost forgot that this was the same city known for decades as a depressing and dirty mill town.

Before going to bed, Carolyn undressed in the bathroom and laid her prayer cloth down next to the sink. She took a hot shower, wrapped herself in a satin robe, and opened up one of the pamphlets the cabbie had given them. A photograph of a copper plate in the one about the Cathedral of Learning caught her eye. Engraved on the plate were these words:

> Faith and peace are in their hearts. Good will has brought them together. Like the Magi of ancestral traditions and the shepherds of candid simplicity, they offer their gifts of what is precious, genuine and their own, to truth that shines forever and enlightens all people.

Faith, peace, and precious gifts.

In the morning, they rose early, taking time to sit for coffee and pastries among throngs of Pitt students ordering their double espressos and dashing off to class. J.R. asked for walking directions one last time, and they made their way over to the massive inner-city complex that was the University of Pittsburgh Medical Center, which every local referred to as UPMC. After walking for what seemed like miles down one hallway after another, they found the appropriate waiting room. Carolyn's left heel was rubbed raw.

"Never mind my head, J.R. I'm going to need surgery on this foot."

"Maybe next time you won't try so hard to impress the doc with your fancy five-inch heels," J.R. said, needling her on purpose.

A nurse led them both back to an examination room.

Carolyn understood the game they played, but she whispered out of the nurse's earshot.

"It's amazing to me that you don't even need a second cup of coffee to wind up your gutter-mouth. You wake up this way."

"It's only because you're meaner-'an-a-snake. I gotta protect myself."

"Puh-lease, J.R. Richards. You act like you're defenseless. It's starting to occur to me that you were born dysfunctional."

"At least I have hair," J.R. said.

"You're balder than I am!" Carolyn yelled back.

"I'm older than you!" J.R. retorted. "I could be your father!"

"Well, hullo there!" a cheery voice interrupted their exchange. "And you must be Carolyn, and Mr. Stager, I presume?" Dr. Ernie Manders gave no indication that he had heard anything previous to his entrance. He gave them both enthusiastic handshakes. Carolyn noticed her small hand disappeared in his.

Still reeling somewhat, J.R. took the opportunity to show himself.

"Most days, you could call me that. But for now, it's just J.R."

Carolyn rolled her eyes and held her tongue.

"J.R., then, I am very glad to meet you today. And how was your flight? Not too delayed I hope? Are the accommodations to your liking? You found everything okay?"

Carolyn and J.R. looked at each other and smiled. They enjoyed everything about their first impression of Dr. Ernie Manders—his warm greeting, his unpretentious manner, even his Canadian accent. They had not imagined that surgeons came quite like him.

After gawking at the enormous size of his hands, Carolyn assessed Dr. Manders' hair, of course—

fair, blondish grey, and windblown. His cheeks were chapped as if they'd been exposed to a strong wind, and his belly looked as though he rarely turned down a good dark beer served alongside warm, buttered bread. His lab coat was open, as was the last button at the bottom of his shirt.

After chatting for a good twenty minutes, Dr. Manders asked to examine Carolyn's scalp. His stream of consciousness style of conversing continued as he inspected her head.

"Whoa, what's this? I see...you've got what I'd call a great big C on the left here, another big defect on the right too. It almost reaches the midline. Oh boy, and here's a challenge—a narrow strip of scalp in between."

"Do you think you can fix it?" Carolyn asked, not knowing what Dr. Manders could do, not wanting to hope for too much.

"Fix it? Why sure I do. You have luxurious hair growth on your remaining scalp. Will it look just as it did before? That's up to your hair follicles. In babies and children, they tend to multiply, may even grow some new ones. But being the lady full of life and experiences that you are, we just don't know yet. You see, one of the first primitive examples of reconstructive surgery through regeneration was through tissue expansion to grow more scalp. That's what we're going to do here, grow more scalp."

Carolyn felt smarter just listening to Dr. Manders. It was clear he liked to teach. His tangents were infinitely fascinating to her. The feeling was mutual. Dr.

Manders was clearly interested, not just in Carolyn's "defect," but in her story of survival as well as her life in Oklahoma. Dr. Manders took a series of photographs and jotted down more first-hand history from Carolyn.

"So, your plans this afternoon? I hope you won't be leaving in a hurry. Did you see the Cathedral of Learning? It is a *marvel*. Nothing like it in the world. One-hundred twenty rooms designed by as many countries. You must see it."

"We'll be glad to go," J.R. said, "if you'll allow us to take you and your wife to Carolyn's favorite steak house in the world."

Dr. Manders beamed.

"Well, why not? We're going to get to know each other over these next many months and years. That's so very kind of you."

So began Carolyn and J.R.'s friendship with Ernie and Sandra. Although Carolyn had never imagined a relationship with a physician outside the clinic door, the connection seemed perfectly natural. They dined at Ruth's Chris Steak House in downtown Pittsburgh: buttery appetizers, buttery bread, buttery steak—even the chardonnay was buttery. The Manders insisted on driving the two of them to the airport that evening.

Ernie and Sandra asked Carolyn and J.R. all kinds of questions about their upbringing, how they met (J.R. cleaned up the story a bit so as not to embarrass Carolyn on their first day together), and, of course, the particulars of the tornado. It was immediately clear that Ernie and Sandra valued their children, their travels, and every person they came across. They seemed to explore the landscape of the Earth as much as they did the hearts and minds of people. They were curious about the world and everyone in it, and they had covered quite a bit of it. Ernie would fly from a conference in Brazil to a meeting in Vermont to a clinic in China all in one month.

But there was nothing puffed up about the man. He shared with them the story of his father, who worked in a paper mill and developed a way to produce paper fifty percent faster. Dr. Manders himself said he perfected the crescent-shaped expanders that he would be implanting under Carolyn's healthy scalp. He talked about his own business with one of his sons, where they created a graft from cadaver skin that heals terrible wounds.

"The Army's been using Gamma Graft in Iraq. It's wonderful stuff. Soldiers can dress their wounds with it right on the battlefield, and save themselves a skin graft later."

"Cadaver skin, you say?" J.R. asked. He took the check from the waiter and gave him a credit card without looking at the total.

"Marvelous stuff. It protects the wound just long enough to get it to start healing, then it curls up like a pork rind and simply falls off."

"Tasty little midnight snack, sounds like," J.R. joked under his breath.

Carolyn shot J.R. the look.

"You won't be putting pork rinds on my head, will you?" Carolyn asked, pretending not to care, but feeling a little sickened by the idea of a dead person's skin on her own. She was grateful that this conversation was happening while they were on their way to the parking garage, rather than over dinner.

"You betcha!" Ernie said with gusto. "Lots of it. In fact, if you'd had Gamma Graft in the ER, you wouldn't have needed those skin grafts."

"Buffoons and fools," J.R. said, letting his personality show more and more by the minute. "Why don't they have the stuff in every burn center in America?"

Ernie smiled as he opened the car door for Sandra and then for Carolyn.

"Some hospital burn centers use it, but they find it cuts down on their profits because instead of a ten-day stay some patients can go home in two."

"Like I said, buffoons and fools," J.R. repeated.

"A wise man, you are," Ernie said.

Just then, Sandra grabbed her husband's elbow so that he would not drive the wrong way down a one-way street.

"Sounds like you and your father were both inventors and scientists," Carolyn observed. "I'm hoping that miracle-worker is in the genes too."

"I will not let you down, Carolyn," Ernie said. Carolyn believed him as though she had just heard a promise from her best friend.

Dr. Manders smiled in the rearview mirror at Carolyn, and his wife had to take the wheel before he slid into the Rental Car Return lane.

"That's what a Harvard education will get you," Sandra said. "A genius who can't parallel park."

"Too much time bashing heads with big men while

hiking footballs, my dear," Ernie said kindly. Sandra pinched his cheek.

In the airport, Carolyn and J.R. had a few minutes to kill. A jewelry store caught her eye, and she peeled away from J.R.

He yelled after her.

"If you find something shiny that costs more than a grand, I'm telling the pilot to leave without you."

Mixed emotions filled Carolyn as the plane took off in darkness toward Chicago—confident that she was in the right place, eager to get started, and disheartened that Dr. Manders could not operate on her until spring.

J.R. looked down at Carolyn's naked ring finger.

"Oh, thank God."

Carolyn disregarded his comment.

"Dr. Manders and Sandra are so sweet to each other, don't you think? And after all those years." She leaned back in her seat and let her head fall gently on the head rest. With eyes closed, she thought she heard J.R. talking.

"I'd be sweet to you, too, if you'd agree to be Mrs. Richards. It's exhausting for me playing the role of Mr. Stager all the time."

"Are you kidding me?" Carolyn laughed. Ever since meeting J.R., she had seesawed back and forth, asking herself if she wanted to marry again or not. Mostly it bothered her that he had never asked. But then she would come to her senses and realize that they would probably make each other miserable. *Exhausting* was the right word; their verbal assaults wore each other out. Plus, what kind of proposal was that? *I'd be sweet to you if*… There was never a guarantee that he would be sweet.

"I'm not falling for that trap," she said.

"That crap? Crap? You're unbelievable. That's what you think about marrying me?"

"No, J.R., that's not what I said. The prenup you'd write up would be longer than the Old Testament. Self-preservation is not exactly the key to a trusting relationship."

"Well you haven't been deceived like I have. See, this is why—" J.R. was gearing up for a tirade, mostly for his own enjoyment.

The plane dropped sharply as it came into some turbulence, and the jolt awoke Carolyn suddenly. She looked over at J.R., his head on an airline-issue pillow, fast asleep. She realized that the conversation in which she had taken part happened only in her imagination.

As the plane touched down in Tulsa after midnight, J.R. drove Carolyn back to his place. They rode in silence, too exhausted to say anything more. Carolyn chose not to say anything about her dream. To her, even unspoken, everything about it was real and true.

The closing for Carolyn's new home had been pushed back because of various legal issues involving the previous homeowner's surviving family members. She wanted to get in it and start stripping wallpaper off the ceiling, pulling up shag carpet from the floor, and putting on layers of richly-colored fresh paint.

Sadly, she knew her home would not be ready for Christmas. Ever since her children were born, Carolyn's house was the heart of the celebration. Even though Christi was married and Nathan was seriously dating a sweet, loving, and talkative young woman named Marci, Carolyn's kids chose to follow their mother's tradition rather than start their own. Typically, everyone would spend the night at Carolyn's place on Christmas Eve. Carolyn would rise early and fix a breakfast of pancakes, a sausage and cheese casserole, ham, bacon, turkey, "reindeer" (which Christi believed it was, until at age fourteen she discovered the rest of the deer), Sarah Leona's melt-in-your mouth cinnamon rolls, and chocolate pudding with homemade biscuits crumbled on top. The feast would take half the day, but the moment it was over, the kids would change out of their pajamas and head out to see their in-laws, other family, and friends. J.R. often took part in the routine too, spending the rest of the afternoon with his family in Tulsa.

It would be the first departure from that tradition in many years.

Carolyn distracted herself by putting in too many hours at the office. Whether she did it to take her mind off a disappointing Christmas season, or to keep herself occupied while she waited impatiently for spring to come, she was not sure.

A dusting of icy snow covered the ground one December morning, and Carolyn woke up in darkness. She had been dreaming about a baby who let out a wail so real that it startled her out of bed. She shuffled to the kitchen to start her morning coffee, not terribly quietly, as Sarah Leona could not hear her anyway, and Pappy was still snoring. A lump in her throat would not go away, and she realized that Abby was on her heart. In years past, she had not understood why people suffered depression around the happiest time on earth. But this morning, emptiness overwhelmed her. She stared blankly at the sleet falling in the morning light. As the sky cried, it appeared to her, she let her own her tears fall.

Carolyn held her hand over her heart, and suddenly she seized up with anxiety. Her prayer cloth was still in Pittsburgh.

Emptiness turned to heaviness, but Carolyn did not let anyone at the office know. She called the hotel in Pittsburgh, but the hotel manager said that housekeeping had been through the room and that no square of cloth had been found. Likely, he said, it had been thrown away and was long gone. Carolyn was sick about it. She smiled with her colleagues during their holiday party, even brought a tray of her mother's warm cinnamon rolls to share. They disappeared in three minutes flat. None of the treats looked appetizing to Carolyn.

The same day a woman who was somewhat familiar to Carolyn was standing in the entryway near the front desk.

"Becky?" Carolyn asked tentatively.

"Becky Woodie. I'm Senator Glenn Coffee's executive assistant."

"Of course, of course. Did Glenn need something?" Carolyn asked.

"No, but I think you might."

Carolyn led Becky to her office where they both sat down. Becky began with her own tale of May 3: how she had been so unaware a storm was coming that she stopped by Braum's for a gallon of milk, then the bank to make a deposit. By the time she arrived home, her son was panicked.

"Where have you been?" he asked desperately.

"Just running errands. Why?"

"Oklahoma City blew away."

"It did?"

After he described what he knew about the path of the storm, Becky realized she had been—unknowingly—blocks away from the destruction.

"I was almost in that."

She felt a tremendous sense of guilt, like an unworthy survivor. *I was almost in that.* People who had taken shelter had been killed. People who prepared for the storm had lost their homes. *I was almost in that.* And she had been driving around town like it was just another day.

The next few days at the capitol, the tornado was the buzz. No one talked about anything else, and everyone seemed to know someone who took a direct hit. But Carolyn's name came up most often. *Blonde, a lobbyist.* Becky could not place her. *Dragged around her driveway by the tornado,* they said. Month after month,

Becky would hear news about Carolyn, but still could not put a face to her name. *The lady in the hats* finally jogged Becky's memory.

"You've been on my heart ever since I heard about what happened to you and your family," Becky said. "It's nearly Christmas now, and I felt called to give this to you."

Becky handed Carolyn a small square of white material.

"It's a prayer cloth. Has anyone ever given you one before?"

Carolyn was speechless.

She gave Becky a hug and let joy flood her completely. Several minutes passed before she could explain how the prayer cloth that had meant so much had gone missing that very day.

"Divine coincidence, I'm sure," Becky said.

Carolyn sat alone at her desk, fingering the cloth with amazement. Attached to it with a safety pin was a small piece of paper with this quote:

"Peace I leave with you, my peace I give you."

Carolyn knew the rest of the verse by heart.

"Not as the world giveth, give I unto you. Let not your heart be troubled, neither let it be afraid."

This time, she pinned the cloth to her bra, and pressed her hand to her chest, feeling the pulse of her heart through the tiny cloth.

Having been given such a special gift on a day that she needed it more than ever, Carolyn was determined to pay the graciousness forward.

The next day she visited a jewelry store in Oklahoma City called Silver Accents. Carolyn zeroed in on a silver cross lined with tiny pearls. Of all the pendants in the case, its glow drew her closer. When the clerk let her hold it, the warmth and heaviness felt right in her hand. She bought ten of them, not knowing whom she would give them to. But she knew she would not keep them; they belonged to those who had helped her in special ways.

    She wrapped up one of the crosses, knowing who needed to receive the first one. This person was unknown to her before the storm. It was a person who brought her unexpected gifts in both meanings of the word; a person who showed her the quiet power of God's love; a person who would never expect to receive anything back from her. Carolyn mailed the cross to Cyndy, Dr. Janssen's wife—the woman she first knew as a stranger, who once called Carolyn an angel; though to Carolyn, the reverse was true.

Beautiful

He will be a joy and delight to you, and many will rejoice because of his birth, for he will be great in the sight of the Lord.

Luke 1:14–15 (NIV)

"You guys can sine die all by yourself, because I'm outta here!" Carolyn announced as she left her office. With her strong Oklahoma accent, you would hardly know that sine die, or as Carolyn said it, "sigh-nay dye," was a Latin term for the close of the legislative session. A busy year had kept her mind off the fact that, due to an international conference where he would be the keynote speaker, Dr. Manders needed to push her first surgery back until July.

It was the last day of the legislative session, and even with the governor's threat to reconvene in the summer, she used the Latin term they all threw around Okie-style when the gavel went down. Sine die literally meant "without a day," but to the lawmakers and lobbyists it meant "hello, vacation."

It was a big day for Carolyn and the family, much bigger than the adjournment of state government.

As Carolyn stood among the same fifty or so

friends and family that had gathered eleven months earlier for Abby's birth, her nerves swirled around in her stomach. Everyone tried to pull off small talk, but no one was fooled. The moment of truth had arrived, and it was taking forever.

All Carolyn knew at this point was that Christi's water had broken the night before, and that she had gone into labor as Mydonna drove her and Roman to the hospital. Roman told her that they sped by DCH without giving a second thought to stopping. This time, Christi had hand picked an OB-GYN at Mercy Health Center in northwestern Oklahoma City who specialized in high-risk pregnancy.

By the time they pulled into the emergency lane, Christi was ready for an epidural. Both Roman and Christi fell asleep until her contractions woke them both up the next morning. Roman picked up his cell phone and spread the word.

Christi was in the care of a nurse they knew well. Madeleine Smith's son-in-law, Dave, was the one who had advised Roman and Christi on the day of Abby's funeral that the hurt of losing a child is only healed by birthing another one. Roman and Christi deliberately chose Madeleine as part of their birth plan. They viewed her as the calmest person on earth. She had eleven kids and probably birthed all of them naturally—Mother Earth incarnate. They trusted her.

But when Madeleine checked the baby monitor, she looked at Roman with concern. She had the benefit and burden of knowing exactly what was at stake.

"Oh, shoot. This is not good," she said urgently as she grabbed the telephone.

Roman grabbed her wrist.

"What's going on, Madeleine? I want to know," Roman blurted out. "Do not let this happen again."

"Roman, let go. Calm down. The baby's heart rate is dropping. I'm calling the doctor in for a C-section. I will not let this happen again."

She wrested her arm away, turned her back, and spoke into the phone.

"Get them in here immediately. We're taking this baby this second. We're taking it right now."

Madeleine pushed Christi's bed down the hallway, and Roman followed closely behind. There was no time for him to let anyone know what was going on.

In the blur that passed, Carolyn thought she recognized Christi's hair and Roman's gait. Immediate family members rushed to Christi's room, only to find it empty. They each took a seat; except for Carolyn. She paced the floor, sick with worry over Christi.

Less than hour later, a nurse wheeled Christi into her room. She was lying down on a gurney, rather than in a wheelchair, and shaking so violently, Carolyn thought she was seizing. Christi's face was ashen. There was no baby.

Carolyn was overcome with nausea, weakness, and then darkness. For the first time in her life, her knees buckled under her and she went unconscious; only Don's arms kept her from collapsing onto the floor.

Roman sprinted into the room, out of breath.

"Roman!" Mydonna demanded. "Where's the baby?"

Roman wiped his bloodshot eyes and looked at Carolyn, who was slumped over in a wheelchair.

"She okay?"

"Fine, fine," Carolyn answered wearily from under a washcloth on her forehead. "Worried about Christi."

"Yeah, I wanted to check on her. Doctor said she was reacting to the meds. She should be okay in a bit. I'll be right back."

"Wait!" Mydonna screamed after him. "What about the baby?"

But Roman had run off. Mydonna shook her head.

"My friend has nine grandkids. Can't I get just one?"

"You have one, Mydonna," Christi managed to mutter. "You have one."

An hour earlier, in an ice-cold operating room, a terrible pressure on Christi's chest roused her from her stupor. She focused her eyes on Roman, who was leaning in toward her, with one hand on her shoulder.

"What's going on?" Christi asked sleepily.

Before he could answer, the two of them heard a cry, a loud, staccato cry that sounded something like a lamb.

"It's a boy!" one of the doctors said.

Roman let out a sob as he watched a team of neonatal nurses and specialists carry his son to the warming table.

"Everything okay?" Roman asked.
"He's just fine," someone answered.
"Are you sure? Is everything okay? You sure?" Roman repeated himself, unconvinced.
"He's nine and a half pounds and healthy as a horse."
"He's breathing?"
"Don't you hear him? He can't cry if he can't breathe."
Moments later, Christi's body began to quiver. Several nurses tended to her and took her back to her room while Roman stayed with their son.
After Christi's shaking had settled some, Roman reappeared with the long-awaited tiny bundle in his arms.
"Hey everybody, sorry for the delay," Roman announced. "Here he is! Roman Dale Duren Junior!"
Oohs and ahhs, tears, and cheers filled the room.
"So beautiful, isn't he?" Christi noted quietly.
"He better be! Looks just like me!" Roman yelled joyfully. He gave Madeleine a kiss on the cheek. "Tell Dave he's a genius."
One by one, sets of arms cradled baby Roman until he had been passed around the entire room twice.
Mydonna felt like her son had been handed to her once again.
Carolyn patiently waited her turn, but she was dying to get her hands on him, and did not want to let him go.
Roman's aunt Terri approached him and Christi, and said in a respectful tone, "You know, I did some

research on kids being named juniors, and living in the shadow of a senior. The French just call them Beau."

"B-E-A-U, like short for beautiful?" Christi asked.

"Or BoPeep's little Bo?" Carolyn asked while gazing at her grandson, asleep in her arms.

"No, just Bo! B-O! I like it!" Roman announced.

Carolyn stood up from the wheelchair to give baby Bo to his mother. Christi almost laughed when she realized where Carolyn had been sitting.

"Just like old times, right Mom?" she said drowsily.

"We've got to find new places to have fun," Carolyn said.

Carolyn smiled, overwhelmed with joy, gratitude, love, and, most of all, relief. She took her daughter's free hand, the one without IVs running through it, and pressed it to her own cheek.

"This was the scariest day of my life, BoPeep. But to see you get your dream—to see God bless you with a healthy baby boy—now it's the greatest."

Carolyn prayed, not just for baby Bo and his parents, but for all of them. She prayed that he would grow up to be one of the most fun-loving boys ever known, that he would bring them the laughter that was missing. She prayed that he would help their hearts heal in a way they thought was not possible, and that he would give them more evidence that God made man in his own image. Carolyn prayed for what she knew would be true about Bo Duren—that this nine and a half pound baby would restore their faith in the good.

Surgery One

Do not be afraid of those who kill the body but cannot kill the soul. Rather, be afraid of the One who can destroy both the soul and the body in hell. Are not two sparrows sold for a penny? Yet not one of them will fall to the ground apart from the will of your Father. And even the very hairs of your head are all numbered. So don't be afraid; you are worth more than many sparrows.

Matthew 10:28–31 (NIV)

Carolyn pulled up the last bit of shag carpet from the new house, which had cleared the courts in the spring to make way for a closing in May and a move in June. Her first purchase was a queen-sized bed, which felt excessively luxurious in comparison to the couch she had spent the last year of her life sleeping on. She filled her home with the gifts given at the shower and took great pleasure in unwrapping them one by one, re-reading the cards that accompanied them. Sarah Leona was thrilled to see all the boxes and bags vacate her storage space, but she ached the moment Carolyn closed the front door behind her, as if she had left home for the first time all over again. With Bo's birth and Carolyn's surgical journey, Sarah Leona understood, above all, that a new chapter in their lives had begun.

On July 6, one year and two months after the tornado, Carolyn was ready to begin the reconstruction of her scalp and the creation of a new head of hair. She had total confidence that the first part could be done. The other part would require a combination of a surgeon's skill, the luck of Carolyn's genes, and a lot of prayer.

Carolyn thought she knew what she was embarking upon. Without surgery, she would spend the rest of her life hidden under wigs, hats, and scarves. Her head revealed large islands of skin next to unsightly patches of hair, looking more like a Halloween costume than a woman's head.

The idea seemed simple enough. Dr. Manders would insert a series of expanders under her good hair to grow more tissue. The expanders would have external ports, to be filled by Dr. Walker or Rosemary with saline twice a week so that they would enlarge like water balloons. Eventually, Dr. Manders would remove the leg graft from her head, and pull the newly expanded skin over as a cover instead. Hopefully, the hair follicles would cooperate.

The Southwest Airlines flight made two stops on its way from Tulsa to Pittsburgh. Once at their destination, J.R. and Carolyn rented a car—so as not to impose on the Manders—and drove themselves to a Hampton Inn. They chose the hotel for its shuttle service to the hospital, which saved them any worry about directions. They dined at an Italian restaurant the hotel manager recommended called Abruzzi's and realized they had never really tasted an authentic Italian meatball in Oklahoma. After a full day of travel and a satisfying number of delicious carbohydrates, all Carolyn needed was one glass of Chianti to knock her out for the next eight hours.

The next morning, J.R. and Carolyn arrived at the hospital's registration desk. While Carolyn filled out some last-minute paperwork, J.R. glanced at the intake nurse.

"Lolita Love? That's seriously your name?"

"My mother had a sense of humor."

"With a name like that..."

Carolyn gave J.R.'s abdomen a hard elbow before he could insult her.

He whispered to Carolyn, "What? I was just going to say she could make a whole lot of money if she..."

"Hush!"

"...wrote romance novels or something," J.R. trailed off as he changed his joke midstream.

Carolyn and J.R. sat in the waiting area for the next two hours. Both of them were antsy; their growling stomachs did not help ease their discomfort. Just when J.R. was about to search for the nearest cafeteria, Carolyn was called back.

"I'll be right here when you come out," J.R. said.

Just as planned, Dr. Manders inserted one large expander outfitted with a drainage tube under Carolyn's scalp in an hour's time. She spent a long time in recovery, vomiting twice, having discovered violent reactions to both the anesthesia used in surgery and the painkiller given after it.

J.R. accompanied Carolyn as her nurse wheeled her from one hospital to an entirely different one, all within the labyrinthine University of Pittsburgh Medical Center complex. The surgery took place at Montefiore, but Carolyn was kept overnight for observation at Presbyterian. The distance between them felt nothing short of a half-marathon. Carolyn found her room at six thirty in the evening, curled up on her side, and spent a typical night in the hospital with medically necessary interruptions every few hours.

"Good morning, pleasant lady!" Dr. Manders announced the next day. "Pleasant lady" was the way Dr. Manders described Carolyn, even in her charts, rather than the standard terminology of writing a person's name or just referring to them as "patient." Instead, he would write, "This pleasant lady has undergone a large expansion." Everywhere he went he was followed and revered by a team of eager interns. They smiled when he called her a pleasant lady and stared as he checked the drainage tube attached to Carolyn's head. They could not imagine there would be enough painkillers in the world to numb the effects of pulling that tube out, which would happen in two or three days.

"Your head is chock full of staples and stitches, Ms. Carolyn. At this point, I'd say you can get your shower."

Carolyn had no interest in getting anything. She did not want to move, not even one hair on her head.

After noon, J.R. convinced Carolyn to try a shower.

"How was that?" he asked.

"Heavenly," she answered, and she was not exaggerating. Amazing to her, the warm, clean water made her feel alive again.

On the way out, they stopped by the pharmacy for antibiotics and pain pills. Carolyn took a nap before dinner. She awoke to J.R. staring out the window.

"What's wrong?" she asked.

"My aunt...she died. I wish I could get back tonight. I called Southwest, but we're already on the next flight out."

"I think we should drive next time," Carolyn said, half-asleep.

"Do you know what you just said? That oughta be an eighteen-hour trip by car."

"It's almost as long by plane. And if we had our car, we could leave right now. I'd curl up in the back seat—probably sleep the whole way—and not know the difference."

J.R. shook his head, figuring Carolyn was still drugged up and not thinking clearly. But she felt well enough to know she was starving for well-known paella at a local Spanish restaurant. She could not make it through to the flan, however. Her head pain was excruciating.

J.R. took Carolyn back to the hotel, supporting her in the elevator, and finally carrying her back to their room. She began to shake uncontrollably, as though she were freezing, but she was not at all cold. For a moment she felt transported back to Mercy Hospital, as if she were the one recovering from an emergency C-section. One of her medications mentioned tremors as a side effect, but J.R. called Dr. Manders at home just to be sure.

"Jeez, sorry to hear it, J.R.," Dr. Manders said with concern, and J.R. imagined him scratching his windblown hair. "You know, anxiety would not be out of the question."

J.R. mouthed "anxiety" to Carolyn, but she shook her head slowly.

"She says she doesn't feel anxious."

"She ought to be! It's unnerving to have stuff sticking out of your head. I think she just needs rest at this point."

Again, Carolyn curled up on her side to avoid lying on the back of her head, and J.R. sat down next to her. Gently, he rubbed her back, just as he had done years before.

Inside her throbbing head, Carolyn focused on a silent prayer of thanks to God for a successful first surgery. *One down, five more to go. With you, all things are possible.*

An early morning flight got them into Tulsa by evening, just in time for dinner with friends. Carolyn could not eat, however; all of the medication made her constipated, and she could not decide whether her head or her stomach hurt worse.

Realizing her limitations for once, she spent most of the next day in bed, save for a knock at the door. Expecting it was J.R. announcing his presence as he entered the room, Carolyn did not respond, and lay there with her eyes closed.

"Mom?"

Carolyn thought she might be dreaming or hallucinating. Then she heard a baby's whimper.

"Mom? Someone's here to see you."

Carolyn sat up to see Christi holding Bo, who was sucking a blue pacifier with gusto.

"Little BoPeep! And Baby Bo! What a wonderful surprise."

It was no surprise to Carolyn that the pain that had consumed her for three days vanished when she took Bo into her arms.

"Christi, he really is a doll baby."

"We thought you might like some company on the drive home tomorrow."

"You thought right."

Carolyn drove to Oklahoma City the next day with baby Bo in his safety seat in the back. She soaked in his sweet cooing all the way home. They skipped Carolyn's exit and headed for Sarah Leona's place for a little post-surgery TLC. Just when Carolyn thought she was ready to take care of herself the surgery set her further back physically than she had imagined. She made the mistake of verbalizing guilt over missing her old workout routine.

"You're going to make yourself sick walking on that thing," Sarah Leona complained.

"I'm starting back easy. Just ten minutes, Mother. Trying to get back into shape."

"Your ten minutes is everybody else's hour. You

think I was born yesterday," she muttered as she walked away.

Carolyn decided she would not set an alarm and just see how she felt in the morning. At seven o'clock, she sat right up, took a shower, and drove into work. She spent her lunch break with Christi, who had a four-hour appointment with the hair dresser.

"Four hours, baby? You think it'll take that long?" Carolyn asked Christi while she was getting her long curls washed.

"I'd rather be here than pushing a walker around," Christi said. Her leg injury made her limp terribly, and her post-partum weight had not yet come off. "How's your head?"

"It's okay," Carolyn said. She did not tell her daughter, but she was nervous about her first injection appointment with Dr. Walker on Monday.

"New hat?" Rosemary asked with a smile as Carolyn walked into the office donning a straw hat with leopard trim first thing Monday morning.

"I don't want to scare the neighbors," Carolyn answered.

Dr. Walker's office had been faxed instructions from Dr. Manders to remove Carolyn's stitches and staples and inject 25 cc's of saline into the balloon.

Rosemary gently removed the stitches one by one, while asking all about the surgery. Focusing on Rosemary's questions took her mind off of the prickling feeling in her head.

Dr. Walker walked into the exam room empty-handed.

"Carolyn, I hate to disappoint you," he said. "I planned to do injections today, but I don't think the needle I have is small enough."

She was, indeed, disappointed. With five more surgeries remaining, and dozens of unforeseen delays like this one, it would be an interminable two years. But Carolyn was not eager to force a fat needle in her head either.

"Small sounds good to me," Carolyn said.

She was the first appointment the very next morning. Dr. Walker gave Carolyn several painful shots to numb the port area, still tender from surgery. Rosemary supervised as he injected two vials of saline into the balloon.

"I know you're a superstar," Dr. Walker said, "but you need to lay off the treadmill for a couple of days."

"Dr. Walker, is it possible that my head feels heavier? This is going to give my neck muscles a workout."

"Heavier, perhaps. Tighter is probably the sensation."

No, Carolyn's head definitely felt heavy, something she had not anticipated.

She would lay off the treadmill for one day and tried hard to limit her pain pills.

On August first, Carolyn went in for her second injection. Already, Dr. Manders wanted the cc's upped to thirty. Rosemary did the injections this time, and Carolyn thought her slow administration was kinder.

"Want to try to push past thirty?" she asked. "The

more you can tolerate, the quicker you'll cross the finish line."

The balloon felt tight, and the pressure made her head throb already.

"I'm usually aggressive in most areas of my life," Carolyn answered, "but for this I want to proceed slower." She literally sensed her head was growing larger. A few of her hats were already too tight.

"For some reason, speeding doesn't appeal to me today. The pain threshold is a little higher than I imagined. My head feels like it could explode at any minute."

"We'll do our best not to let that happen. You are your own best judge, Carolyn."

"What's the goal anyway?"

Rosemary checked the letter from Dr. Manders.

"Seventeen to nineteen centimeters. About seven and a half inches of skin. A lot, huh?"

Seven and a half inches.

"Too bad Dr. Manders can't just give me a little face lift, and take all *that* extra skin."

Rosemary raised her eyebrows as if she were considering the exchange.

"You don't have an inch to spare, much less seven and a half."

In August, Rosemary did all of the injections, nice and slow, and Carolyn found herself looking forward to their time together. It became the equivalent of a weekly coffee break, with a shot of saline rather than espresso. If she were running late, Carolyn would bring in two "non-fat with whip toffee nut lattes" to make it authentic, if not to sweeten the appointment.

One afternoon, Dr. Walker popped his head in to say hello, and Carolyn was surprised to see him somewhat disheveled in a sweatshirt and jeans.

"I'm on leave," he explained without Carolyn asking. "See you at seven, Rose?"

"Mmmm ... a big date with Dr. Walker?" Carolyn risked the personal question after he had gone.

"Tim? Oh no, we have some office administration issues to iron out. We haven't been an item for more than seven years now."

"An item? You two were an item?"

"My mistake. More than an item. Married. We were married. Oh, ah!" Rosemary shouted.

She had been pushing past thirty cc's of saline into one of the balloons, trying to get to thirty-five, but it squirted back out.

"Married?" Carolyn asked. "I didn't know you two were married. How can you work together?"

"Oh, when we divorced, we became much better colleagues. And friends. Sorry, Carolyn, but your head doesn't want any more."

"I'm kind of stunned. You've both always been so professional, but I thought there was something more to the way he calls you Rose."

"I don't typically tell patients because I want them to feel they can say anything about me or Tim. But you're stuck with us for a while."

"And I'm ready for the next surgery, Rosemary."

"I know you are, but your head has a mind of its own."

They laughed at Rosemary's accidental double entendre.

"I should hope it does!" Carolyn said, smiling. "Have you heard from Dr. Manders about when he wants to do it?"

"Let's not get ahead of yourself, Carolyn." For some reason, the inadvertent references to Carolyn's cranium seemed especially funny to both of them on this day.

"Let's see how close you are," Rosemary said as she pulled out the tape measure for the weekly check to chart Carolyn's progress. "Sorry, toots. Just nine centimeters."

Nine centimeters. Ten more to go.

Late in the summer, Carolyn felt well enough to travel to Fayetteville, Little Rock, Nashville, and Manhattan, Kansas, mostly for work-related conferences and one wedding.

But by September, Dr. Walker wondered whether she had not been overdoing it. In early September, the expander felt soft, and Dr. Walker suspected a leak.

"I could be wrong, but what if I'm not? I'd rather take the sunny path," Rosemary said. She disregarded his diagnosis and forged ahead with fifty cc's, the most Carolyn had ever taken.

That night, an internal hammer pounded Carolyn's head. As she looked in the mirror, she worried. Her hair growth on the expanded skin was nil. She had not been to a hairdresser in months, knowing coloring it could cause an infection. Her head was certainly growing; she had outgrown all but two hats, a straw one with a black band, and a red baseball cap. As her head grew, it itched, but she took care not to irritate it. She swallowed two pills for the pain, washed her hair with baby shampoo, and collapsed on her pillow. In the morning, she checked the pillowcase to make sure it was dry.

The next week's appointment confirmed Rosemary's optimism. Carolyn's scalp was expanding. It measured thirteen centimeters. There was no leak. Carolyn gave a prayer of thanks for growth, for comfort, and for speed. She was on a roll. She felt thankful for the hair she did have, which easily covered the rear-most expander, and for God's watchful eye.

But the following Monday, Christi called to tell her that Bo was sick and needed to see the pediatrician. Carolyn was scared to death. Getting him here had seemed like the greatest challenge. Now even something as small as a cold threatened to darken their lives once again.

The three of them went to both appointments—to Bo's doctor and to Carolyn's. Rosemary fussed over Bo and told Christi how happy she was to finally meet her.

But by the time Carolyn had walked to the parking lot, the top of her head throbbed with a deep and new pain. She tried to conquer it with mind over matter, but the ache only intensified. She stared at her burrito platter, not able to eat, wondering how she would drive home. Nathan had joined them at their favorite

Mexican restaurant, and he offered to take her right away. But Carolyn did not want to go home.

She paged Rosemary, something she had never done before. Had they not shared such fun and somewhat intimate conversations over the past months, she was not sure she would have done it.

"I'm so sorry to bother you, Rosemary," Carolyn said through tears. "I've never had this much pain. I can barely function. Should I go to the ER?"

"Meet me at the office in fifteen minutes," Rosemary said.

It was 7:45 p.m. when Nathan helped Carolyn walk from the empty parking lot to the dark office building. Rosemary met them at the door, unlocking and disarming their way to the office. She worked with great speed, sucking out 25 cc's of fluid with a syringe. The relief was instantaneous.

"I'm a big wimp I know," Carolyn said.

Rosemary shook her head.

"Too much pressure, Carolyn. Perfectly understandable. Let's measure."

"You're at fourteen."

The tears rolled down Carolyn's cheeks, and Nathan found a tissue. Something profound had changed in the way Carolyn viewed Rosemary. In her mind, Rosemary crossed over from being a conscientious nurse to a devoted friend. Carolyn was overwhelmed by her compassion.

October treatments continued to be painful, but nothing like the last one. Rosemary would add fluid, then take some out, add more, then take some out, all during one appointment. Her measurements were beginning to show a range, from fourteen and a half to sixteen.

"I'd better call Dr. Manders and make sure I've been doing this right," Rosemary said one afternoon.

Carolyn's stomach dropped.

"Can't we just go with sixteen? Three more and we're there!"

The next visit, Carolyn asked Rosemary to measure right away.

"I know we just measured, but can we do it again?"

Rosemary obliged.

It was as though they were measuring a pregnant belly. Carolyn was, indeed, expectant. Her surgery could happen any day now.

But it would not happen until after Thanksgiving per Dr. Manders, although neither Carolyn nor Rosemary had any luck pinning down how long after Thanksgiving. Christmas? New Year's?

Carolyn alternated between having lively visions about the life of her new tissue and disheartening ones. She pictured the nerves connecting, the blood flowing, and the hair follicles growing like wild flowers in a field. Dr. Manders had said that children can grow new hair follicles, but that someone her age would likely not. What good would more scalp be if it didn't have hair? Carolyn knew that she needed her scalp to be intact, but the idea of so much sacrifice for a partially-bald head depressed her.

It had been nearly a year and a half since the

tornado blew their lives apart, and for the first time Carolyn looked back and wondered, *Did I do something to deserve this? Have my shortcomings, much more numerous than the hairs of my head, taken hold of me? Is this why my head is heavy, why I cannot hold it up? Have I not been faithful enough? Are my sins so great that I deserve this struggle?*

Carolyn's thoughts turned to J.R. and how conflicted she was about whether he was the right partner for her. Her thoughts then drifted to Charlie, Christi's biological father, and how she never married him, how he disappeared from Christi's life, and how he re-entered during the time she needed him most. And then Carolyn settled on the most painful of all her thoughts—Christi's own difficulties with her weight, her depression, and her marriage, and whether Carolyn herself had unintentionally passed them on to the daughter she loved with all her heart. She knew from reading the Bible and from life itself that both blessings and burdens are passed on to future generations.

As Carolyn drove south to Ardmore, these thoughts consumed her. A group of doctors' wives had invited her to speak at a luncheon about her ordeal. At first she tried to graciously decline, explaining that she was just beginning the reconstructive phase of her recovery. But the hostess, Regina Turrentine, a doctor's wife who had served with Carolyn on the Keep Oklahoma Beautiful board, convinced her that the women would be fascinated by the medical aspect. To this point, Carolyn had not spoken publicly about May 3. She prepared herself by writing out note cards, reminding herself of the chronology of events, and bringing photographs of the old neighborhood. But she still was not sure what message she would ultimately share.

No one could possibly want to hear about bald heads and a dead baby and sins of the past, could they?

As Carolyn walked into the room, her heart thumped in her chest. The faces of about twenty lovely women dressed to perfection greeted her eagerly, which Carolyn took to mean their expectations were high.

Carolyn set aside all of her note cards except for one. With ease, she talked about the initial impact, the news of her scalping, and the first surgery. She gave some details about the care of her tender head, and the expanders hidden under her hat. As promised, the doctors' wives showed interest in all of these topics. Then, with difficulty, she told them about Christi, Abby, and Bo.

She picked up the one card she needed. Up until this point, she had not decided whether she would share what was written on it. She could not be sure if this audience would want to hear what she believed. She looked down at her "God" card and scanned each point, numbered one through five.

"Looking at life through the rearview mirror," Carolyn said, "I've learned more than ever that the most important things in life are not things; they are relationships. I haven't succeeded in all of them, but I know they matter more than my coin collection, my sock of jewelry, my house.

"I've learned that all glory is fading, and that the moment you think you're grand, you'll be taught what is.

"I've learned that even if you're in pain, you don't have to be one." This comment got a lot of laughs.

"Only God is in the position—literally—to look down at other people. I've learned that my goal, since I've been given a second chance at life, is to leave not a title, but a testimony. When people die, the survivors don't talk about degrees or promotions or the things that seemed to mark success. They certainly don't have these things to talk about when a baby dies. Instead, whether you're young or old, they talk about how that person impacted their life.

"In the end, I want to be remembered for walking the sunny path." Carolyn paused, wishing Rosemary could hear her own words spoken aloud in a new context.

"I want my story to be a message of hope—a testament to God's love and faithfulness. After all, only God cares to know how many hairs are on your head. He alone can count them—just to prove to you how valuable your every fiber is to him. Nothing is too small or too big to trouble God. Just as your grandchild is your delight, so you are his. The God who loves you enough to count the hairs on your head will never fail you. Thank you."

To Carolyn's surprise, the women jumped to their feet to offer her a standing ovation and closed in around her. Most of the women were wiping tears from their eyes, and each of them hugged Carolyn as they thanked her.

When she arrived home, she had a message from Rosemary that Dr. Manders wanted to schedule the next surgery two days after Thanksgiving.

On the twentieth, the eve of Carolyn's forty-sixth birthday, she underwent her nineteenth procedure with Rosemary, the last one before her second operation in Pittsburgh.

"And that makes it 465 cc's altogether," Rosemary announced with pride. "That's a bunch of liquid, Carolyn. Incredible. Want to know how much we got in just today?"

Carolyn shook her head. The count did not matter. God—and, to a degree, Rosemary—knew how much she could take. Her skin had stretched. She was there.

Surgery Two

Now faith is being sure of what we hope for and certain of what we do not see.

Hebrews 11:1 (NIV)

The day after Thanksgiving, Carolyn and J.R. packed up and headed out before sunrise. On this journey, they would travel through Nashville, and nothing said Nashville to them like the Grand Old Opry Hotel.

J.R. and Carolyn were accustomed to getting lost in and out of Pittsburgh, but never had they lost their way inside a hotel before. The Opry was gargantuan, a veritable city inside a hotel. The billions of tiny, white Christmas lights mesmerized and fascinated them. The months it must have taken to string them all up! Carolyn marveled at the greenery, the waterfalls, the pathways, the shops, the restaurants, and the throngs of people moving in and out of them.

"They ought to have something like this in Oklahoma City," Carolyn said to J.R.

"I think Las Vegas has about fifty of them already," J.R. answered.

"Is it possible to run out of interesting towns in between Pittsburgh and home?" Carolyn mused.

"If we compare them all to this circus, yeah, it's possible."

"And by circus you mean one of the most fascinating places in our country, right?" Carolyn loved the hotel and could have spent a week there.

They left for Pittsburgh early Saturday morning and arrived by evening. They spent Sunday touring the rivers of the city and wandering through an old train station.

On Monday morning, Carolyn and J.R. checked in with a nurse a little after ten in the morning. She told them it was going to be a while, and they knew based on the last experience that could mean hours. So they took a walk, exploring Presbyterian hospital, and paging through magazines. J.R. ordered a bagel and coffee. Before he had a chance to take a bite, a nurse came running over to their table. Dr. Manders was ready to go, earlier than they expected. She was desperate to get Carolyn back upstairs and prepped for surgery.

Despite their disappearance, Carolyn and J.R. were greeted happily by Dr. Manders—his smile warm as ever, his hair and cheeks still wind-blown, and his hug oversized. He immediately inspected Carolyn's head and pronounced it a grand success. Carolyn thought he was downright giddy going into surgery. He reminded Carolyn that her skin grafts were too thin and not a sufficient cover for her skull. She needed a better protective covering, and the newly-grown skin would supply most of it to the right side. First, two more expanders needed to go in; one over her right brow and the other in the back of her head. Dr. Manders' joy over the procedure was contagious. Physically, Carolyn felt better today than she had since the last surgery—a feeling she knew would be short-lived, but she enjoyed the temporary euphoria nonetheless.

As a nurse wheeled her in to the operating room, she heard a head-banging tune that sounded like it might be coming from an eighties rock band.

"Who gets to decide on the music?" Carolyn asked in mock disgust.

"Whoever carries the biggest needle," teased the anesthesiologist.

"You guys just want me awake in here so I have to hoist myself on to the bed. Here I am, a walking miracle, and apparently, I'm doing all the work."

The surgical staff liked Carolyn. She was not the typical patient, there for a vanity operation to enlarge breasts, lift eyes, or suck out fat.

Over a bowl of vanilla ice cream, Carolyn winced at the post-surgery pain. The drainage tube dripped more than the last surgery, and Carolyn could not find a comfortable position around it. Her head hurt, she felt nauseated, and the Hydrocodone only worsened her symptoms. She had already forgotten that eighteen months ago she took the same painkiller and had the same reaction. She chastised herself for not remembering by now what she could and could not take.

The shower that revived her the last time was not so magical this go-round. The problem that remained was the awkward drainage tube sticking out from

Carolyn's head, which Dr. Manders had no trouble yanking out soon after the first surgery. The tube prohibited her from pulling a shirt over her head. It ran down her shoulder and emptied blood and excess fluid into a bag hidden in Carolyn's chest pocket. The whole contraption repulsed her.

Carolyn convalesced in her hotel room as J.R. dutifully ran out for pizza. Nothing tasted right, not even her favorite supreme-style pizza, and Carolyn hoped she might lose a few pounds before the holiday smorgasbord began. When J.R. returned, he was covered in a white powder—it took Carolyn a few moments to recognize it as snow! Carolyn rose from her bed, upsetting her pile of half-written thank you notes and stared at the city under a soft white blanket. The streets and buildings looked spotless and bright, just about the opposite of how Carolyn felt. In her mind, she thanked God for the purity of the view, for the reminder that his care is tender and perfect.

Dr. Manders was certainly kind-hearted, but tender and perfect did not come to mind when he jerked out the offending tube. Tears welled in Carolyn's eyes. She was not in any shape to stay for a steak, and clouds threatened more snow, so J.R. drove sixteen hours straight back to Tulsa while Carolyn rested her sore head full of staples and stitches on pillows, her body under a down comforter. J.R. offered to stop, but nothing sounded better to Carolyn than home.

On Sunday, Carolyn prepared to meet Christi and Bo at their church while Roman had to work at the plant. Carolyn was used to seeing the two of them without Roman for various reasons. This week he had missed out on family activities due to a sick stomach. Christi had just overcome the symptoms and feared that if the culprit was not food poisoning it was flu.

Carolyn thought she had escaped the roving bug on Monday when she checked in with Dr. Walker. While Dr. Manders was normally the effusive one, Dr. Walker was so impressed with the look of Carolyn's head that he declared her the simultaneous poster child and supermodel for Ernie.

Covered by a new hat, Carolyn ventured out to a Christmas party at the Governor's mansion, and then an Investment Club cocktail hour the next day. Everywhere she went, people asked about her account of May 3, and they would chime in with their own experiences about where they had been and what they had seen. Knowing they shared a common experience bonded them in a way that was similar to the camaraderie formed after the Oklahoma City bombing. Everyone knew just where they were, what they heard and felt, and whom they lost.

Early Thursday morning, Carolyn awoke to violent diarrhea and vomiting. The flu gripped her body forcefully, and by noon she was in the ER with an IV in her arm to treat dehydration. The hospital staff sent her home by evening, but two days later she returned with an infection at the IV site. The week went down as the most miserable lead-in to Christmas in all her life.

By Christmas Eve, all was forgotten. Carolyn's kids, including baby Bo, spent the night at her place, and on Christmas morning she felt healthy enough to prepare her elaborate breakfast buffet, from the infamous smoked reindeer to homemade biscuits crumbled in chocolate pudding.

The second day of the new year, Carolyn underwent her first treatment with the second balloon. Rosemary started off with a bang, filling it up with 60 cc's. The balloon was squishy to the touch and did not hurt Carolyn's head, a relief after the struggles over the last month.

The balloons seemed to enlarge Carolyn's scalp faster this time. She thought she might be imagining what she desired, but she decided to believe it anyway and celebrate by buying a two-hundred-dollar sassy blonde wig. The hair was longer than any of her other wigs with bangs and a flip at the bottom. Between the Oklahoma winter wind and her wish to never look at another hat again, Carolyn enjoyed her new look.

At the end of January, Carolyn stole away from the Oklahoma ice storms and treated herself to a three-day vacation in Scottsdale, Arizona. She stayed with her friend, Marilyn Herbert, but also enjoyed the company of her old boss, Jill Kennedy, and her family: Hunter, Kendra, and Ryan. J.R. asked if she wanted company, but she chose to go alone, taking her time in the shops and with friends. After one especially long and relaxing shower at Marilyn's, Carolyn noticed an irritated spot on the top of her head near the rear expander.

When Carolyn returned to the cold of Oklahoma City, Dr. Walker showed concern about the infection and treated it with an antibiotic cream. For the first time, he refused to do an injection in the rear balloon, claiming the risk of further infection was too great. He explained that the transplanted area did not yet have a proper blood flow to quickly heal a small irritant. Unfortunately, he put a temporary stop to the sassy wig.

Carolyn had no choice but to trust Dr. Walker, even though she suspected that Dr. Manders would not have skipped an injection. While Carolyn's hometown surgeon approached his medicine conservatively, her remote surgeon took a far more aggressive tack. Carolyn understood that she probably benefited from having both men caring for her. She also recognized that surgeons are as human as anyone, and just because one thinks he is right does not mean that there is only one truth.

By February, Carolyn was cleared for an injection, and she had never felt so happy about that fact. When she complained of pain on the lower right side of her head, Dr. Walker explained that the expander could be pushing on nerve endings. Carolyn admitted to herself that she might need a regular dose of painkillers to get through the next month. She did not like the fact that in the last seven months, she had taken eighty-five pills. Eighty-five seemed like a large number.

To address the pain issue, Rosemary suggested that Carolyn come twice a week for injections rather than just once a week. She thought the pressure would be less intense with an expedited result. Carolyn also asked her to keep the measurements to herself and her chart. The last time Carolyn focused so intently on the size, the time crept by at an agonizingly slow pace.

"Do you at least want to know how many cc's I've got in so far?" Rosemary asked.

"Sure," Carolyn said indifferently.

"You're about to be more excited than that—245 cc's total."

Carolyn raised an eyebrow.

"I'm halfway there already?"

Nothing erased Carolyn's discomfort like an evening with baby Bo. She carved out time to see him several times every week, and recently Sarah Leona had been complaining about not getting more face time with her great-grandbaby. So, "Great"—as she began calling herself ever since Bo's birth—baked an apple pie to entice them all over to her house, and it worked.

On the first of March, Carolyn's friend, Michelann Ooten, the public information officer for the state Office of Emergency Management, called with what Carolyn was sure was a practical joke.

"This just in," Michelann teased as she continued in a serious newscaster voice, "Brian Williams from NBC News New York just called for you."

"What? The anchorman?" Carolyn asked, not certain she heard correctly.

"He's looking for tornado survivors and wants to talk to you, Christi, and maybe even Nathan and Roman."

"Brian Williams called for me? He picked up the phone to talk to me?"

"Yep. And I hope you don't have any plans tonight, because a film crew is showing up at your house at eight p.m."

Carolyn called her kids immediately, but only Christi could come. Both of them frantically fixed up their makeup and hair. Christi's looked long and lush, curly and blonde. Carolyn tied her thin strands of blond hair into a low ponytail, and donned her favorite leopard cap. A crew of four out of Dallas arrived at Carolyn's home that night and shot for two hours. They had also stopped in Norman, catching interviews at the National Weather Service's Storm Prediction Center and Severe Weather Lab earlier in the day for additional footage. The story ran the very next night, and sure enough, Williams fronted the piece.

BRIAN WILLIAMS: NBC NEWS IN DEPTH TONIGHT...AS WE HERE ON THE EAST COAST BATTEN DOWN THE HATCHES FOR A POSSIBLE NOREASTER...ANOTHER PIECE OF BAD WEATHER NEWS...IT'S THE OFFICAL START OF TORNADO SEASON.

IN AN AVERAGE YEAR, ONE-THOUSAND TWISTERS HIT ACROSS THE COUNTRY. SO FAR THIS YEAR, THERE HAVE BEEN MORE TORNADO-RELATED DEATHS THAN NORMAL, AND THAT PUTS EVEN MORE PRESSURE ON SCIENTISTS TRY-

ING TO DEVELOP A BETTER EARLY WARNING SYSTEM FOR TORNADOES.

IN DEPTH TONIGHT, HERE'S NBC'S KELLY O'DONNELL.

O'DONNELL: CAROLYN STAGER AND HER DAUGHTER KNOW THE TERROR OF TORNADOES, NATURE'S MOST VIOLENT STORMS.

THEY LIVED THROUGH ONE OF THE FIERCEST EVER.

IN 1999, FORTY-SEVEN OTHERS DIED. STAGER'S HOME WAS FLATTENED. SHE SUFFERED PERMANENT HEAD INJURIES AND BARELY SURVIVED.

Carolyn: "Instantly you could hear and feel the windows being sucked out of the house, and then just instantaneously you can feel your whole home being sucked out... your whole body being tossed about."

O'DONNELL: THIS MONTH MARKS THE START OF THE MOST ACTIVE PART OF THE TORNADO SEASON, NOW THROUGH JULY. ALREADY THIS YEAR—TWENTY-ONE. NOT SO MANY, BUT WITH A HIGH DEATH TOLL—TEN SO FAR—POINTING AGAIN TO THE URGENCY OF GIVING AS MUCH ADVANCE WARNING AS POSSIBLE.

O'Donnell: "Ten years ago when a tornado was coming, the government was able to give only about six minutes' warning to get sirens going and news reports out before the storm hit. Now it's a little better, ten minutes on average. But today the government says it wants to improve even more."

O'DONNELL: AN ARMY OF RESEARCHERS WORKING, RELEASING INTRUMENT-LADEN BALLOONS, CHASING TWISTERS.

Natural Sound: We have a big tornado!

BUT SCIENTISTS SAYS THEIR BEST HOPE IS BETTER DOPPLAR RADAR. THEY'RE SPENDING 25 MILLION DOLLARS TO CREATE A STORM- WATCHING VERSION OF A RADAR USED BY NAVY SHIPS TO SCAN FOR ENEMY WAR PLANES. IT SENDS OUT MANY BEAMS AT ONE TIME, COULD BE SIX TIMES FASTER AT DETECTING DEVELOPING TORNADOES, AND THEY'RE WORKING ON ANOTHER KIND OF RADAR BEAM TO VASTLY IMPROVE ESTIMATES OF THE DENSITY OF RAIN IN A STORM AND WHETHER THERE'S HAIL—ALL VITALLY IMPORTANT IN RECOGNIZING WHETHER A THUNDER STORM CAN SUDDENLY BECOME A TWISTER.

GOVERNMENT RESEARCHER, JAMES KIMPLE

Kimple: "Our goal is to get the lead times into the twenty to thirty minute window, say, in the next ten years."

BUT DESPITE ALL EFFORTS METEOROLOGISTS ARE UNABLE TO FORECAST WHETHER A WHOLE TORNADO SEASON WILL BE BETTER OR WORSE THAN NORMAL. THE HEAD OF THE STORM PREDICTION CENTER, JOE SCHAEFFER

Schaeffer: "We don't know enough yet to make long-term forecasts. I wish we could, and we're working hard at it, but right now the knowledge just isn't there."

AND FORECASTERS CANNOT SAY WHAT THE REST OF THIS YEAR WILL BE LIKE, LEAVING UNCERTAINTY IN TORNADO ALLEY AND REVIVING BAD MEMORIES FOR CAROLYN STAGER.

Carolyn: I thought I was dying. I mean, I did think I was dying. I knew that my body could not stand much more abuse.

A RACE AGAINST THE ELEMENTS NOW TO WARN PEOPLE SOONER—WHEN EVERY MINUTE MEANS SAVING LIVES. KELLY O'DONNELL, NBC NEWS, NEW YORK.

Surgery Three

He is able, more than able
To accomplish what concerns me today.
He is able, more than able
To handle anything that comes my way.
He is able, more than able
To do much more than I could ever dream.
He is able, more than able
To make me what He wants me to be.
   (Rory Noland & Greg Ferguson, "Prayer Song")

The next week, Rosemary measured Carolyn's expansion, and she had reached nineteen and a half centimeters in record time. *Faster and better than ever! Let's go, go, go!* Anxious to move forward, Carolyn made Rosemary promise she would fax a report to Dr. Manders, believing he would be willing to do the surgery early.

The month of March passed without a word from Dr. Manders' office. So Carolyn took it upon herself to call. The nurse explained that Dr. Manders had been out of the country but that his schedule looked open on Wednesday, May 30. Carolyn asked her to book it.

Carolyn approached her expansion appointments with renewed vigor, knowing that she was one month away from her third surgery. The more she thought about the amount of saline that had been injected into her head, the more she wondered how she had avoided looking like a giant beach ball. She had no doubt that Dr. Manders would be able to cover much of her head with the newly stretched skin. The light at the tunnel's end was in sight.

And for the first time in her reconstruction, she experienced a month of pain-free treatments. She was not sure whether she had become accustomed to the feeling or whether the adrenaline from her own determination masked the discomfort. Whichever it was, everything seemed to be going her way.

Carolyn spent the anniversary of the May 3 tornado planning out her road trip through Pennsylvania—Gettysburg, Lancaster, and Hershey—for Civil War history, quaint Amish towns, and chocolate.

One week before the surgery, Carolyn called Dr. Manders' office manager to request a private meeting with him first to go over the long-range plan prior to going under the knife again. She thought she remembered Dr. Manders saying he would accomplish full coverage on the right side of her head and partial coverage on the left, the most dramatic changes yet. But Dr. Manders was not there.

"He has to go to Brazil," his office manager said over the phone.

Carolyn sighed.

"Brazil? When is he going? When will he be back?"

The manager paused. Carolyn imagined her scrolling lazily through Dr. Manders' jam-packed calendar on the computer.

"Back in a few weeks. Actually, he left a message about your surgery. He wants to reschedule it for the twentieth of June."

Carolyn's disbelief converted to fury. *Was someone going to let me know about this before I arrived in Pittsburgh?* She wanted to shout it, but she held her tongue and instead decided to call Dr. Manders directly—at home.

The only other time Carolyn had resorted to direct contact with Dr. Manders was when J.R. called him, concerned about her reaction to post-operative pain medications. But this time, she sensed that her determination and stamina were for naught. She could barely see the numbers on her cell phone as she punched in Dr. Manders' home telephone number.

"Carolyn, you pleasant person, you're not bothering me at all. How can I help you?"

If Dr. Manders' had said something along the lines of, "Why are you disturbing me during my lunch hour?" Carolyn might have been able to yell at him. But he would never dream of insulting a patient, and his forever gentle and kindly manner disarmed Carolyn right away, although she did not plan to back down entirely. She explained how she had been counting the minutes until the May surgery, only to be let down at the last minute and put off for another month. She nearly broke down just thinking of returning to Rosemary and Dr. Walker for bi-weekly injections for four more weeks; she feared waiting any longer meant a higher risk that Dr. Manders would be called away for a more important surgery or patient or conference in a very distant land.

"Carolyn, I'm simply knocked over by this," Dr. Manders said as genuinely as ever. "I'm just as surprised as you are. This must be so distressing for you, and please know I'm sorry. I do have time, I do. Let me see—"

Again, Carolyn imagined Dr. Manders' calendar, but this time she could hear the actual shuffling of papers. He was not the kind of slick surgeon who carried a Blackberry. *So he does have time? Why doesn't his office manager know that? She must not be doing her job very well.* Now Carolyn found herself redirecting her anger and wishing she had called Dr. Manders in the first place.

"In fact, yes! I could do it this week! Absolutely!"

"This week?" Carolyn thought about having to tell J.R. to drop everything and drive for two days. She knew he would have a choice response. "But, aren't you leaving for Brazil?"

"I am. I am. I leave Thursday evening, so we could do it Wednesday and then give you the okay the next morning. What do you say?"

Now Carolyn felt like a schmuck.

"Dr. Manders, I don't want to press you into this. And at risk of sounding like a choosy beggar, I'd feel better if you weren't in Brazil the day after surgery. I know you're the best, but..."

"Complications happen to even the best. Wise

you are, my dear. Of course, of course. You're absolutely right. I'll be back on Thursday, June 7. Let's do it on the eighth."

Carolyn began to understand why her surgery had been pushed back. Dr. Manders was clearly busier than she had imagined. The last thing she wanted to do was to set him up for a misstep. After all the bluster, she was willing to give him an out.

"You won't be too tired? Jet-lagged?"

"No, no, no, no, no! Your surgery is fun and easy. How about this? Let's plan our pre-op meeting on Friday the eighth, enjoy the weekend, then suit up on Monday morning, yes?"

Dr. Manders' enthusiasm made Carolyn want to laugh.

Emotionally and mentally, Carolyn was beyond ready for the next surgery. But physically, her head had other ideas.

On Monday, May 28, what would have been two days before the original surgery date, a seam along Carolyn's head became infected. Rosemary treated it with a topical antibiotic cream, but by the weekend, the spot had grown bigger and bright red. Rosemary met Carolyn at the office for another emergency visit, applying Silvadine to protect the infected area, draining nearly 100 cc's of fluid, and with Dr. Walker's approval, giving out a round of antibiotics.

"Good thing your surgery was rescheduled, Carolyn," Rosemary said. "I wouldn't want you to go to Pittsburgh looking like this."

"You know what they say," Carolyn said. "People plan and God laughs."

By Sunday, Carolyn felt well enough to go to church. She wanted to believe that the drugs had taken hold and the redness was diminishing. When she craned her head around, the spot looked to be the size of a quarter. In reality, it was much larger.

"It's about the size of a grapefruit, Carolyn," Dr. Walker said as he cleaned her scalp. "The transplanted skin is breaking down." He lifted a mirror to show her the big, bloody mess. Carolyn felt sick to her stomach. Dr. Walker noticed the color drain from her face. He put the mirror away.

"Blood is good, Carolyn. It'll be flushed out, and then start to heal. Of course, it could take three to four weeks to heal..."

"Three to four weeks?" Carolyn asked, shocked.

Dr. Walker continued. "Which means your surgery will likely be delayed again..."

"Delayed?" Carolyn could not say anything more. *For how long?* she thought. *We've already missed one date. I'm going to have to call Dr. Manders again. This cycle could go on forever.*

The bad news, coupled with every round of anticipation and disappointment and each roller-coaster ride of record-breaking progress and the worst-ever delays, drained the well of tears that had been building up for the last two months.

Carolyn wanted to hibernate from the world for the rest of the day, but as always, her schedule—not unlike Dr. Manders'—was full of appointments with people who counted on her. So she went about every task with a brave face and a tissue in hand. Her good friend, Saundra, was going to be sworn in as mayor of Edmond, and she had promised to be there. Carolyn chose her most elegant scarf to hide her wounded head. She stood by her friend with a smile to mask her wounded heart.

For the rest of the week, Carolyn wrestled with her decisions over the past two years. She began to question herself in a way she had never done before.

Am I walking down the right path? Should I have chosen a world-class surgeon who spends so much time with the world? Do I have the strength to see this through?

She realized that in focusing on herself, rather than on God, her prayers had become off-center, her confidence off-balance. She came to the conclusion that while she doubted her own ability to see herself through this challenge, she never disbelieved God's.

I may not be able, but he is. He is more than able...

The thoughts took her back to one of her favorite prayer songs from church.

He is able, more than able, to accomplish what concerns me today...

The words of the song calmed Carolyn's mind enough for her to make room for the unexpected: gratitude. The May surgery date was not meant to be. J.R. had encouraged her to stay with the planned surgery in early June, infection or not. Her head could possibly heal just in time. Carolyn felt herself giving thanks to God for his perfect plan, for her newly discovered capacity to accept a timetable different from her own.

So during the first week of June, somewhere along their third road trip to the city of Pittsburgh, J.R. deviated from their written directions and took a northbound highway.

"Scenic route?" Carolyn asked from the passenger seat, her head resting sleepily on her trusty traveling pillow.

"Nah, change of plans. I want to go to Terre Haute."

"Indiana? Why?"

"They're going to fry Timothy McVeigh this week, and I want to try and talk to him."

Carolyn sat bolt upright.

"Have you lost your mind, J.R. Richards?"

She asked the rhetorical question so often that she knew the answer.

As they pulled into town, Carolyn found herself surprised at its vitality. She saw signs for a number of universities and colleges, and thought the town itself had an appeal similar to Oklahoma City's. She sensed a revival of the historic downtown, with new businesses opening up next to stately buildings from the turn of the century. She took a picture of the Clabber Girl corn starch sign, amused to see an actual storefront. They stopped for an early dinner at a Texas Roadhouse—J.R.'s choice, because he liked what he called "the manliness" of getting to eat peanuts and then toss the shells on the ground.

J.R. drove two miles outside of town, and in that

short distance, the charm of Terre Haute faded away as they approached the desolate grounds of the federal prison, home to the country's only death chamber for federal capital punishment prisoners. The sea of TV satellite trucks from around the country reminded her of the days after the bombing in downtown Oklahoma City, where the cathedral parking lot north of the old Murrah Federal Building was crammed with TV trucks. At that time, no one except a co-conspirator or two knew the name Timothy McVeigh was connected to the worst act of terrorism on American soil. But he came to personify evil in Oklahoma, and in the country for that matter, and six years later (three months shy of the attacks on the World Trade Centers on 9/11 which would dwarf McVeigh's destruction), all the trucks, reporters, photographers—and J.R.—appeared once more to see the "devil get his due."

"Honestly, J.R., I'd rather be tasting chocolate in Hershey about now," Carolyn said.

"Are you kidding me? This is damn history in the making. The Feds haven't toasted a prisoner since the mid-seventies. And there's no better jerk to do it to."

"Don't you think God should control who lives and who dies, not us?" Carolyn knew better than to engage J.R. in a serious debate. Sparring was his game. "Technically, McVeigh won't be 'toasted.' He'll be given lethal injection and drift off to sleep."

J.R. frowned.

"Shooot, they should stick him on the tenth floor of a glass building and not let him know when it's going to blow up. Let him get a taste of his own TNT."

"You mean fertilizer. Anyway, is this supposed to make me feel better?" Carolyn asked, but J.R. ignored her as he looked for an opening between the trucks.

"Just checking," Carolyn said with a sigh as she plunged her head back on to her pillow.

Carolyn's mind drifted back to April 19, 1995. She was in her office, the legislature was in session, and they were wrestling with the unions. The explosion was thunderous; Carolyn made a flippant comment about an unhappy party to the negotiations dropping a bomb on her office. When they turned on the television to see what had happened, they were stunned and horrified, and Carolyn felt sick that she had made light of it. Several friends of hers had been in harm's way, it turned out, but miraculously, all of them had escaped. A friend from kindergarten, Jean Martin Fraley, had been across the street in the Journal Record building. A friend from Tulsa, Ann Domin, had been inside the Murrah building, but she unknowingly saved her life as she ran late to a meeting by stopping in the ladies room.

J.R. stopped the car and got out his cell phone.

"J.R., what are you doing?" Carolyn asked.

He waved her off.

"Hello, J.R. Richards here, from Oklahoma. Wanted to see if I could talk to one of your prisoners, a Tim McVeigh."

Carolyn shook her head and turned away from him. Even though no one could see them, she felt her cheeks turn red with embarrassment.

What bothered Carolyn most about the bombing,

the part she still held on to year after year, was the suddenness of death. One-hundred-sixty-eight people were gone in a flash, and yet McVeigh had six years to prepare for his departure from the world. *Those innocent adults and children took so much to the grave,* she thought, *never getting the opportunity to say goodbye to loved ones.* Carolyn knew that if any of her children or grandchildren had died in the bombing, her first response would be to hope the perpetrator would succumb to a death as terrible as the one he had caused. Yet, staying alive, only to be confined forever, and having to deal with what was left of his conscience forever, seemed to her a harsher punishment. *Dying is the easy part,* she thought. *Living with what you had done would be torture.*

J.R. clapped his phone shut.

"Said he's not allowed any phone calls. I can send a letter though. It'd have to be overnighted."

"You're unbelievable."

"This is what I would've told him," J.R. continued, "life's short and if it were up to me, he wouldn't get this quick end."

"What happened to blowing him up?"

J.R. continued.

"Life in prison is what I want. I'd like to see him suffer. You just can't take innocent people's lives. So, my vote, I vote against injection. I vote for suffering for the rest of his life."

"So, you want him to live?"

"Well if you're asking me if the S.O.B. was standing in the road here, would I run him over? Yes, with pleasure. But since he's in the pen, and probably not having that much fun, I think he ought to stay there making license plates and fending off sex offenders. Now I think I'm ready to find a vodka."

J.R. found one at their hotel and Carolyn found a fresh pillow. Her favorite parts of being on the road were the way she slept after a long day of travel and the food.

They started off with pancakes in Terre Haute, the best little burgers in Richmond, Ohio, and then a chocolate-dipped ice cream cone in Wheeling, West Virginia. They would have made it to Pittsburgh before dark if J.R. had not been stopped by police. The officer was suspicious of J.R. for driving with his bright headlights on, and he was harsh at first, but before long J.R. had charmed the officer so much that he escorted them to their hotel in downtown Pittsburgh.

The next morning, Carolyn skipped breakfast, just in case Dr. Manders wanted to do the surgery right away, instead of waiting all weekend.

But on their way to the appointment, Carolyn got a call from the hospital. Dr. Manders had missed his flight out of JFK airport in New York, and would be arriving at 2:30 p.m., or three, or as late as five.

Carolyn took the news in stride. She and J.R. killed time at the Carnegie museum, touring an exhibit on light, and since surgery that day was out of the question, sitting down for lunch.

Dr. Manders blew into the clinic at four, cleaned Carolyn's wound, applied Gamma Graft, scheduled surgery for Monday, and invited Carolyn and J.R. to dinner at Ruth's Chris steakhouse.

"Weren't you in Brazil today?" Carolyn asked with admiration.

"Today? I think so ... yes." Dr. Manders ran his hand through his rumpled hair. "Or maybe it was technically yesterday, but we have to eat, after all!"

At dinner, Dr. Manders drew a map for Carolyn and J.R., to guide them to his favorite places along their intended route. He made a detailed sketch of battlefields, museums, a cemetery, and an Amish restaurant known for its "plain and fancy" country style shoo-fly pie. Carolyn wondered how there was room in his head for so much information. She also marveled how he was still functioning after sleeping on one flight, missing another, and holding hours at his clinic, all within twenty-four hours of leaving a different hemisphere.

Even if they had not stopped for pie, Carolyn would have been intrigued enough by reading the signs along the highway, particularly "Bird In Hand" and "Intercourse" (J.R. pretended to jerk the steering wheel off the highway). They passed Amish families traveling in horse-drawn buggies on the side of the road, cutting their yards with push-mowers, plowing their fields with teams of horses, and drying their clothes on lines in the sun. To Carolyn, the simplicity of it made her feel as though she were a witness to colonial life or to Hollywood-directed scenes from the movie by the same name.

Even the basic highway signs diverted Carolyn

from fretting about her impending surgery. This way to Washington, D.C., that way to New Jersey, this way to New York City. It was all right there.

They spent the night in Hershey, and spent the next day discovering how chocolate is made. Carolyn convinced J.R. to ride a small roller coaster that cleverly dumped them into a candy store. She bought bags of candy and chocolate-colored t-shirts that read "KISS ME" for the kids.

The third surgery went well. There was, indeed, enough excess skin to cover the right side of Carolyn's scalp and some of the left. Dr. Manders inserted a new expander, hoping to get twenty-two centimeters of skin out of it by the next surgery. He put in a second expander, but with the infection and the anticipated success of the first expander, he thought better of it and took it out.

"Spot on!" Dr. Manders' declared after the surgery. They were more than halfway finished.

J.R. met Carolyn in recovery, an area where surgical patients were lined up like sardines in a can. Carolyn came to after a short while, and she told J.R. she was ready to move. J.R. had been annoyed by the crowded conditions, and he became less tolerant of them as the hours passed.

"Hey, I'm that jerk from Oklahoma," he announced to one of the nurses. "I'd like to visit with the head nurse."

Invariably, the head nurse would have more important tasks than deal with J.R., so he would pester anyone in scrubs he could find.

"This isn't our first rodeo. Carolyn's been in recovery too long. If you don't get me a private room in thirty minutes, I'm going to call Dr. Manders and start chewing on him. I don't think he'd like that very much, would he?"

Raising Cain was an art form for J.R., partly because it got results.

Carolyn was confined to the hotel room for the next twenty-four hours, mostly because the drainage tube from her head to the vial in her pocket kept filling up. It was too gross to go out in public. Even J.R. raised an eyebrow when Carolyn asked him to help her squeeze the bloody liquid through the tube. But he was a trooper, and mostly did what he was asked.

Carolyn's post-op appointment was scheduled for Thursday, four days after the surgery. Again, the timing turned out to be fortuitous. Initially, she had hoped to leave Pittsburgh and get on the road by Thursday morning, but she awoke with tremendous swelling in her head. Dr. Manders said he would have been alarmed had her head not been swollen. He removed a few staples, the Gamma Graft, and the drainage tube. As grateful as Carolyn was to get rid of it, the divesting process was a miserable one.

Before they departed, J.R. thought to ask Dr. Manders to draw a detailed map, much like the one that took them through Pennsylvania Dutch country, to get them out of Pittsburgh. As many times as they had driven in and out of the city, they could not get a picture in their minds of the city's street map. Unlike Oklahoma City's grid, Pittsburgh's streets wound around in all kinds of directions, as though city planners simply paved over the circuitous horse and wagon trails from the 1700s. Despite Dr. Manders' sketch, the two of them managed to take twice as long as any native driver to get out of the city.

Back in Oklahoma City, Carolyn chose to recuperate at her mother's house for a few days. The "spot-on" surgery left the skin on her head throbbing and feeling terribly stretched. Carolyn tried not to complain out loud, but Sarah Leona could see the pain every time her daughter moved and winced.

In the kitchen one evening while preparing supper, Sarah Leona whispered to Pappy, "I'm worried about Carolyn this time." Of course, being so hard of hearing, Sarah Leona could not be certain that her whisper was indeed quiet. But she did not want Carolyn to hear just how concerned she was. "She's done this so many times before. But this time is different, and she really doesn't feel well. I wonder if that infection has gone to her blood or something."

"Honey," Pappy answered with simple honesty and loudly enough for the neighborhood to hear, "would you feel good if you had that thing in your head?"

Without meaning to, Carolyn burst out laughing.

"Mother," she yelled, "I know *you* would make sure everyone knew you were feeling bad!"

The healing came slowly. Dr. Walker, ever conservative in his approach, did not clear Carolyn for injections until the beginning of July. Carolyn wrapped her head gently in scarves, donning a wig only for special dinners out with the family. Wigs were a good cover for dirty hair, since Carolyn could not over-wash her head, but the dried pieces of Gamma Graft made them fairly uncomfortable. Carolyn treated herself to a facial by Farrah; she wanted another chance to thank Farrah for recommending Dr. Walker to her in the first place. Farrah gave Carolyn a sympathetic smile.

"I'm glad he's been working out. Are you almost finished with him? Or, he with you?"

Carolyn thought her question was curious.

"Not quite. I wish. Not that he's not perfectly lovely. It's just a long road."

"Oh, Carolyn, I hear he's going on sabbatical next year."

"Really?" Carolyn was surprised. Her mind began to spin. Who would take over her care? As long as Rosemary was around, she would be all right. Carolyn decided to dismiss the rumor as salon talk and not worry about it until she could confirm the information for herself.

But it was not salon talk, and the truth was worse.

Surgery Four

Do you see this woman? I entered your house, and you gave me no water for my feet, but she has wet my feet with her tears, and wiped them with the hair of her head. You gave me no kiss, but she, since the time I came in, has not ceased to kiss my feet. You didn't anoint my head with oil, but she has anointed my feet with ointment. Therefore I tell you, her sins, which are many, are forgiven, for she loved much. But to whom little is forgiven, the same loves little.

Luke 7:44 (WEB)

Carolyn knew it was not humanly possible to pray for everything, but she figured that her most critical bases were covered. She sent up daily prayers of healing for Christi and herself, of protection for baby Bo, of fulfillment for Nathan, of thanks for her family and friends, as well as intercessions for their needs. But there was one prayer she had left out, one that never occurred to her to ask for; she had assumed that there was no need for it, that it would always be there.

On the second Monday in July of 2001, Carolyn was sitting where she had nearly every week, and sometimes twice a week, for more than a year—on an examination table in Dr. Walker's office. Rosemary had the unpleasant job of trimming the dried Gamma Graft from Carolyn's head, although she treated it like she might overgrown fingernails. The crispy pieces fell on the floor and still looked—to Carolyn—ridiculously and disgustingly like fried pork rinds. But did they ever work.

Carolyn felt a nervous flutter tickle her stomach. She already had one long-distance surgeon. She chose Dr. Walker in the first place because he was, in her opinion, the best in Oklahoma City. Casually, she said, "I heard last week that Dr. Walker is going to take next year off. Is that true?"

"Yep. That's in the works. Don't worry, he'll have someone very capable covering for him."

"I don't mean to sound selfish," Carolyn said, "but selfishly, I'm so disappointed. You've both been so good to me. I just always pictured that you and Dr. Walker would be there until the end—to take credit, if nothing else!"

"I know," Rosemary said sympathetically.

"At least I'll still have you," Carolyn said. "Thank God."

"Carolyn..."

Carolyn could tell by the tone of Rosemary's voice that something was wrong.

"I'm leaving too."

"What? On sabbatical? Together? Are you eloping this time?"

Both of them laughed—a natural cover for doubt.

"I'm moving to Washington, D.C. Remember I

worked at Walter Reed Hospital? I've always wanted to go back and live in Georgetown. My daughter being in New York is the icing on the cake."

"I understand," Carolyn said, "but I'm blind-sided. Here I prayed to get my surgeries over with quickly, for the doctors to keep me in good health, but I never thought to pray for you *not* to move. That one never entered my mind. I wish it had."

"A prayer in this case would not have made a difference, Carolyn. I'm a big city gal with a Midwestern heart. You probably weren't *supposed* to pray about this. You've got bigger prayers to make. You're going to be just fine," Rosemary said through glassy eyes. "That's not to say I'm not disappointed I won't get to walk this walk with you until the last day. Truly, though, you don't need me. You are rock solid."

The news about Dr. Walker was unsettling enough, but to know that Rosemary would be gone as well felt like a punch to the gut. Carolyn was surprised how much she had come to depend on Rosemary, not just for her gentle touch, her reliability no matter the hour, and her wise medical advice, but for her friendship.

"What do you think?" Rosemary asked as she handed Carolyn a mirror, as though she had just given her a haircut.

"Do you need to get that piece right there?" Carolyn asked Rosemary, referring to one small piece of dried and curled graft.

"Nah," Rosemary said, "it'll probably fall out when you're giving a speech or something."

"I don't care if the next nurse doesn't know a thing

about expanders," Carolyn said. "But you'd better make sure she makes me laugh."

Carolyn refused to let Rosemary's move bring her down. Besides, she knew she must be happy for her friend. The power of positive thinking had brought her this far, and she did not want to take a step backward. She knew exactly what pick-me-up was in order. She called her kids and invited them to lunch.

The next morning, Carolyn fixed a casserole, set her dining room table, and was still baking two dozen cookies made of oatmeal, caramel, nuts, and chocolate chips when Nathan and Christi showed up. The kids walked in to their mother's house with the ever-familiar and always-welcoming scent of bronzed sugar and butter. While Carolyn thought of herself as changing bit by bit, month after month at a slow pace; she felt like her children were rapidly moving in opposite directions.

Christi was spiraling downward. While she did not talk about her home life, Carolyn could see through her façade. Christi's hair was perfectly coiffed and her makeup applied just right, but her spirit was lifeless, as if she were going through the motions: functioning, but numb. The contrast between Christi the woman and Christi the young teenager was too stark to ignore. She had been a national cheerleading champion whose energy, athleticism, and beauty were incomparable. Carolyn wondered where that girl had gone and whether she could ever come back. Carolyn knew her daughter was in pain, but had not a clue how to touch it. She simply put her arms around Christi and let her know she was loved, and Carolyn hoped that was enough.

Nathan was rocketing upward. Here Carolyn raised two children in the same home, under similar circumstances—at the very least, the same amount of love; yet he had grown into the opposite of Christi. While Christi carried the weight of the world, he floated around like he had not a care in the world. Ironically, this trait worried Carolyn for years. She wondered whether it would mean as an adult he would be unfocused or undisciplined. While Christi had no issues finding a good government job where her superiors valued her, Nathan struggled to get the job he had set his heart on—a firefighter. He had earned his college-level safety engineering degree, taught EMTs how to be first responders, served as a volunteer firefighter, but getting paid to work as a firefighter seemed harder than winning the lottery.

Carolyn often told herself that watching her children struggle was harder than surviving an F-5 tornado. She could not let her angst rule her life. It helped her to imagine wrapping up her concerns in a little box tied with a ribbon and handing it to God.

Please take it away. I can't give it to anyone else, and I have to loosen this grip on my heart. The sooner I let go, the faster I will have my serenity back. Fretting, orchestrating, trying to control any of it is futile. I don't control a lot, I realize this. So I am offering this up to you, as a gift to myself.

It turned out, Nathan was disciplined, focused, even driven. Carolyn realized that she had misinterpreted his lax attitude. It turned out to be self-confidence. Nathan never doubted himself, never doubted that life would work out for him. In fact, he had just met a girl named Marci whom he felt sure would be his wife. A few fire departments showed interest in him. All was right in Nathan's world. Christi, however, was in the midst of uncertainty, discovering how much could go wrong.

The three of them sat down at the table. Nathan turned to his mother and made a request.

"Mom, mind if I bless the food before we eat?"

The moment hung in the air. Carolyn sat speechless. While she had always blessed the food, even in restaurants, Nathan had never asked to do it. Carolyn soaked in every word of his prayer of thanks. Before any of them took a bite, she felt fully satisfied from her head to her soul.

The Gamma Graft held on until early August, when the last piece crashed to the ground in the middle of a vigorous workout on her home treadmill. She realized that even though she felt like a teenager inside, singing along the words to Billy Joel's "Movin' Out," believing that nothing on her aerobics or yoga or Pilates tapes was beyond her ability, she was limited by the reality that her head remained precariously stitched together.

Normally Carolyn welcomed the passage of time, except that a new infection festered and made her wish Dr. Manders traveled to Oklahoma like he did Brazil.

Dr. Manders can't watch over me 24/7, but God can. I will put my trust in him. I will.

Carolyn's head was too big and bloody to wear wigs anymore, and she was already down to her last hat. Dr. Walker decided that more Gamma Graft was needed, but it would be days before Dr. Manders' office would mail it out.

Nathan inadvertently took Carolyn's mind off of her latest medical setback; he had the flu. Carolyn babied him at home with roast beef, fresh-squeezed orange juice, and a new bottle of Tylenol. They sat on the couch and watched with deep sadness and pity the news coverage of the day. Two planes had flown into the World Trade Centers in New York City *on purpose.*

In the blink of an eye, the Oklahoma City bombing was no longer the worst terrorist attack on American soil.

Just like that, Carolyn thought, *comes the thief in the night. Just like that, what is destroyed will take years, if not ages, to rebuild, recover, and restore what was lost. But inherent in restoration is the way that God uses us to re-story the ending. The ending can be tragic—it can cause tears and heartbreak and blame and unspeakable sadness, until we give it a new ending, which is a beginning again.*

Carolyn was determined to get there.

"How much does Dr. Manders want before the next surgery?"

"One thousand cc's," Rosemary answered as she checked her chart. "You've done four hundred so far."

"Let's get more aggressive. Tell your new gal, I'm ready."

Rosemary observed the appointments through the month of October, guiding Dr. Walker's new physician's assistant, Robyn. Although her timid nature made Carolyn nervous, there was nothing wrong with Robyn, she was perfectly pleasant to borrow Dr. Manders' favorite phrase, but Carolyn did not have the energy to grow close to her as she had to Rosemary.

In November, Rosemary moved out of her house and took Carolyn up on her offer to stay at her home while her furniture went east. Carolyn was amused to discover that Rosemary was even more down-to-earth out of the office than in. She sat cross-legged on the floor in front of Carolyn's flickering fireplace, enjoying a Chardonnay with her favorite patient. Having unfettered access to a nurse-in-residence for a few days was a treat for Carolyn too.

"Your next surgery is in December, right?" Rosemary asked.

"December fifteenth. Twenty-two days to go. Not that I'm counting."

"I'd like to go. Do you think Dr. Manders would let me watch?"

"Are you serious?" Carolyn asked. "I bet he'd be delighted—and probably will use that exact word."

Carolyn spent much of November tending to the recurring infections on her head. By early December, Dr. Walker decided the last of the Gamma Graft needed to come off, as moisture had accumulated under it and undermined its effectiveness. Dr. Walker apologized for cutting off a cluster of Carolyn's hair to better access one infected area.

"I know how hard you work for every strand, Carolyn."

Don't worry, she prayed, *it'll grow back. Surely it will grow back a hundred-fold.*

Carolyn decided to accept it as though her head were a sick tree in need of pruning to ensure its long-term health and survival. Carolyn wished more than ever that Rosemary were still around, but knowing she would see her in Pittsburgh for the fourth surgery gave her something else to look forward to.

For now, however, her head wrapped thickly in gauze, Carolyn embraced the wound as progress. She even gave in to her Clematis Club girlfriends who convinced her to pose for a group picture with Santa, although she stopped short of agreeing to sit on his lap. The big hat with gauze peeking out from underneath it was asking for enough unwanted attention.

J.R. and Carolyn packed up his Suburban and headed out midway through December. Knowing they both wanted to save their vacation time for Christmas, this trip would require a quick turnaround. They drove straight through to Pittsburgh, arriving Sunday morning.

Seeing Rosemary in the lobby of the Hampton Inn felt natural, as if the three of them had always gone into surgery together. Rosemary's palliative care had meant much to Carolyn, and it soothed her further to know that she would be standing in the OR, observing Carolyn's fourth out-of-state surgery.

Carolyn's surgery was scheduled for Monday at four thirty in the afternoon. The hospital was packed with patients. The pre-op holding area was so crowded that the privacy curtains that hung among them were useless; Carolyn could see everyone else's IVs and bandages. She passed the time trying to figure out what kind of surgery each of them would undergo. J.R. overheard a nurse advise a patient to get on the waiting list for space in the recovery area.

Rosemary watched with great interest as Dr. Manders focused on the left side of Carolyn's head, inserting two new expanders—one in the back, and other in the right forehead. The expanders were large enough that they required three drainage tubes, which would cause Carolyn more pain than any of the previous surgeries.

Carolyn also reacted badly to the anesthesia. Crawling into a little ball and sleeping for a week sounded like the only viable solution.

J.R. slept in Carolyn's private room, which they had requested months ahead of time. Rosemary stopped by to give her version of events in the OR. Of the hundreds of surgeries she had observed or participated in, she had never seen anything like Carolyn's.

"Doctor Manders is a genius. He does beautiful work."

"Not feeling so beautiful at the moment," Carolyn said. "All I want is a shower. Maybe pizza." J.R. ordered a supreme pizza, knowing it was Carolyn's favorite, but she could not eat it.

"I'm zapped, J.R.," she said as her lids drooped and then closed for the night.

Wednesday morning, Carolyn considered opening her eyes, but only one of them cooperated. Her right eye was purple and swollen shut, a hazard of intense work around her forehead. With her black eye and three tubes protruding from her head, Carolyn took a reviving shower, and surprised even J.R. when she agreed to venture out of the hospital for lunch.

"Medusa has nothing on you, sweetheart," J.R. said unreassuringly.

"Watch it, J.R. Richards," Carolyn shot back, "I may just kill you with a look."

"Baby, you slay me once a day."

"Oh, don't act like you care that much," Carolyn said with a smile. "At least no one can ever call me vain. Maybe they'll think I won the fight."

Carolyn was not sure about whether she was in fact winning. Even after her surgeries were finished, there was no guarantee that her hair would grow back. All of the drainage tubes, miles of road, and flat out pain could be for nothing more than to make sure her skull had a proper covering. If the hair did come back, it could return spotty and patchy, like a dog with the mange.

As Carolyn expected, the removal of the tubes from her head was more painful than ever before—at least three times more. On the verge of tears, she held back, wanting to be strong in front of Rosemary and for Dr. Manders. He had done so much for Carolyn, and was giving her hope for her future; she could not ask for more from him.

"That ought to do it," Dr. Manders said, washing his hands. "How about a movie matinee?"

"Seriously?" Rosemary asked, eyebrows lifted in surprise.

"Yes, absolutely, yes," he answered. "Takes her mind off her head, so to speak. We have this wonderful IMAX theater downtown and just now they are playing this spectacular film about Sir Ernest Shackleton, his courageous crew, and their tremendous journey to claim Antarctica for England in the early nineteen hundreds. Just marvelous, I understand."

Carolyn had no idea what Dr. Manders was talking about, but she was incapable of turning him down. She feared that, as enthusiastic as his asking was, his disappointment if she declined would be more intense. J.R. answered for her.

"We'll be there. Carolyn needs an excuse to get out of the house."

"Great then! It's settled! Sandra and I will pick you up—oh, jeez—in an hour and a half? How about we just pick you up in front of the hospital? Rosemary, will you join us?"

Rosemary declined politely, as she had a flight to New York to catch. She planned to visit her daughter before returning to D.C.

"I wouldn't mind if you showed me how to find my car though. I'm afraid I'm a few miles from where I parked."

Rosemary gave Carolyn a gentle hug goodbye,

and Carolyn felt sad to watch her go. She would like nothing more than to have Rosemary help her recover from this surgery back in Oklahoma.

Carolyn could hear Dr. Manders' and Rosemary's chatter fade as they trotted down the corridor.

Carolyn looked at J.R.

"Sir Shackleton?"

J.R. answered.

"Shackle-somebody. Whatever. Come on, Manders is a hoot. He wouldn't drive us over a cliff."

J.R. was right. Carolyn had never been to an IMAX theater, but the moment the sound pulsed through her body and the sweeping images filled every space, she forgot herself. As the story moved across the ice of Antarctica, Carolyn swore the temperature in the theater dropped to freezing. Yet her hands sweated as the narrator recounted the harrowing 635-day journey, crossing the frozen continent on foot without today's modern equipment. Their mission ultimately failed, but Sir Shackleton and his crew left behind a greater legacy than success might have—the indomitable human spirit.

"By endurance, we conquer," read the narrator, citing Shackleton's family motto and the inspiration for his vessel, *The Endurance*.

By endurance, we conquer.

Over seasoned steak and cheesy scalloped potatoes at their mutually-beloved steakhouse, Carolyn could not get those words out of her head. *By endurance, we conquer.* If she counted the days of her journey since May 3, 1999, she had already surpassed 635 days.

Granted, very few of those days had been as death-defying as an early Antarctic expedition, but she saw parallels in her story and that one. She witnessed this truth: that it is man's nature during protracted and difficult missions to experience disappointment, uncertainty, and even failure as part of the greater journey.

As they left the restaurant, the cold wind whipped them, and all but Carolyn found their hair being blown straight up. On their way out of downtown, they drove by a busy ice-skating rink, and Carolyn felt grateful that Dr. Manders had encouraged her to get out of bed and keep moving.

Five days before Christmas, J.R. and Carolyn left the snow flurries of Pittsburgh behind. They bought coffee for the road, as they often did, and headed in the wrong direction (north), as they always did.

J.R. spent a lot of the holiday hunting while Carolyn played hostess at her house. Over the years, her favorite tree had been a fresh pine flecked with white paint to look like snow. But this year, she understood her limitations, and so she bought an artificial tree for the sheer convenience of it. To her delight, no one's spirit appeared diminished by the swap. While many people complain of exhaustion during the holiday run-around, Carolyn was energized by the parade of pancakes, presents, and the people she loved. It was no small joy to reclaim a role she cherished.

The next week, Dr. Walker removed stitches from Carolyn's forehead, her face still bruised and swollen. The staples would have to wait another week to come out; Carolyn's head was just too tender.

By endurance, we conquer.

If *her* goal, *her* mission to have her old head of hair back, were to fail, Carolyn could still win by simply moving forward and enduring. Although in her heart, she knew she had done much more than endure. By leaning on what she believed was God-granted—the strength to stay positive—she had inspired.

With This Ring

For this reason I kneel before the father, from whom his whole family in heaven and on earth derives its name. I pray that out of his glorious riches he may strengthen you with power through his spirit in your inner being, so that Christ may dwell in your heart through faith. And I pray that you being rooted and established in love, may have power, together with all the saints, to grasp how wide and long and high and deep is the love of Christ, and to know this love that surpasses knowledge—that you may be filled to the measure of all the fullness of God. Now to him who is able to do immeasurably more than all we ask or imagine, according to his power that is at work within us, to him be glory in the church and in Christ Jesus throughout all generations forever and ever. Amen.

Ephesians 3:14–21 (NIV)

In Oklahoma, they call it "Texas Caviar," even though to anyone else in the country it looks remarkably like a big old bowl of black-eyed peas. The name is meant to slight Oklahomans' rivals to the south, that Texans are not sophisticated enough to discern between Beluga fish eggs and fat peas. The dish sat unpretentiously among a ham, a roast, mashed potatoes and gravy, corn, green beans, rolls, and Sarah Leona's famous apple pie. The New Year's tradition of Texas Caviar on the table carried new meaning for Carolyn, and it was not a pleasant one. Every flavorless pea reminded her of her own black eye, still sunken in and swollen as the blood and vessels took their time settling back into place. J.R. got a few more laughs than normal telling everyone that Dr. Manders had been forced to punch out a sedated yet still defiant Carolyn mid-surgery. Everyone laughed harder when, with a takes-one-to-know-one tone, Carolyn reminded J.R. that the only person who knew her as a feisty little cuss was him.

Concerned about her eye, Carolyn asked Dr. Walker to email photographs to Dr. Manders.

"Please ask him," she said, "in bold letters, IS THIS NORMAL?"

Try as she might, she could not muster her energy as she usually did. Mentally, she ached to get back on her treadmill routine, but her body ached worse. Ever the conservative, Dr. Walker wrote Carolyn a prescription for antibiotics to fight back infection.

On Saturday, Carolyn, Christi, and Bo watched Nathan coach a team of young wrestlers at Del City High School, in the same small gym where Nathan competed a few years before. As Carolyn watched the boys twist each others' heads and unnaturally bend their limbs, she was reminded why she used to pace the hallways and rub her sweaty palms on her jeans during Nathan's own matches. While other mothers worried about broken bones, Carolyn worried about suffocation. Because of Nathan's asthma, she found herself praying, "Please, God, let him breathe long enough to get through this whole match." Much to Carolyn's dismay, Christi informed her that Bo would likely be a wrestler too. Thinking about some muscle-bound bully contorting Bo's little body into a pretzel made Carolyn feel sick to her stomach.

By Monday, a ringing nagged at Carolyn's plugged-up right ear which was now too tender and sore to sleep on. Dr. Walker referred her to an ear, nose, and throat specialist, whose appointment book was too crowded to work her in until Thursday. Carolyn went to work anyway, gritting her teeth and hiding her discomfort, as she could not imagine missing the start of the 2002 legislative session.

Privately, Carolyn worried about feeling so unwell. She did not like to worry, because to her it indicated a misplaced focus of centeredness—trusting in herself rather than in God. In her mind though, she could not fight back thoughts that she might have to return to Pittsburgh because something just was not right. Lethargy weighed down her days, and pain plagued her nights.

The specialist found no signs of infection. He guessed that the expander near that eye and ear was pushing on a muscle, creating the resulting tenderness. The good report had a psychosomatic effect. Carolyn laughed at herself and began to feel better at once, well enough to go to Roman's birthday party at Chelino's, his pick for dinner. Roman was his usual boisterous self; and Christi seemed cheerful enough, though her mood changed after a spurt of goofiness that reminded Carolyn of the old Christi, to which Roman responded, "Don't act so stupid." Carolyn noted the insult, tucked her anger away, and focused her attention on the ever-energetic Bo, who had recently learned to barrel into everything.

In late January, Carolyn returned to Dr. Walker for his first injection in the back balloon. He pushed hard, so different from Rosemary's slow, smooth, and gentle touch. The balloon felt tight right away, forcing Dr. Walker to withdraw a few cc's. Before the expander grew too large, Carolyn pulled out her old blonde bobbed wig again; she knew she would have a few weeks until her head would outgrow it.

The next week's session with Dr. Walker went more comfortably. Apparently Rosemary had called him, making sure he was going easy on Carolyn after such an involved surgery. He did, and his new assistant watched wide-eyed as Carolyn thought, *I'm sure he'll get better. He has to because I'm not letting her near my head.*

Carolyn missed treatments for the next two weeks because of a wicked winter storm. Temperatures dropped below freezing, and then came the rain. It rained for two straight days, coating everything in ice. A pine tree in Carolyn's front yard bent all the way over so that its tip touched the ground. The capitol building lost electricity and the rest of the city shut down.

Carolyn told herself that the forced delay would

give her more time to heal. She had begun her fourth round of antibiotics for the infection still aggravating her ear and for the one that had taken over her sinuses. It was clear to Carolyn that her immune system was shot, and the best medicine—rest—was the hardest to come by. She gave a prayer of thanks that God cared about the little colds as much as the big infections.

Progress would move as it wished at a snail's pace. By mid-February, Dr. Walker was still not able to tap into the front expander.

"I think you're going to need to put the wigs back in the closet, Carolyn. Looks like this area around the port has been rubbed quite a bit. It's seriously irritated."

"So am I. I guess it's not true that blondes always have more fun," Carolyn said. "The hair was nice while it lasted. Back to hats, I promise."

At the end of the month, Dr. Walker managed to get a little bit of liquid into the front expander. Carolyn was not sure why she had not thought of it before, but having a lump in the back of her head and in the front was going to look very bizarre.

Within two treatments, the front of Carolyn's head was stretching with lightning speed. Or perhaps she noticed it more because she could see it clearly when she looked in the mirror. Headwear was getting challenging, but also more necessary than ever. When another infection broke out near the back expander, Dr. Walker ordered more Gamma Graft.

The remainder of the spring was like that—up one minute, down the next—for not just Carolyn, but her whole family. Sarah Leona was hospitalized with a blood clot. The doctors said it was a matter of adjusting her blood pressure and heart medications, but it scared Carolyn to see her mother attached to so many tubes and monitors. Carolyn and Patty took turns relieving Pappy, who seemed not just lonely but lost without Leona on his arm.

Then Nate came bursting through the door with two wonderful pieces of news. He had landed an interview with the Moore fire department, with the very same firefighters who had helped rescue tornado victims in Carolyn's old neighborhood, and he had asked Marci, the pretty long-haired blonde with doe-like eyes, to marry him. She had said yes.

Carolyn relied on pain pills more heavily this time, careful to use them as an aide and not an addiction. She alternated between hurting from an infection or from the expanders themselves, so tight and uncomfortable. Nothing had felt right since the surgery, and she wondered whether the skins of her head were in rebellion.

Suddenly, just as Carolyn wished time to slow itself so that she would be physically ready, the next surgery approached rapidly. One month from that day, on May 30, she would be on Dr. Manders' operating table once more. Three weeks after that, possibly bandaged and likely bruised, she would be holding flowers at her son's wedding.

Two weeks before the surgery, Carolyn's dear friend Becky Woodie gave her another prayer cloth, her third but most powerful yet. She wrote a few lines of scripture that Carolyn had always loved on an accompanying card about God's power to do immeasurably more than any human mind can fathom. Carolyn had lost both of the cloths given to her, the first in a hotel room and the second to an ever-stealthy dryer, a small symbolic reminder that while God is powerful, man is not. Becky reassured Carolyn, explaining how she knew that the tiny patches of material were easy to lose.

"Each cloth serves a purpose for a time and a prayer," Becky said, and this one was, in her words, "fierce." Becky said the cloth was hot when she and her pastor prayed over it, and as Carolyn tucked it into her bra, she felt an electrifying jolt against her breast.

Becky laid her hands on Carolyn and said, "There is a victorious surgery to come, we know this, Lord; your handiwork will baffle even the doctors." How Becky divined such knowledge, Carolyn was not certain, but she knew Becky was right.

The weekend before the surgery happened to be Memorial Day. The holiday traffic would be horrendous, so J.R. wanted to wait until the first wave of travelers was off and the last minute had arrived to make the drive to Pittsburgh. They stopped in Joplin, Missouri, for a coffee break, where J.R. announced he wanted to detour over to the store Sutherlands, purportedly to look for a leather sofa. J.R.'s friend Neal worked there, a dealer of fine furniture and diamonds.

While in the store, J.R. motioned for Carolyn

to join him and Neal, who was holding a tray of big, bright, and shiny diamonds.

"Which one do you like?" J.R. asked with a grin.

"They're all pretty," Carolyn said.

"Well, you don't seem too excited."

No bended knee, no words of undying love, not an ounce of romance in the whole deal. *We're standing in a furniture store in Joplin, for goodness sake.* It was just about the most anticlimactic moment of Carolyn's life. She thought back to her all-caps question to Dr. Manders earlier in the year: IS THIS NORMAL? She knew the answer. Carolyn had dated J.R. longer than he had been married to number two, but for whatever reason, J.R. had held out asking for her hand. Perhaps he harbored some misgivings of his own.

There was no doubt that J.R. was loyal, kind when he wanted to be, and mostly unselfish. The trips to and from Pittsburgh were evidence enough of that. It was just that, as strange or wonderful as this may sound, Carolyn wanted a boyfriend or husband just like her son—a man as kind, loving, and spiritual as he was handsome.

Carolyn assumed that J.R. dropped the whole notion of a ring, and neither of them talked about it as they drove into Pittsburgh.

"I'm a little rusty. Been on vacation. Sorry if this stings," the anesthesiologist at Montefiore told Carolyn as she prepped her for surgery. "You're not a tough stick, are you?"

Carolyn thought she was teasing her, and hoped she was, because with each needle stick and each surgery it did seem tougher and tougher to get IVs started. Something about the body learning what is coming, and nerves causing veins to shrink and disappear from view.

Carolyn's chest felt warm and she thought she was flush from anxiety, until she realized it was the prayer cloth she had pinned to her hospital gown. She looked back at her hand and saw that the IV had gone in without the slightest twinge. She smiled, knowing she and J.R. and the anesthesiologist and a whole slew of people she loved all had doubts about each other, but there was no doubt in her mind that God guided everyone and everything, even that sharp little needle.

Dr. Manders reported that the giant frontal expansion that had caused Carolyn so much anguish had paid off. The two most troublesome expanders were taken out, a small one went in, and the next surgery could happen in just three months. Nearly every part of Carolyn's scalp was newly covered, save for two small strips in the back of Carolyn's head on the right and left.

The good news was tempered by the fact that the hospital recovery area was full, meaning Carolyn would spend the night in a semi-private room next to a stranger instead of J.R. But late in the evening, a patient unexpectedly checked out, freeing up a private room for Carolyn and J.R.; an unexpected blessing, another reminder of that untold power.

The next morning, Carolyn felt well enough to be discharged. The contrast from the last surgery was striking. She looked forward to a refreshing shower, insisted on skipping the wheelchair, and had enough energy to stop by the pharmacy on her way out. Seeing her wrist tag, the pharmacist asked if she were just now leaving, and if so, did she know that she missed all the action.

"What action?" Carolyn asked.

"A brutal wind, a shower of hail, and then a tornado," the pharmacist said.

"Are you sh—kidding me?" J.R. caught himself. "I thought everybody around here said you never get tornadoes."

The pharmacist shook his head.

"Caught everybody off-guard. Blew through the Kennywood amusement park and actually killed a lady."

"I guess no place is safe," Carolyn said.

The unusual and deadly tornado dominated the news coverage that night, and the only upside might have been that Carolyn and J.R. felt like they were actually home.

On Sunday, Dr. Manders dropped by the hotel to remove Carolyn's single drainage tube. It was nine in the morning, and he had just finished up a grueling surgery with a patient who had been injured in an early morning car accident.

"Carolyn, there's something unbelievable going on here. I'm simply stunned."

That sounded like a good thing to Carolyn,

although she could not find a word to respond as she focused on the tube exiting her head.

"Somehow, it appears to me, you are growing *more* hair in the newly expanded scalp. I know I've told you about children before—their follicles most always come back, but not adults. Not adults. I had thought our modest hope here was to have your old hair cover up the bare spots. But feel this. It's positively lush!"

Carolyn ran her hand through her hair. Dr. Manders was right. So was Becky.

There is a victorious surgery to come, we know this, Lord; your handiwork will baffle even the doctors.

From that point forward, Carolyn could not pass a mirror without taking a second look. Oh how she wished she could count the follicles on her head—count them just to make sure! But there was only one who could, and she credited him with each miracle, both small and quantifiable, and vast and immeasurable.

J.R. teased Carolyn with all her talk of miracles.

"The anesthesiologist was just that good—what else do you expect? You're still not as bald as I am. The real miracle is that we got to get out of Pittsburgh without getting lost!" On that last point, Carolyn had to laugh in agreement.

Most of June seemed a month-long celebration. If Carolyn was not shopping for her mother-of-the-groom dress, she was buying a nightgown for the bride. She dropped in on Christi and Bo, who welcomed Carolyn with a rousing, "*It's my Mo-mo!*" and Carolyn felt sure her heart would burst.

Although the legislature had gone home for the

summer, Carolyn needed to end the week there for a grand ceremony to top the new dome on the capitol building. Senator Kelly Haney, a Seminole Indian and a great artistic talent, had sculpted a twenty-two-foot bronze of an Indian to stand guard atop the statehouse. Kelly described "The Guardian" this way: "The image is of standing one's ground. I feel it embodies values shared by all Oklahomans. It represents the deep love of family and home we all share, and the desire to protect them." Carolyn could not help but feel it was yet another strong symbol of the value of endurance.

The Guardian stood in great contrast to another famous statue of an American Indian, created eighty-seven years earlier, now housed at the old Cowboy Hall of Fame. That Indian had no name, only a title: "The End of the Trail." Seventeen feet high, formed out of white plaster, he sat slumped on his horse, exhausted and defeated, evoking the artist's sympathy for the suffering of native people. Carolyn never passed him by without stopping. She would have walked away with a profound sadness with each visit if the statue were not so exquisitely beautiful.

On the ground, "The Guardian" was arresting, majestic, and powerful. His ears were as large as her two hands. His long hair flowed gracefully down his muscular neck.

His chin tilted up, his eyes focused on the distance, and his demeanor evoked strength, pride, and expectation. As Carolyn walked around him, she hoped his power would not be diminished so high in the air. Only those gathered this day, the birds, and God would see the finely-sculpted details up close. She made a mental note to remember his features well enough to tell Bo what he would never see at this close range.

The capitol building had come so far from the days when a former President Pro Tem of the Senate let workmen paint the brass knobs black, believing they would be easier to maintain. Today, the structure shined from the inside out, from every foot of marble down to every inch of brass. With each passing year, Carolyn watched out her office window as the capitol grew more beautiful. When Christi asked her why she wanted to spend such a beautiful day stuck inside dealing with politicians, Carolyn told her, "It's an awe-inspiring place. I'm there every day of half of the year, and have been since you were about Bo's age. Everything that affects us happens there. You can't imagine how many issues live or die by just one vote—just one vote! Ideas matter in that glorious building."

The rest of the month was a blur. The air conditioner at home died and cost nearly a thousand dollars. Workers dumped a load of dirt for landscaping, and Marci brought her bridesmaids over to spread it around before they flew out to Las Vegas. Dr. Walker removed all the remaining stitches and staples and gave pointers on scrubbing off scabs. Then Carolyn locked her keys in her car, making her late for an eyelash dyeing appointment, forcing her to bobble a friend's birthday package, breaking the contents. And finally, at eighty miles per hour in the left lane of the Kilpatrick Turnpike to Tulsa, on the cell phone gabbing, while driving nearly as fast as she had been running—*POP!*—her tire blew out.

Steady. Steady now.

She dropped her phone and held the shuddering wheel; forced her foot far from the brake, and slowly weaved through rushing traffic to the only shoulder off the far lane, where she continued to tremble and hyperventilate for a few minutes. Two good Samaritans saw it happen and pulled over to help. There was nothing left of the tire. When they affixed the spare and subsequently refused cash, she made sure to get their addresses for gifts to be sent by mail.

Before starting up again, Carolyn sat idling in her car a little longer. She closed her eyes, prayed thanks to God for keeping her safe, and apologized for going full throttle ahead with reckless disregard for the fragility of life, as if she expected she would be handed a third victory over death.

The speedometer's needle remained at fifty-five the rest of the way.

"I'm so sorry I'm late," Carolyn announced, sweaty and shaken. As she walked in the door of J.R.'s house, she managed to hand him a box without dropping it. "Happy birthday," she said, hoping he could not see the stress of the journey in her sweaty brow or trembling hands.

Dinner was long over, but J.R.'s mom—sweet little Mammie—had set aside a plate for Carolyn. She heated it up while J.R. poured her a glass of Chardonnay.

After supper, Carolyn apologized for needing to run one more errand. J.R. offered to drive her so that she could drop off materials at a local hotel for an upcoming conference. Carolyn felt a wave of relief that she did not have to get behind the wheel once more tonight.

On the drive over, J.R. handed Carolyn a small black box.

"I thought it was *your* birthday," she said.

"I got you a new nose-picker," he said.

Inside the box, a perfectly round two-karat solitaire diamond on a platinum band sparkled back at Carolyn. But it did not shine.

It did not shine in the way that love should. With young love, it should be a fountain of euphoria, rushing upward and outward from every crevice. With mature love, it should be a river of peace, filling the soul that you did not know existed until this person showed it to you. In either case, the size of the diamond or the quality of the ring makes no difference whatsoever. When it reflects love that is true, it shines.

Calling it a nose-picker did not help.

"Why did you wait so long to do this?" Carolyn asked.

"What do you mean, 'wait so long'?" J.R. asked. "What's the problem, not big enough?"

I love you. I want to do your perfect will. I want to serve you, honor you, and be better because of you.

Carolyn said those words with ease to God. But she could not utter them to J.R.

"J.R., you could buy a ten-carat ring, and I'm not

sure it would mean anything. The ring without the relationship just feels empty."

"Without the relationship? *Without the relationship?* What have I been doing driving your butt cross-country and back every six months, picking up scabby pieces of your head?" Carolyn started to protest, but J.R. sighed dramatically. "Just, just keep it. See if you change your mind in the morning." Under his breath, J.R. muttered, "If you aren't the most ornery woman on earth. If only I'd known how much trouble that little parking lot chick was going to cost me—"

The diamond ring sparkled in the sunlight on Friday, June 21, 2003. Carolyn wore a long black skirt with high slits up the front and back, a metallic silver top and a black jacket piped in white. It was not your average gown. Carolyn would feel snazzy wearing this outfit to Carnegie Hall. Snapping her out of feeling too glamorous was the wig on her head. At least it was new, short, blonde, and did not—her best friend Cheryl assured her—look too "wiggy."

A range of emotions, all within the realm of thrilled, enveloped Carolyn as she watched her only son make his way toward his bride. Their grins set the chapel on fire. Carolyn could not help herself as she thanked God for their union and prayed for grandbabies, lots of healthy grandbabies. (Prayer answered: a spunky, strawberry-blonde baby girl named Manning, or Mimi for short, would arrive nine months later) Carolyn wept as she watched Marci dance with her daddy; then she cried a little harder when the little hunk she had raised to be a loving and faithful husband asked his mama for a turn.

The Last Cut

But if a woman has long hair, it is a glory to her, for her hair is given to her for a covering.
                    1 Corinthians 11:15 (WEB)

"What would you say if I got a divorce?" The question came about halfway through the trip, somewhere outside of Shreveport. Their summer Southern swing ran from Oklahoma City to Dallas, Montgomery, Shreveport, Birmingham, and Memphis. Carolyn planned the trip around her favorite conference in Montgomery, thinking that she and Christi could use the mother-daughter time away from home. And no one alive enjoyed riding in a car more than Bo Duren. His presence did create some interesting juggling acts for Christi and Carolyn; at the Isle of Capri, a Louisiana hotel, the women alternated popping in and out of the casino as they took turns entertaining Bo. Another challenge was Christi's eating regime. She was trying, once again, to lose weight, a constant struggle considering her bad leg never properly healed, forced a limp, and prevented her from a convenient form of exercise. Already she had lost six pounds on Weight Watchers, and Carolyn admired her daughter for dutifully counting points as she considered the myriad of the southern-fried and sugared options.

"Are you and Roman talking about it?"

Bo was sleeping soundly in his car seat in the back, but Christi whispered just in case.

"Looking at Nathan and Marci at their wedding, it just showed me what we don't have. We're so unhappy, Mom. We're miserable. It's not good. It's like he hates me, and Bo sees it. And the thoughts I have about him. None of it is healthy."

Carolyn wanted to tread very carefully through these grounds. She knew the chances of Christi ever leaving Roman were slim. Their relationship could improve in a week depending upon their moods, and Carolyn did not want to say anything she would regret. She also wanted to consider her own part in her daughter's failing marriage, in her child's unwillingness to insist on her own happiness. As she fiddled with the ring on her finger, Carolyn felt sure that her semi-engagement to J.R. did little to clarify Christi's confusion about the enduring qualities of any relationship.

"You know Dad and I just want you to be happy. I'm sure Mydonna and Steve want the same for Roman. You two need to come to terms with whether life would be better together or apart."

"I worry about Bo."

"You're going to worry about him whether you're together or not," Carolyn said. "What kind of example is he getting from the man of the house? Do you want him to grow up to be like either of you? What do you show him by staying?"

"Loyalty. Endurance."

"Are they worth it?"

Christi's mind drifted back to a terrible fight they had the week of the anniversary of Abby's death. She considered it the moment of truth.

It started with Roman, who whispered, "If you'd listened to me, we wouldn't be here." He looked down, feigning to pick dirt from under his fingernails.

"What? What did you say?" She heard him, and felt a fire ignite inside her.

His eyes narrowed.

"If you'd done what I told you, she'd be alive."

She met him.

"How dare you—"

"Am I wrong? *Tell me I'm wrong!*" As he screamed, spit streamed from his mouth.

"God doesn't work that way. I know it..." Now she was crying.

"God can't help a dummy!" he smacked one of his hands against the other, as if he wished it were her face. "And blubbering isn't going to save you!"

She turned her head and wiped her nose with a tissue. Her bloodshot eyes stared blankly out the window. The fire was smoldering, doused with numbness. She let nothingness wash over her.

"What are you looking at?" he asked, wanting a fight more than an answer.

"Nothing," she answered without blinking, barely moving her lips. "Absolutely nothing."

She wanted to throw up, then curl up and go to sleep forever. She wanted to tell him how much she hated the way he treated her, but she did not dare utter the words. She did not have to. Roman already knew.

What he did not know, was that he despised himself even more.

Neither of them could understand where this venom was coming from. They barely recognized themselves and did not understand what was overtaking their words, emotions, and actions. All she felt was guilt; all he felt was anger. Both emotions poisoned their marriage and their lives. Every word toward each other dripped of it, and yet they never discussed it in a civil manner. They could not see through the dark veil of hate smothering their hearts—a veil laid there by a force outside of them.

He believed he had been brave. He had not left the family, thrown his cell phone out the window, and disappeared out west. He had chosen the hard path, to move his two legs forward and face his worst fear—to find his wife and child buried alive. And he had never been rewarded for his courage. His wife had never held him and thanked him for not walking away.

And because of it, he was consumed with anger. He was so consumed with anger that he could not comfort his wife. He could not hold her or tell her how grateful he was that she was spared—how sorry he was that they lost a child. He could barely stand to look at her.

And yet, they would not leave each other. They

stayed together, miserable and poisoned, out of guilt and fear.

Christi did not answer her mother's question: "Are they worth it?"

She knew the truth. She looked out the passenger side window and wiped a tear. Carolyn patted her daughter's knee, knowing nothing had changed.

"That homemade peach ice cream stand looks good about now," Christi said, smiling through her tears. "We deserve it."

The expander treatments in July brought on all kinds of complications, but Carolyn refused to let any of them darken her mood. In two months, all of it—the odd shapes bulging from her head, the painful needles and sore ports poking into it, the sticky, bloody stuff oozing out of it—would be over.

In August, Dr. Walker introduced Carolyn to another new assistant, the third since Rosemary. But Janelle, competent and confident, looked like she might stay for a while, and Carolyn hoped she could see her through to the last injection. She injected five times the normal amount: 100 cc's of saline, the largest expansion to date. Carolyn's scalp had never accepted so much liquid, but Dr. Manders said the balloon could take it. But something was not right. It seemed too strange that such an enormous, practically unheard-of amount of stuff went in and did not ache the way just 20 cc's normally did. And then two days later it would be gone. On top of it all, the skin was not expanding. Was it absorbed? Leaked out? But her pillows remained dry. Where did it all go? Why was it going wrong now?

Carolyn decided that she needed to call on Becky for an immediate intervention, perhaps that evening. But Becky had a knack for divining emergencies, and called Carolyn first.

"Put one hand on the wheel, honey, the other one on your prayer cloth," Becky said with conviction.

"While I'm driving? Should I pull over?"

"You'll be late for Dr. Walker. We're doing a drive-by prayer, and I can promise you God doesn't mind."

Something happened that turned everything around. Dr. Walker acted as though a light bulb had just clicked on, moments before Carolyn walked in, perhaps during the "drive-by." Her case had been on his mind, he said, but he could not figure out how to solve it. He suddenly decided to make several adjustments—switching to a smaller gauge needle, taking his time injecting the saline, and leaving the needle in the port in Carolyn's head for twenty minutes before removing it. Carolyn felt her head swell. *Big head at last,* and Carolyn welcomed the pain. The next morning, the pillowcase was wet with saline, but the expander stayed taught.

Still in her nightgown, Carolyn dashed off an e-mail to Dr. Manders. She recapped the leakage issue and the results today as irrefutable proof that prayers make miracles happen.

He wrote back instantaneously, "If prayer works

like that, we need to get a patent, because I had no idea how to plug a leak that big without another surgery."

The measurements in August continued to astonish them. Halfway through the month, Dr. Walker pushed 180 cc's into her head, and they held, except for one drop.

"Carolyn, I saw that with my own eyes," Dr. Walker said. "That drop didn't come from a bag; it came from your head."

Instead of fearing the path of the saline, and trying to sort it out scientifically, she accepted it as part of the order of the universe. If she tried to rationalize what happened, nothing made sense. When the balloon went flat, there was no liquid visible. But when the balloon began to work, the liquid wet her pillows. Why the balloon began to function was a mystery that Carolyn received as a sign of grace. With every shot, Carolyn imagined the breath of God blowing into her body. Just as life springs from moist and fertile ground, so would growth come from her well-watered head and well-nourished soul.

But none of it was nearly that pretty.

At the end of August, Dr. Walker discovered that an expander was exposed.

"It's only the size of a dime, but your scalp is not covering it. I can poke it if I want to."

"Please don't," Carolyn said, crumpling up her face. "That is so gross. It creeps me out."

It worried Dr. Walker, who called Dr. Manders right away.

Dr. Walker did not want to risk more saline or the

expander would further open up Carolyn's head. Dr. Manders wanted to know the measurements because, he explained, some expanders can work under those conditions. He encouraged Dr. Walker to proceed.

Dr. Manders' judgment paid off. A hairy scab, the size of a dime, covered the exposed area. Only a sliver of balloon poked through.

"At least it has hair on it!" Carolyn exclaimed.

They scheduled the surgery for early September, the fastest turnaround yet, the last surgery of all.

Carolyn and J.R. drove overnight to Richmond, Indiana, the most direct route they could surmise. There would be no touring on this final operation, no closing act. Carolyn went through the motions, and before she knew it, she was lying in a bed in the crowded recovery area.

"*We hit a home run!*"

Dr. Manders had said it before, but never quite like this. The first time it was opening season. Today it was the World Series.

Three medical students trailed Dr. Manders as he moved closer to Carolyn's bed. Her euphoria—and possibly the high level of painkillers—kept her from hearing much more than long-awaited key phrases like: everything is covered, expanders are out, head is full of hair, you're port-free.

It was over.

Although not untrue, "full of hair" was an exaggeration. Among the old hair, new growth, and fresh stitches and staples, it was thin and patchy, coming in blond like a child rather than silver like the middle-aged woman she was. But all of it belonged to Carolyn.

Carolyn spent no fewer than ten hours in recovery, listening to all the moans and groans of patients in pain. For the first time in this hospital, she could concentrate on praying for other peoples' problems; her ordeal was over. They were suffering, but she was not. She wanted to tell each of them to hang on, that healing happens sooner than they can imagine. She wanted to run down the hallway and ride back to Oklahoma City that night, but first she needed to sleep.

After the morning shower and checkout, J.R. took Carolyn back to the hotel. She was refreshed but exhausted; the three-year emotional ride was pulling into the station. J.R. picked up her antibiotic, a painkiller, and a sandwich from Arby's. Carolyn prayed over it for a long time.

"Go on, girl, it's just roast beef," J.R. prodded.

"It's like the feeding of the five thousand," Carolyn said.

"Naw, that's barely enough for you at a buck twenty."

"Only when God is in control of the equation does a little become more by separating it, dividing it, and multiplying it. I'm living proof—a walking witness of a miracle."

"Are you still talking about one stinking sandwich?"

"I'm talking about my hair, J.R."

"Of course you are. Why don't we lay off the pain pills for the rest of the morning?" In truth, J.R. fully understood where Carolyn was going with this, and he did not disagree with her. At times, he was just as awed by her progress as she was. He was simply having fun reeling her in and seeing how far he could take her.

"Who would think that you could take a patch of hair, one little patch, and stretch it again and again until it's so thin you can see through it, then sew it together, and then it multiplies? It's miraculous."

On Wednesday night, the first anniversary of September 11 attacks; Carolyn and J.R. shared their last Ruth's Chris steak with Ernie and Sandra. The Manders offered an open invitation to use their condominium in Oregon. Carolyn gave them a thank you basket full of Oklahoma-made products—barbeque sauce, chocolate-covered potato chips, cow patties, and a sweet and edible version of cow pies.

"I wanted to stick some lamb fries in there, but they're nasty cold," J.R. teased.

"They're nasty warm, too," Carolyn said.

"Oh, my," Sandra smiled, as if she understood. And then asked innocently, "What are lamb fries?"

Ernie roared with laughter, and Carolyn soaked in his chuckles. *What a glorious instrument of God you are,* she thought. She was going to miss these steak dinners.

Carolyn was starving the next morning, a sign that she felt really good. She craved a double burger with cheese, a bag of "skinny" fries, and a Coke at Steak 'N Shake. It was just a plain fast-food joint, but she did not have one in Oklahoma City, and she felt nostalgic about it already. From there, they were home free.

The staples came out a week later, and even though her scalp was red and tender, Carolyn thought it was time to make an appointment to have her hair styled for the first time in three years. Her scarred, half-bald, and patchy head was gone. Carolyn's hair was not thick by any means, but there was just enough hair—enough dishwater blonde, baby fine, shaggy hair—to give it some shape. Only Carolyn knew the remaining imperfections—places where hair might never fill in—but she intended to hide them with a fabulous hairstyle.

Her hopes were very high. For a woman who used to have a trim and style every five weeks, she enjoyed the fresh feeling after a good cut and color. She planned to have her picture taken afterward, and email them right away to Dr. Manders, just to remind him of his handiwork. She walked into the salon giddily, her eyes sparkling under a ball-cap which she planned to throw away in celebration. No more hats, scarves, or wigs. Tia, Christi's stylist and Roman's cousin, told her to put her purse away, because Christi had already paid for the special cut. They spent time talking about what style would work best and settled on bangs with a few layers. Carolyn wiggled in the chair like a bride about to get a fancy updo.

The cut was a disaster. Carolyn could see in Tia's face that she felt responsible, but they both knew the fault lay with time. There had not been enough of it for the hair to grow in, and the cut actually brought more attention to the imperfections on Carolyn's head. Dejected, Carolyn put the ball-cap back on her head, and did not let Tia see the tears that came in the car. She told herself that pouting for the next few days was perfectly reasonable.

Later, Carolyn tried again, with her usual stylist, Terry Frazier, whom she had not seen since before the tornado. She worried that if she had gone back to Tia, the pressure for perfection would have been unfair. Truthfully, if Tia failed to coax Carolyn's hair into a cute style a second time, Carolyn would have blamed herself for putting both of them through it.

This time, her locks were ready. Terry hugged Carolyn in celebration and refused to let her pay. As Carolyn stepped out of the salon, she caught her reflection in everything—the shop window, the bumper of a car, her windshield. The Oklahoma wind gave her a shove, and she instinctively put her hand to her head to keep her head-covering of the day from flying off. Instead she touched her own hair, soft and silky as a newborn's or an angel's—almost like Abby's. Carolyn walked out into the world looking and feeling not like a tornado victim or a storm survivor but more like a woman who was sure of her core.

Revelations

"O Death, Where Is Your Victory? O Death, Where Is Your Sting?" The sting of death is sin, and the power of sin is the law; but thanks be to God, who gives us the victory through our Lord Jesus Christ.
1 Corinthians 15:55–57 (NAS)

C hristi walked up to the counter.
"Hey, Christi. Need something?"
Christi swallowed hard and averted her eyes.
"Abby's death certificate."
"Of course, of course. Eight years ago, right? Nineteen ninety nine? Hang on. I'll get it for you."
Without looking at it, Christi took the copy of the small white card back to her desk. She sat down, took a few deep breaths, and laid it out in front of her. She stared at the bold black print.

CERTIFICATE OF FETAL DEATH (STILLBIRTH)

STATE OF OKLAHOMA— DEPARTMENT OF HEALTH

NAME: ABBY DAWN DUREN

DATE OF DELIVERY: JUNE 13 1999

HOUR: 11:10 AM
SEX: FEMALE
WEIGHT OF FETUS: 3 LBS. 7 OZS.

Christi read the information over and over again, letting it sink in. The details were as uncomplicated as the emotions had been complex.

IMMEDIATE CAUSE (a): Intra Utero Fetal Death
DUE TO (b): Suspect Umbilical Cord Accident

But to question number nineteen: *"When Did Fetus Die?"* There were *two* boxes marked:

BEFORE LABOR and UNKNOWN

Dr. Perry had never said he did not know when Abby died, not that she remembered, at least. He had said her umbilical cord was wrapped around her neck. For eight years, Christi assumed her baby had been thrown around so violently during the tornado that the cord twisted in a way that suffocated her to death.

Christi did not say anything to Roman that night. She lay in bed, staring at the ceiling fan turn in the dark. She awoke earlier than usual, before the alarm, and left Roman a note asking him to take Bo to school.

She turned on the lights in the office. She pulled the death certificate out of her purse, and placed it on her desk again.

UNKNOWN.

She picked up the phone and dialed.

"Dr. Perry? It's Christi Duren. I wasn't sure you'd be at the clinic this early."

"Oh sure. Had an emergency c-section two hours ago."

"I need to ask you something about Abby, my baby who died after May 3."

"Sure, sure. I remember. Cried that night. This ole Catholic boy had some serious anger at our Creator."

"I thought I remember you saying her umbilical cord was wrapped around her neck. But the death certificate says the death of the fetus is unknown. Didn't you believe she died after the tornado?"

"As I recall, that cord was wrapped around her neck, her body, a few times. She was wrapped tight."

"So tight she couldn't breathe? She couldn't thrive?"

"If you're asking, is that what killed her... you know what? Let me pull your records. Can you hold on just a minute?"

Dr. Perry put the phone down, rather than on hold. He had been birthing babies for a long time, including both of Carolyn's babies, and his practice seemed old-fashioned to Christi. As Christi heard Dr. Perry's footsteps grow louder, her heartbeat thumped her chest harder.

"Okay, says here you had three general anesthetic surgeries for a right calf debridement and plastic repairs... that on June 11th you reported no fetal movement... the nurses found no fetal heartbeat... are you sure you want me to read all this information? I could mail it to you."

"No, no. If you have time. I need—I'd like to hear it now."

"We induced labor at three a.m. on June 13 ... you'd been given a med that was essentially the French abortion pill, which can take a day and a half to work. So at 11:10 a.m. you delivered the baby. She was moderately macerated—"

"Macerated?"

"Means the skin would wipe right off. She'd been dead for a while. And, yes, this was amazing. There was no evidence of a blood clot or placental separation. Christi, I don't understand why that didn't happen in the tornado. That would've taken her in minutes, and you in a few hours. Looks like I took a culture. There was no sign of infection either. Want me to keep going?"

"Please."

"Okay, here we go, she had the classic cord around her neck, wound tightly. That happens all the time, mind you. It was under her armpit and around her trunk too. And there was a knot in the cord. The problem was, that made the cord too short from the placenta, so she couldn't get her nourishment. That's where the failure to thrive comes in."

"So, all that happened because of the tornado? I mean, would she have been fine if I had been somewhere else?"

"Regardless of the tornado, Christi, it would've happened. Very likely, she was just about gone by then. It didn't have anything to do with the tornado. You know, I've been doing this a long time. There are things we just can't do anything about. It's got to be divine design, although, like I said, the trauma on mama made me so mad..."

Regardless of the tornado, it would've happened.

Christi did not hear anything Dr. Perry said after that.

"Christi? Honey, you there?"

After another long pause, Christi asked, "Dr. Perry, you're saying I didn't cause Abby's death?"

"Good God, child. Of course you didn't."

"Thank you. Thank you, Dr. Perry. Thank you so much."

Christi told the secretary that she was going home sick. In a daze, she walked out of her office, took the elevator down to the garage, sat in her car, and cried for an hour.

She decided to get a copy of her records from Dr. Perry. She drove by the clinic before heading home.

Roman walked through the door around three o'clock, having finished up his yard service work for the day. For the last few years, Nathan had been running the business to supplement his firefighter's income, but ever since his daughter had started to walk, he felt uneasy about keeping the chemicals in the garage. Nathan sold all of it to Roman at the beginning of the summer.

"What are you doing home early, Sis?" Roman asked. Christi was sitting at their dining room table with several papers spread out in front of her. The skin around her bloodshot eyes was blotchy. She looked up at him, her cheeks wet with tears.

"What's going on? Where's Bo? Is he okay?" Roman asked urgently.

"Bo's fine. I asked Mom to take him for the rest of the day. I need to tell you something."

"Okay, then, blurt it out."

"Read this."

Still standing, Roman scanned the death certificate, but took his time looking over Dr. Perry's notes. He read them twice. When he was finished, he looked up at Christi.

Roman shook his head.

"Unbelievable. This is unbelievable."

"He says it wasn't my fault."

"No, it doesn't look like it was."

Roman took a seat at the table. He turned to his wife and said, "I've been so damn mad at you for so long. I blamed you. I blamed you for choosing to go to your mom's house instead of my uncle's where it was safe. I blamed you for nearly dying. I blamed you for Abby. I blamed you for putting me through it."

Christi looked indignant.

"You through it? You?? How could you—"

"Just hear me out," Roman interrupted. "I've got a lot I want to say."

Christi folded her arms and sat down on the living room couch.

"Somebody calls into the Dayton locker room that night, talking about a killer tornado. I crack a joke about it, and then they're like, 'No, seriously, people are dying.'"

"I know all of this, Roman," Christi said.

"So I stand up and say, 'I'm going home. My wife's pregnant.' And my boss says, 'You walk out that door and you're fired.' Then they lock down the whole plant and keep us hostage 'til after seven.

"When I finally get out, I turn on the radio in the truck. The weather guy says, 'If you're not in a shelter, you're dead.' Just like that.

"But I think, well, everybody's safe because they're in a shelter. Everybody but Nana and Papa. So I worry about them. I drive there first.

"Half a mile from the neighborhood, everything is fine. I cross 29th street, and there's a cop standing there, blocking the road. Everything looks fine. I ask him what's going on and he says no one's getting through. That's not stopping me. I'm getting to my grandparents, not even thinking about you, because I know you're safe. So here comes the part you don't know."

Roman took a breath, and to Christi's surprise, he was tearing up.

"I drive around the corner, and I'll never forget. I see this friend of mine from high school and he's shivering. 'Roman,' he says, 'there's nothing left.'

"Alarm bells ring in my head. Nana and Papa are dead. I just know they are. I drive up to a debris pile and run to their house. Half of the house is still standing, the other half is gone. 'Boy, it was bad,' Papa says, 'but we're okay. Everyone's okay,' he says. But Nana kind of acts funny. 'Nana,' I ask, 'what's going on?'

"That's when she tells me. She says, 'Christi didn't go to the shelter. Your mom and dad think she's at Carolyn's over there.' I look in the direction where she's pointing, and I can't even tell where Carolyn's house is. I start running, across a creek, over a hill, the smell of gas is sickening.

"And there is nothing left. And I mean nothing. I just know you're dead. I know that you and Abby and your mom are gone. No way could anyone have survived. You know what my instinct was? To throw my cell phone and wallet out the window and drive west to Washington to my aunt Pam and uncle Ronnie's place in the mountains. Just start over without ever having to face my dead wife and dead child.

"Then I see my mom. She says, 'Roman, you're white as a ghost.' I fall to my knees, bawling like a baby, screaming into my hands, I can't go in there. She's on her knees holding me. Mom says, 'You have to, son. You have to go in there and help your father get them out.' Dad's the fireman, he rushes in. Me, I want to run away. I hate that about myself, but I want to run so fast in the opposite direction. I could not do your funeral. I could not bury my wife.

"Then my brother Paul comes running over yelling, 'Roman, we found them.' I don't even have a chance to ask if you're alive. Paul takes off running back toward you, and I can barely keep up.

"I get to where you are and they're screaming, 'They're alive! They're alive!' Dad tells me, 'Don't let

Christi look at Carolyn because she might not make it.' I'm here thinking my wife is going to see her own mother die before her eyes. Dad lies to me and tells me your leg is real bad. You know my queasy stomach. I can't even think. I don't even look at you. I don't know what I was looking at.

"Dad tells me and Paul to get two doors to carry you and Carolyn out, and we run into Nathan. And he's screaming like someone tore his arm off. That's my mom! That's my sister! That's my baby niece! My mom's trying to calm him down, and I'm thinking we're all in hell.

"Once we get you moving, you're covered up, and I try to talk to you, but you're seeing houses that aren't there. I hold your hand and stay with you while we get to the hospital, and if it wasn't for Dad flagging down pickup trucks, we'd still be lying at the side of the road with your leg bleeding to death.

"So the nurse tells me this, she says, 'We may have to give Christi stuff that will kill the baby. Do we have your consent?' I hesitate, and say yes. 'Give my wife whatever she needs to survive. Do what you have to do.'"

Roman cried harder.

"I didn't think they'd do it. I didn't think they'd hurt Abby. It was just a miracle that you were alive, and so I just believed that she would make it too. I thought the worst was over. But it wasn't. And when I lost Abby, I hurt. I hurt real bad. I was so angry at the world, and so angry at work for not letting me out earlier to get you and Abby to a safe place. And angry at myself. I gave consent. I let them do things that took Abby from us. The guilt is unbearable. And you. Yes, you were injured on the outside, and everyone could see your scars. Mine were invisible, so no one asked about me. Not even you understood that I went through trauma too. That I wanted to walk away, that I could've walked away, but I didn't. You were thrown into the mess, but I chose to stay.

"So I haven't cared for you or held you or comforted you like I should have, because I couldn't, because I blamed you most of all. It was easier to blame you than myself. I was so mad at you; I couldn't even hold our daughter. To this day, it's my biggest regret, that I never touched her. When I looked at her, all I saw was you. Blonde, big-eyed, and beautiful, just like her momma. I told myself I didn't want to get attached. And I think I've been saying the same about you, and we're alive living in the same house. I don't want to get attached. I'll just get hurt again. That's no way to treat your wife. All because, I told myself, it was all your fault.

"And now, what can I say? What can I say, Sis?"

Roman put his arms around Christi and sobbed in her hair. After a while, he looked up longingly at Christi, both of their faces wet with tears, and they kissed passionately. Roman pulled his head back, still holding Christi tightly, and pressed his lips against her ear and whispered, "I'm sorry."

One Decade Later

> Listen, I tell you a mystery: We will not all sleep, but we will all be changed—in a flash, in the twinkling of an eye, at the last trumpet.
>
> 1 Corinthians 15:51–52 (NIV)

Mydonna had just taken Bo out for a strawberry milkshake when they passed by Sunnylane cemetery. A small flowering tree had grown up in the place where the infants would not; it had been planted to honor the children lost on May 3. Mydonna saw the tree out of the corner of her eye and made a point to look away. But Bo stared at it and said, "That's where my sister is buried. Someday my mom's going to take me there to see it."

The simplicity and the truth of the words that came from her seven-year-old grandson took Mydonna's breath away. She did not know that Christi and Roman had told him.

Later, Mydonna shared the story with Carolyn at one of Bo's baseball games. As the wind blew through Carolyn's hair and the boys kicked up dust on the diamond, she soaked in the setting sun and Bo's red-cheeked exuberance, and could not imagine a day without him. He was all the little man she would ever need.

As for the man she had needed throughout the ordeal of her surgeries, J.R. was no longer in Carolyn's life. She sold the ring. She spoke kindly of him when Dr. Manders or anyone else asked. He had supported her during the most critical time of her life. But Carolyn believed that people come in and out of each other's lives for reasons and seasons, and she accepted that their season had come to an end. She was grateful for all of the gifts J.R. had represented in her life, and while he wasn't the man she would eventually wed, she would always be grateful for their friendship.

On the eighth anniversary of the May 3 tornado, a local TV reporter whom Carolyn had known for many years called. Dozens of survivor stories had been told in Oklahoma City over the years, but for some reason, Carolyn's never had.

"Are you sure you're ready to do this?" she asked Carolyn.

"I'm ready," Carolyn answered.

FIRST REPORT: UNTOLD STORY TEST OF COURAGE, HEART.

ANCHOR LIVE: YOU'RE ABOUT TO HEAR A SURVIVAL STORY FROM May 3, 1999, THAT HAS YET TO BE TOLD.

WE WANT YOU TO TAKE A CLOSE LOOK AT THE TWO WOMEN LYING DOWN HERE. WE TOOK THIS VIDEO MOMENTS AFTER THE F-5 TORNADO SHREDDED

THE NEIGHBORHOOD WHERE THEY LIVED IN DEL CITY AND JUST BEFORE THIS MOTHER AND DAUGHTER WERE RESCUED.

EYEWITNESS NEWS FIVE'S KIMBERLY LOHMAN IS LIVE IN DEL CITY. AND KIMBERLY, THAT'S WHERE THEIR HOUSE USED TO STAND?

REPORTER LIVE: EIGHT YEARS AGO TODAY. AND IF YOU'LL TAKE A WALK WITH ME, THAT SPOT YOU JUST SHOWED US, THIS IS THAT SPOT TODAY. YOU CAN SEE THE FLOWERS HAVE GROWN BACK—SO MUCH HAS CHANGED IN THIS NEIGHBORHOOD—ESPECIALLY THE WOMAN AND THE DAUGHTER FOUND LYING HERE.

Carolyn: "It was a test, I mean, it was a test."

REPORTER: SOMEWHERE IN HERE WAS A CLOSET, WHERE THE TEST OF THE HEART BEGAN.

Christi: "One moment I even felt like I was being buried alive."

Carolyn: "What I was feeling like is that I was being run over by something."

REPORTER: THEY ENDED UP—ALL THREE—SOMEWHERE IN THE BACK YARD.

Christi: "I just remember looking up and thinking, 'Lord I love you and I'll see you in a minute,' because I could just feel my body losing the life out of it."

REPORTER: CHRISTI'S BODY HAD LIFE INSIDE IT—SHE WAS SEVEN MONTHS PREGNANT.

Christi: "I remember just laying out there, and I thought I was all alone. It appeared to be a dressmaker's dummy, a mannequin, just lying on the ground. And as I continued to yell, that's when she started to move, and I realized it was her."

REPORTER: AT CHRISTI'S FEET—THAT MANNEQUIN—WAS HER OWN MOTHER, CAROLYN STAGER.

Carolyn: "Every time someone came around, they were not giving me eye contact; they were looking at my head, not realizing at that point that I'd actually been scalped."

REPORTER: THE SCALPING APPEARED TO BE THE WORST TEST OF THE DAY.

Carolyn: "They said a piece of paper could become a lethal weapon that night because of the velocity of the wind."

REPORTER: THE STORM ALSO SHATTERED CAROLYN'S RIGHT HIP; CHRISTI NEARLY LOST HER RIGHT LEG.

Christi: "It was over 50 percent chance that they were going to have to amputate."

REPORTER: WIND WHIPPED CHRISTI BLACK AND BLUE BUT LEFT HER BELLY UNTOUCHED. THEY HAD HOPE FOR THE BABY SHE HAD ALREADY NAMED ABBY.

Christi: "My doctors were even amazed that my placenta hadn't gotten knocked loose during the tornado, but they said it was a miracle; I would've bled to death instantly."

REPORTER: THIS WAS THE STORM THAT TESTED THEIR FAITH.

Christi: "For a long time when I was in the hospital, I felt like I made it to be Abby's mom, and so for her survival. But then as it was, now I think that he allowed her to keep me; he allowed her to stay with me through the hospital to help keep me going until he knew I was stable enough to let her go."

ANCHOR LIVE: JUST AN UNBELIEVABLE STORY. THAT FAMILY CERTAINLY HAS A LOT OF STRENGTH.

AND WHAT COMES TO MIND IN ADDITION TO THE STRENGTH IS THE FAITH THE STAGERS HAVE.

REPORTER LIVE: ABSOLUTELY, AND WHEN THEY LOST THE BABY SIX WEEKS AFTER THE STORM IT WAS DEFINITELY THE LOWEST POINT FOR THIS FAMILY. BUT THIS STORY DOES NOT END THERE, AND YOU TOUCHED ON IT—THIS TEST ONLY STRENGTHENED THEIR FAITH.

WE'RE GOING TO TALK MORE ABOUT THAT COMING UP AT SIX O'CLOCK.

SECOND REPORT: TORNADO VICTIMS STILL RECOVERING—AN UNTOLD STORY

ANCHOR LIVE: EVEN IF YOU LIVED THROUGH IT, IT IS HARD TO IMAGINE THAT ANYONE DIRECTLY HIT BY THE May 3, '99 TORNADO COULD'VE SURVIVED. BUT CAROLYN STAGER AND HER DAUGHTER CHRISTI DID. ON ONE SIDE OF YOUR SCREEN, STAGER'S DEL CITY NEIGHBORHOOD BACK THEN ... ON THE OTHER SIDE TODAY'S VIEW AND WHAT IT LOOKS LIKE NOW, A VERY DRASTICALLY DIFFERENT SCENE.

KIMBERLY LOHMAN IS LIVE THERE— WHERE IT TOOK SO LONG FOR THE PEOPLE THERE TO RECOVER THEIR HOMES AND THEIR PSYCHES AFTER SUCH A DEVASTATING EVENT.

REPORTER LIVE: FOR CAROLYN AND CHRISTI STAGER, THEIR ADDRESS, 3324 DEL AIRE PLACE DOESN'T EVEN EXIST ANYMORE. IT USED TO BE WHERE THAT HOUSE IS NOW. BUT FOR ALL THEY LOST, THEY SAY THEY'VE FOUND SO MUCH MORE.

Carolyn: "Sometimes you have to endure situations because otherwise it's hard to relate to people going through devastation."

REPORTER: THIS IS A WOMAN WHO NOT ONLY ENDURED THE LOSS OF HER HOME, AND EVERYTHING SHE OWNED, SHE ALSO LOST PART OF HER SCALP, SHE ALMOST LOST HER DAUGHTER, WHO DID LOSE HER UNBORN CHILD.

Carolyn: "I look at myself where I am today and sort of feel like Job. There were so many losses and so many challenges. And I will say that my faith is stronger today. And I've just decided, as bad as it gets, I can never complain of a bad hair day ever." (SMILE.)

REPORTER: FOUR YEARS OF HATS AND SCARVES AND NEARLY ONE HUNDRED MEDICAL PROCEDURES LATER, CAROLYN'S SCALP IS RESTORED.

Carolyn: "Was this the tree?"

REPORTER: CAROLYN STAGER SAYS SHE HAS TWICE TODAY WHAT SHE HAD EIGHT YEARS AGO.

Neighbor: "I think we were the only people in this whole section that had a wall standing."

REPORTER: CAROLYN MOVED AWAY, BUT THE NEIGHBORS BOUGHT HER LOT AND REBUILT THEIR HOME. THEY HAVE ONE REMINDER, A FRAMED LIFE MAG-

AZINE FEATURING CAROLYN'S DAUGHTER'S CAR.

Christi: "It had gotten wedged up against the neighbor's tree and wrapped around it, and we feel it might have saved their life because it protected the corner room where they were."

REPORTER: ONE OF DOZENS OF MIRACLES, BUT WHAT TRULY HELPED REVIVE THE FAMILY'S FAITH—AFTER CHRISTI LOST HER BABY ABBY SIX WEEKS AFTER THE STORM—

Bo: "That's the tornado."

REPORTER: BO CAME ONE YEAR AFTER ABBY DIED.

Christi: "She'll never be replaced, but he's definitely my pride and joy. (LAUGH.)"

Carolyn: "Every day you pick up the paper, you turn on the news, and you see people are enduring the same; and if they could find hope in our story, in our situation, and realize that as bad as it is today, the end result can be great and wonderful so you've got to keep holding on."

REPORTER LIVE: SUCH A STRONG FAMILY, AND CAROLYN LIKES TO TALK ABOUT HAVING TWICE TODAY WHAT SHE HAD TWO YEARS AGO AND THAT INCLUDES HAVING TWO TIMES THE NUMBER OF GRANDCHILDREN.

Mimi: "It's upside down! How did it do that upside down?"

Carolyn: "Tornado did that."

REPORTER LIVE: NOW THAT IS MIMI STAGER, CAROLYN'S OTHER GRANDCHILD, BORN A FEW YEARS AGO. WE WANTED TO SHOW YOU HER AND LITTLE BO DUREN BECAUSE THEY'VE HELPED THIS FAMILY HEAL—HELPED GIVE THIS STORY A HAPPY ENDING. REPORTING LIVE IN DEL CITY, KIMBERLY LOHMAN, EYEWITNESS NEWS FIVE.

ANCHOR LIVE: ONE MORE HIGH NOTE TO SHARE WITH YOU. AFTER CAROLYN WAS SCALPED IN THE STORM, SHE WENT TO A PLASTIC SURGEON IN PITTSBURGH, AND HE NOT ONLY RESTORED HER SCALP—YOU SAW HOW SHE LOOKS TODAY—BUT HER OWN HAIR GREW BACK AFTER THE ACCIDENT... AND DOCTORS SAY THAT MAY BE THE MOST MIRACULOUS PART OF HER RECOVERY.

More miraculous news followed in the fall of 2008. Christi was pregnant again. Her due date: May 2, 2009.

Epilogue: The Last Word

But you, brothers, are not in darkness so that this day should surprise you like a thief. You are all sons of the light and sons of the day. We do not belong to the night or the darkness. So then, let us not be like others, who are asleep, but let us be alert... For those who sleep, sleep at night... But since we belong to the day, let us be self-controlled, putting on faith and love as a breastplate, and the hope of salvation as a helmet. For God did not appoint us to suffer wrath but to receive salvation through our Lord Jesus Christ. He died for us so that, whether we are awake or asleep, we may live together with him. Therefore encourage one another and build each other up, just as in fact you are doing.

1 Thessalonians 5: 4–11 (NIV)

The moment I gripped her neck with a solid stranglehold, I smelled my prize. I tore her scalp from her skull. Her piercing cries pleased my ears. I sucked out her last breath, felt it vacate her body. I knew with all certainty that I had successfully snatched what I had sought—her life.

"But when she lived, much to my dismay, I remained determined to kill, and so lusted after the next best thing—her hope. Because a body without hope is simply a body.

"All around her, my claws found ways to tear away at the people she loved and destroy the things she valued. I started with the ones dearest to her, her own flesh and blood, the first and second generations of her womb. Luckily for me, they were most vulnerable.

"I shattered her home and every precious item and memory in it; although mysteriously, that unconquerable book bearing a cross reappeared. No matter, I lay down many traps, set off a number of tricks, and deliciously, a few targets needed little prompting to let hate, doubt, fear, and best of all—blame—poison their hearts. Blame is far better than guilt. A person burdens himself with guilt, a self-imposed punishment. But blame he tends to place squarely on another, as if he himself is clear of it. They thought it was a tornado that wrecked their lives, never suspecting a thief, or that they could become thieves themselves. I grabbed their throats again and again; stuffed down hot, angry words; filled their heads with murderous thoughts; and iced over their hearts so much that one or two of them nearly joined me by choice.

"But try as I might, this woman could not be touched. Maddening! It was as though her very head were protected with a helmet. But I saw her blood! And still, she was saved. I ripped the ground out from beneath her, and yet, she stood firm. No, more than that. In her quiet way, she fought back powerfully, like a courageous warrior, scalped yet steadfast. The words she uttered (to whom I do not acknowledge) ran like swords through my gut. She carried an invisible yet impenetrable shield; neither profanity nor pain, uncertainty nor death, not even death, could separate her from the love she claimed. It claimed her back, satisfied her every fiber, and left no room for blame. By the example of her stubborn, unfaltering walk of faith, those around her sensed not war but peace, and so they gathered strength, and fell in line behind her.

"Even as I prepared myself for the sweet victory of taking the life of an unborn child, infuriatingly, I was foiled. I knew that if I could steal the most innocent among them, after they had convinced themselves the worst was over, the bonds of their belief would be undone. But in the moment that I moved to capture the child, she vanished from my clutches; an unseen power, greater than my own, pried open my fingers with no more effort than a whisper, and swept her far from my grasp. Where she went I cannot say, for the light that followed blinded me and destroyed my ambition.

"What is worse, the infant's mother discovered this unfortunate turn of events. During the time that grief and guilt consumed her and the one she pledged to have and hold forever blamed her; I enjoyed their suffering. But by some miracle that only the prayerful are capable of knowing, the truth revealed the child's purpose in her life. And the truth gave her enough hope to journey onward, love again, and the worst possible outcome from my perspective—create once more.

"Disgusted and deceived, my work left unfinished,

I turned my back on all of them, the whole brave, shining lot, in search of cowards under dark storm clouds whose souls could be stolen," said the thief.

In the twinkling of an eye, he was gone.

No, in all these things we are more than conquerors through him who loved us. For I am convinced that neither death nor life, neither angels nor demons, neither the present nor the future, nor any powers, neither height nor depth, nor anything else in all creation, will be able to separate us from the love of God...

Romans 8: 37–39 (NIV)